Indian Giving

Economies of Power in Indian-White Exchanges

DAVID MURRAY

UNIVERSITY OF MASSACHUSETTS PRESS

Amherst

Copyright © 2000 by the University of Massachusetts Press
All rights reserved
Printed in the United States of America
LC 99-088274
ISBN 1-55849-243-7 (cloth); 244-5 (pbk.)

Designed by Dennis Anderson
Set in Janson Text by Graphic Composition, Inc.
Printed and bound by Sheridan Books, Inc.

Library of Congress Cataloging-in-Publication Data

Murray, David, 1945–
    Indian giving : economies of power in Indian-white exchanges / David Murray.
        p. cm.—(Native Americans of the Northeast)
    Includes bibliographical references and index.
    ISBN 1-55849-243-7 (cloth : alk. paper)—ISBN 1-55849-244-5 (pbk. : alk. paper)
        1. Indians of North America—First contact with Europeans—Northeastern
    States.   2. Indians of North America—Commerce—Northeastern States.   3. Indians of
    North America—Northeastern States—Economic conditions.   4. Barter—Northeastern
    States—History.   5. Ceremonial exchange—Northeastern States—History.   I. Title. II.
    Series.

E78.E2 M87 2000
303.48'2'08997—dc21

                                                                                99-088274

British Library Cataloguing in Publication data are available.

Contents

Acknowledgments

MUCH IN this book questions the claims made in the name of giving and generosity, but, of course, the book itself and my capacity to write it have relied on the generosity and help of countless people. A semester's study leave was funded by the Humanities Research Board of the British Academy, who also co-funded a month's research at the Newberry Library in 1998. I am grateful to Fred Hoxie and the staff of the library, and to the scholars at the Darcy McNickle Center there, in particular, LaVonne Brown Ruoff, for their help and interest. A Paul W. McQuillen Memorial Fellowship allowed me to spend two months at the John Carter Brown Library in 1997. Norman Fiering and his staff gave invaluable help, and the sense of shared scholarship and enthusiasm among the other researchers there, particularly Hilary Wyss, Richard Rath, Rebecca Bach, Susan Niles, Karen Graubach, and Jean Charles Benzaken, was a memorable experience.

Earlier versions of sections of chapter 6 have appeared in "David Brainard and the Gift of Christianity," *The European Review of Native American Studies* 10, no. 1 (1996): 23–29, and "Spreading the Word: Missionaries, Conversion, and Circulation in the Northeast," in *Spiritual Encounters: Interactions between Christianity and Native Religions in Colonial America*, ed. Nicholas Griffiths and Fernando Cervantes (Birmingham, 1999), 43–64. An earlier version of part of chapter 4 appeared in *Symbiosis* 1 (1997). My thanks to the various editors for their help and for permission to reuse that material here. In developing ideas

I have been helped by the thoughtful and generous responses of more people than I can do justice to here, but some of them are John Strong, Arnold Krupat, Helen Tanner, Charlotte Taylor, Colin Harrison, Kate Shanley, David Moore, Shamoon Zamir, Mick Gidley, Leslie Pinder, Helen Carr, Graham Taylor, and my colleagues in the School of American Studies at Nottingham. I was fortunate to have Laura Murray and Eric Cheyfitz as initial readers of the manuscript, and I am indebted to them for their painstaking and sympathetic readings, as I am to the editors at the University of Massachusetts Press for their care and patience. Finally, and most of all, my thanks to Gill, who, as well as reading sections of it, has lived with this book with her usual patience and generosity, and has given me more than I can repay or properly acknowledge.

D. M.

Indian Giving

Introduction

THIS BOOK is about value and the circulation of value, within and across cultures. More specifically, it is about what was given and exchanged in early encounters between Europeans and Indians and how these transactions were understood and represented on each side. My argument is that these exchanges need to be seen as operating within a set of interlocking economies, which include the realms of the discursive and religious as well as the material. The book moves, therefore, between detailed discussions of particular moments of giving and exchanging, together with the objects and signs involved, and broader arguments about what these instances reveal about the workings of power within and between societies. My justification for this large and sometimes speculative sweep is that it is only by looking at these exchanges, and the idea of economy itself, in the widest available terms that it is possible to see the full imaginative dimensions of the early encounters.

As I worked on this material, though, it also became strikingly clear how much Western societies' thinking about their own political organization and economy since the sixteenth century has been based on a series of implicit oppositions between primitive and civilized societies, and how fundamental the role of exchange and giving has been in these debates. In trying to elucidate specific seventeenth-century instances, then, I draw on later theories of exchange and gift-giving from Marx, Marcel Mauss, Pierre Bourdieu, and others. But it is part of my larger argument that these encounters with Native American cultures, through their representations in Western thought from Jean de Lery and Montaigne onward, themselves play a surprisingly important role in the development of the theories I am applying. While it is easy to identify and simplify this in the seventeenth and eighteenth centuries as the discourse of noble savagery, I argue that the same issues remain crucial in much later debates over primitive economy, gift-giving, and political organization.

Like many other people, I suppose, part of my fascination with Indian history and cultures has been in the endless play of similarities to, and differences from, my own history and culture, and when I began working on this book I had some idea of the contrasting economic and cultural systems I thought I would be exploring. One of the effects of my research has indeed been to find differences and similarities—but not necessarily where I expected them. In trying to explicate instances of exchange, to separate the agendas on each side, I invariably found myself caught up in the process of exchange itself, with its swirl of oppositions and transformations. In trying to disentangle what happened when gifts, beads, words, or ideas were exchanged, translated, transvaluated, and circulated, I was forced to question more oppositions than I expected and to return to fundamental questions of power and sovereignty. This is my justification not only for covering a wide range of topics in this book but also for devoting large parts of the first two chapters to discussions of political representation and sovereignty before I concentrate in the remaining chapters on more detailed instances of exchange.

Though the main focus of the book is on seventeenth-century northeastern America, I want to begin with a couple of classic accounts of first encounters from the late fifteenth and sixteenth centuries. There has been an understandable fascination with the textual accounts of these early encounters as somehow paradigmatic of the fundamental differences between the two sides or at least the terms in which Europeans textualized difference, but there are dangers in isolating one moment or instance for cultural analysis. One temptation, particularly seductive perhaps for the cultural critic or New Historicist or text-based commentator, is that of seeing first contacts as too conveniently tableaulike, setting up clear-cut oppositions and presenting the historical event of contact as a rupture of a whole, sealed timeless culture. As

Neil Whitehead warns, these first accounts are often "also a peculiarly European trope of encounter, feverishly reproduced in the fiction of an 'ethnographic present' and clearly serving the ideology of colonial possession."[1] Certainly, an awareness of the dynamic nature of both cultures and of their economies and circulations is necessary, but we do need to be aware initially of the rhetoric of these early encounters and the prominent role of exchange and the terms in which it is expressed. My chosen instances are therefore intended simply to illustrate and isolate here some of the issues that are developed in the rest of the book. We can begin with the first of the first, in 1492:

> What follows are the very words of the Admiral in his book about his first voyage to, and discovery of, these Indies. I, he says, in order that they would be friendly to us—because I recognized that they were people who would be better freed [from error] and converted to our Holy Faith by love than by force—to some of them I gave red caps, and glass beads which they put on their chests, and many other things of small value, in which they took so much pleasure and became so much our friends that it was a marvel. Later they came swimming to the boats of the ships' launches where we were and brought us parrots and cotton thread in balls and javelins and many other things, and they traded them to us for other things which we gave them, such as small glass beads and bells. In sum, they took everything and gave of what they had very willingly. But it seemed to me that they were a people very poor in everything. All of them go around as naked as their mothers bore them.

This famous passage continues with a description of the Indians' body-painting and cutting themselves on swords out of ignorance of sharp metal and concludes

> They should be good intelligent servants, for I see that they say very quickly everything that is said to them; and I believe that they would become Christians very easily, for it seemed to me that they had no religion. Our Lord pleasing, at the time of my departure I will take six of them from here to your Highnesses in order that they may learn to speak. No animal of any kind did I see on this island except parrots. All are the Admiral's words.[2]

Many elements of this passage were to become paradigmatic of accounts of first encounters, but the more closely we look at the actual moments of exchange, the more they appear to be overlaid with a whole series of assumptions about motivation. One immediate problem is authenticity, since the events are textualized several times over. Even if we accept Las Casas's framing phrases ("what follows are the very words") indicating that this part is verbatim from Columbus's now lost journal, rather than summarized, as are many other parts, we still have problems of interpretation and translation. His son's account of Columbus's life, for instance, which seems to have drawn on the same sources as Las Casas, gives similar details, but with slight differences in emphasis. In his account, at the first exchange of objects Columbus,

> perceiving that they were a gentle, peaceful and very simple people, gave them little red caps and glass beads which they hung about their necks, together with other trifles that they cherished as if they were precious stones of great price.[3]

Antonio Gómez-Moriana has shown how the differences between Las Casas's summary and the version by Columbus's son Fernando Colón already reflect crucial distinctions, in that Colón introduces calculations of monetary value and property into the language of this first exchange that are not present in Las Casas. This reflects a shift of emphasis which, he says, ends up "converting the idyllic scene, the old topic of the *locus amoenus* which dominates the whole scene surrounding the act of taking possession of the utopian island into a market scene of the exchange of goods."[4]

In Peter Martyr's account, the event has changed again, so that the initial encounter is ambiguous in different ways. On seeing the Spaniards, the natives flee, and the Spaniards seize one woman, whom they take on board,

> where they gave her plenty of food and wine and clothes (for both sexes lived absolutely naked and in a state of nature); afterwards this woman, who knew where the fugitives were concealed, returned to her people, to whom she showed her ornaments, praising the liberality of the Spaniards; upon which they all returned to the coast, convinced that the newcomers were descended from heaven. They swam out to the ships, bringing gold, of which they had a small quantity, which they exchanged gladly for trifles of glass or pottery. For a needle, a bell, a fragment of mirror, or any such thing, they gladly gave in exchange whatever gold was asked of them, or all that they had about them.[5]

Here the initial act is one of violence and capture, though this is effaced in the text and supposedly in the woman's mind by the stress on the liberality of the Spaniards, who are presented as giving the first gifts.

The fact that the gifts are reciprocated with gold and the Indians are presented as eager to trade smooths out the complexities of Columbus's journal account to create a simple scenario of benevolent Europeans and grateful and credulous Indians. But in all of these texts it would be dangerous to assume too clear-cut a distinction between economic rationality and reciprocal gifts on the part of the original participants or even in the minds of the later commentators. Gómez-Moriana sees the overlay of what he calls "a discourse proper to an economic bourgeois mentality" on top of the medieval and aristocratic values that preceded it, but it is precisely the entangling, rather than the opposition, of the economic and the spiritual that is my concern and can be most usefully traced in the changing complex of figures and metaphors that surrounds the idea of exchange.

Columbus's comment that, having taken objects of little value, "they became so much our friends that it was a marvel" is translated by Gómez-Moriana as "they ended up being ours to an amazing extent," which he sees as reflecting the fact that "the final result of this commercial exchange consists of the possession of these people."[6] Gerald Sider's reading of the same passage also stresses the problematic nature of the friendship described: "After deprecating the gifts, and the act of giving, to then say that the native people became 'entirely our friends' is to mock and utterly deny the mutuality implicit in the concept of friendship." This is perhaps to overstate the cynicism or insensitivity of the Europeans, but Sider does refer usefully to the description as presenting the meeting as a "paradigm of friendship and inequality," pointing to the complex swirl of deceptions and self-deceptions involved in such scenes.[7] As Stephen Greenblatt puts it in a description of Columbus's "Christian imperialism," "This discursive economy brings opposites into the closest conjunction with one another and yet leaves the heart of their relation a mystery. Columbus takes absolute possession on behalf of the Spanish crown in order to make an absolute gift; he seeks earthly gain in order to serve a divine purpose; the Indian must lose everything in order to receive everything."

Greenblatt shows that this is rooted in a Christian rhetoric of sacrifice, but it also has a wider discursive reach, because it relates to the material and political as well as religious realms. As he puts it, "the rhetorical task of Christian imperialism then is to bring together commodity conversion and spiritual conversion."[8]

Nevertheless it is important not to dismiss these actions and intentions as merely hypocritical, covering over straight mercantile and commercial greed with the rhetoric of Christian benevolence, especially as this maintains a separation of the economic and religious not necessarily recognized by either side of the encounter at the time. The rhetoric is much more than just a misleading disguise for "real" motives and actions and needs to be taken seriously; the challenge is to develop a skeptical reading of European representations of exchange and encounter as textual productions within a discursive field without falling into the trap of dealing with the text entirely in terms of its rhetoric and assuming it cannot give us any information beyond this. This would be to read out of existence the culture being described, in an overscrupulous concern not to assume the text's representational reliability. Texts may also incorporate native categories, perceptions, or beliefs and may be valuable sources of information about both cultures, but there is no easy way of knowing when and how. This is a problem to which I shall return throughout the book.

One particular category of events where the action is interestingly inseparable from the rhetoric is performative speech acts. The most famous of these was the *Requerimiento*, in which the discoverer proclaimed to an uncomprehending audience of Indians the legitimacy and intentions of the colonizing power.[9] Here is perhaps the ultimate example of language being used not to communicate but as a performative act. It did not matter whether it was understood, as long as it was said and legally enacted. We could argue that this element of the performative rather than the communicative was constantly present in situations where language barriers prevented easy communication and power and sovereignty were being asserted. In their accounts, though, Europeans often obscured this element by assuming an understanding or assent that was unlikely to be there.

My second example, from Jacques Cartier's account of his voyage of 1534, demonstrates this. Cartier describes how soon after landing the sailors erect a large cross, with a sign saying "Long Live the King of France," and try to demonstrate its importance to the watching Indians.

> [W]e all knelt down with our hands joined, worshipping it before them; and made signs to them, looking up and pointing towards heaven, that by means of this we had our redemption, at which they showed many marks of admiration, at the same time turning and looking at the cross.

In this short passage we find two words that are scattered across such accounts but rarely explained in detail. The reference to "signs" emphasizes the effort at communication but tells us nothing about the reception and what, if anything, was understood on the Indian side. The "marks" of "admiration" are no clearer than signs, and if we take the word *admiration* (in the original French *admyradtions*) in its earlier sense, as denoting wonder as much as approval, their response is even less clear. The local leader appears to object and points "to the land all around him, as if he wished to say that all this region belonged to him, and that we ought not to have set up the cross without his permission." The giving and exchanging that then take place seem to be a strange mixture of friendliness and compulsion, with the French dictating the agenda.

> And when he had finished his harangue, we held up an axe to him, pretending we would barter it for his fur-skin. To this he nodded assent and little by little drew near the side of our vessel, thinking he would have the axe. But one of our men, who was in our dinghy, caught hold of his canoe, and at once two or three more stepped down into it and made the Indians come on board our vessel, at which they were greatly astonished.

They are assured no harm will come to them and are given food and "every sign of affection." "And then we explained to them by signs that the cross had been set up to serve as a landmark and guide-post on coming into the harbour, and that we would soon come back and bring them iron wares and other goods; and that we wished to take two of his [the chief's] sons away with us and afterwards would bring them back." After receiving clothing and knives, the Indians then "made signs to us that they would not pull down the cross, delivering at the same time several harangues which we did not understand."[10]

The manipulation and underlying force here are striking. We could even see the holding up of an axe and the enforced "invitation" to dinner on board as perfect symbols of the ambiguity of threat and exchange. Equally striking is the way the absolute lack of linguistic understanding, eventually admitted at the end, is effaced in the confidence of the guesses and assumptions ("as if he wished to say"). Such assumptions are almost the norm in such encounters, even when they are implicit rather than explicit, and we need to be aware of the extent to which problems of communication and translation are effaced by performative actions and by being woven into a self-justifying narrative of accord.

I return to the question of language and how much was understood in chapter 3, where I examine the actual Indian words that Cartier includes as a list in his published account; it is enough here to point out that any agreement or accord implied by Cartier is thrown into question by the failures of understanding. The cross, which is there to constitute a claim of sovereignty, is conflated with trade and reciprocal exchange of gifts in a way unlikely to be comprehended by the Indians, and this overlapping and confusion of motives and meanings is typical of many early accounts, in which multiple forms of exchange or translation happen at once. The ideal moment of accord would also be the moment of complete "translation," with Indians converted to Christianity and land transferred to European ownership, in a moment of friendship and complete communication. Failing that, a performative act like the *Requerimiento* or the erection of a cross can be built into a narrative of accord built on "signs" and suppositions to seem to create legal and political legitimacy for the Europeans. Such accounts, though, also often contain other sorts of often contradictory information about the encounters. Apart from the elements that may point to different Indian agendas and perceptions, either directly by reported speech or indirectly, there is also the existence of alternative views of the event from within the European perspective. Paralleling the idea of accord and translation, for instance, is the recurrent idea that the natives have no sense of the value of things and that the idea of a fair exchange, of communication on a shared basis, is irrelevant. Thus we have the regular disparaging references to baubles and trinkets, with which Indians are apparently deceived.

Dealing with linguistic communication, Eric Cheyfitz comments that early travel narratives are "not constituted by accuracy or even adequacy of translation but by a congeries of contradictions that attempt to parade as linguistic coherence by constructing a fiction of translation, which is, however, itself contradictory."[11] Cheyfitz sees the capacity to hold these contradictory ideas together while obscuring the contradiction as the work of ideology. I show how similar ideological operations are at work in the representation of other forms of exchange, most notably the gift, and I follow Cheyfitz in stressing their convertibility and interchangeability. As Greenblatt implies, the circulation of goods is also a circulation of signs, and it is the interpenetration of different systems of value and of language that is my main concern.[12] I shall follow through the representations and figures of exchange, but because of the congruences within the cluster of terms with which I am working—*exchange, gift, metaphor, translation, conversion*—none is necessarily more fundamental or fixed than any of the others, none is necessarily more "proper" or literal or beyond circulation as a sign or a figure. My intention is not to reduce everything to sign, but to show, by reconstructing the whole discursive economy, the full imaginative and symbolic ramifications of relations that are often treated in more narrow political or economic terms.

Because the term *economy* is usually associated with narrow financial and material bookkeeping, to use the word to link all of these terms of exchange may seem to be using economy as a metaphor. In fact, though, as I show, I am also looking at the economy *of* metaphor. In using the term economy, I mean a system in which we find a circulation of signs creating and sustaining a set of values. These signs may circulate as language, religious symbols, clothing, or forms of money, but my interest is not only in the separate semiotic systems but in the way the different realms overlap and interlock, as in the case of wampum and beads, which can be seen functioning at different points in all four of the preceding categories—as linguistic unit, monetary unit, jewelery, and religious symbol. What is often not clear, though, is which system or discursive economy we are in, and my broad use of the term *economy* has perhaps the advantage of suggesting a dynamism, which, as Steven Connor has put it, "allows and obliges the critic not only to order and distribute the elements of his field of study in inert relationships of equivalence and distinction, but also to show the processes of exchange, circulation and interested negotiation which bring these relationships dynamically into being."[13] Indeed it is the process of *exchange* in the circulation and creation of value that is my concern, because rather than dealing with separate cultures or systems, I explore what is carried over, given value, and circulated within the new economy created when these separate cultures meet and begin to exchange. This collision of cultures applies, obviously, to the meeting of European and Native American cultures and the exchanges that took place, but one of the things highlighted by these exchanges is the unstable movement between apparently separate spheres of value on the European side.

If we use the terms of religion to describe money, or describe coins as words, we are moving between what are usually seen as separate spheres by means of metaphoric connections. The metaphor works, then, by tracing apparent similarities and analogies across areas of difference, and this is fundamental to our use of language and our thinking. In this particular case, it works because of the similarities between semiotic systems or circulations of value that I call economies. But my interest in metaphor is not just because metaphors underlie so much of our thinking, and analyzing their use can demonstrate fundamental clusters of ideas in our culture, as William Labov has demonstrated. Rather, it is because the structure of metaphor is itself closely related to my other key terms of exchange, *translation* and *conversion*. Metaphor needs two dissimilar items and a point of contact between them, based on similarity or comparability of some sort. The point at which a metaphor works is the point at which the two terms are present in the mind but turn around each other, exchanging their identities around an axis of resemblance. If we say a man is a ray of sunshine or a rock, we mentally line up the object with the man and use it to isolate those qualities in him of cheerfulness or steadfastness that we conventionally recognize in this metaphor. To look in him for the capacity to burn like sunshine or for growths of moss, as on a rock, would be to allow aspects of the object introduced for the purpose of comparison (the vehicle) to proliferate beyond their proper function. Other elements of difference need to be screened out for the metaphor to effect its moment of exchange and turn momentarily and precariously around its axis of similarity.

Like *translation*, the word *metaphor* has its roots in the idea of carrying over, of moving from one side to the other. As Cheyfitz points out, "the notion of translation and of metaphor both etymologically and ideologically are inseparable." So metaphor depends on a process of exchange and substitution, but it has usually been seen, from Aristotle onward, as privileging one side over the other. When we talk of spreading the word of God as sowing the seed, we retain the idea that the real subject is words rather than seeds. As Cheyfitz reminds us, Aristotle's definition of metaphor involves the idea of "transporting a term from a familiar to a foreign place, from, that is, its so-called 'proper' signification to a 'figurative' sense, with the idea of 'resemblance,' or 'similitude' determining the decorous limits of such transportation."

This means that metaphor depends on a process of exchange and substitution, but only as long as one term is clearly the proper, or home, term and the other the foreign term. Thus "the very idea of metaphor seems to find its ground in a kind of territorial imperative, in a division, that is, between the domestic and the foreign."[14]

This idea of a fixed point of meaning or value, whose stability and "properness" is the basis on which substitutions, exchanges, translations, or conversions are made, can be found beyond the realm of language, and it is important for my larger argument about the overlapping of discursive economies that Aristotle also uses the same normative idea of the "proper" to distinguish between legitimate value, based on use, and illegitimate, based on exchange. This points us to a set of structural similarities between the exchanges involved in the activities which come variously under the headings of *trade, barter,* and *gift-giving* and the operations involved in metaphor and translation. In an act of clear communication, there would supposedly be an agreement about what was "proper" and what was not proper and was metaphorical. This also describes the possibility of communication across languages, where common agreement about the meaning of a term is necessary, but it could also be seen as Aristotle's ideal condition of fair exchange or trade, where there is an agreement about value based on what is "proper," that is, use value rather than exchange value.

In another way, though, trade relies on a disparity of needs, and when the exchange is between groups encountering each other and their economies anew, the disparity between ideas of value comes to the fore. The effect of the discovery and settlement of the New World was potentially to unsettle the sense of what was domestic or "proper" and, paradoxically, also to increase the ideological weighting of these terms in the need to justify and defend ethnocentric values as proper at the same time as appropriating Indian land and property. What we find, then, and what I try to give full weight to, is a dynamic mixing of values and meanings, as different systems collide and change, together with a determined effort to control meanings and values. The whole thrust of a range of deconstructive critiques has been to question what Derrida has called "the reassuring opposition of the metaphoric and the proper" on which so much of Western thinking is based,[15] and these critiques provide the basis of an approach that is, I hope, more attuned to the complexities of exchange in all its forms in the materials I present.[16]

My generalized use of the word *economy* and emphasis on the symbolic should be seen not as a move from the material to the cultural, but as an attempt to take seriously the actual and metaphorical exchanges that operate across all the discourses of value within and across the cultures involved in the complex exchanges of the seventeenth century. Just as my emphasis on the symbolic economy should not be construed as neglect of the material economy, so my emphasis on terms like *exchange* and *encounter* rather than *expropriation, invasion, conquest,* or *domination* should not be seen as lack of concern for the power relations and the inequalities of power that underlie early Indian-European relations.[17] My intention, rather, is to show the complex role of ideas of exchange and giving and their representation, at the time and later, in the legitimation and subversion of power. In this way, I hope to provide a more nuanced view of individual exchanges and a broader picture of how the different realms of exchange—linguistic, material, and religious—are related.

In moving the focus away from the more obvious oppositions of victims and oppressors and toward areas of mutual exchange and negotiation, a middle ground in which both sides have their own agendas, there is one particular danger. This approach can feed too easily into and even reduplicate an ideological operation that occurs throughout the European accounts of such encounters, which is to minimize or efface the role of power in exchange. This is common in the ways in which the linguistic, economic, and religious exchanges I am interested in create fictions of accord, that is, of equal and satisfactory translation, exchange, or conversion. My reference to a middle ground is bound to suggest Richard White's wide-ranging and justly influential account of a specific period of mutual accommodation between Europeans and Algonquians in the region of the Great Lakes. White's middle ground is the place "in between cultures, peoples, and in between empires and the nonstate world of villages . . . It is the area between the historical foreground of European invasion and occupation and the background of Indian defeat and retreat." White's account has a two-century historical sweep, during which initial hostility and nonacceptance are replaced by a search for "accommodation and common meaning," only then to return to hostility, and he gives a densely textured picture of the mixed motives and agendas that went into the precarious understandings and exchanges.[18] Focusing largely on groups and encounters farther east, I do not use this narrative sweep, partly because in many cases there was not time for the process White describes to evolve or be recorded, but mainly because my concern is more with the *representation* of moments of often ambiguous interactions between the linguistic "material" and spiritual economies. As a result, I am more interested than White in concentrating on the slippages—the accommodation and conversions of value but also the blind spots and evasions in the representations that can be used to reveal the underlying ideological investments.

In the first two chapters, I deal with exchange, power, and sovereignty and develop the broad framework in which the more detailed accounts of linguistic, monetary, and religious exchanges of later chapters can be seen. In chapter 1, I outline some of the main debates over exchange and value that have defined the terms in which the colonial encounter has been discussed. Focusing on the potent idea of the gift, I explore exchange in general and concepts of use and commodity as they have been involved in defining value. Such debates over different forms of exchanging and giving have been fundamental and pervasive in setting the terms in which the West has distinguished itself from other societies and thought about its own social behavior, from Montaigne to Marx and on to Mauss, Marshall Sahlins, and Georges Bataille. These themes are taken up more concretely in chapter 2, where I concentrate on specific early accounts of encounters, placing them in the pervasive European discourse on America, which stressed wealth and the legitimation of power and sovereignty. From this base, I move in succeeding chapters through linguistic, religious, and economic themes, emphasizing the interlocking nature of these ideas in the discursive economy of seventeenth-century northeastern America.

At the center of the book in his ability to operate in so many relevant spheres, as linguist, trader, and missionary, is Roger Williams, and his remarkable book of 1643, *A Key into the Language of America*. Explaining the extralinguistic purposes and functions of his book, Williams reminds his readers that "A little Key may open a Box, where lies a bunch of Keys."[19] His image suggests not a single treasure unlocked, but a series of locks and keys, and it is in the interlocking nature of the main elements of Williams's book, the complex exchanges involving religion, trade, and language, that his importance for my own study lies. The *Key* itself needs unlocking, but this unlocking involves showing how, as a text, it is generated out of a set of interlocking discursive economies, and in order to see just what Williams's book opens up, we need to be aware of them. Just as a key locks as well as opens, so the idea of economy, or systems of meaning and value in which objects, words, or ideas circulate, can imply a closed or open system. I am interested in the points where closed systems link with other systems, where the key turns the other way, where translation, conversion, exchange, and transformation of values take place.

Like the key's double function, the gift, with its simultaneous actions of giving and holding, ceding and asserting power, the open palm or the grasping hand reminds us of the complexities and paradoxes of early encounters. Developing my initial discussion of the gift in chapter 1, I attempt in later chapters to bring out the Janus-faced nature of exchanges between Europeans and Indians. In chapter 3, I concentrate on the complex functions that the inclusion of native words can perform, and this provides a context for the fuller treatment of Williams's *Key* in chapter 4. My examination of his interlocking concerns of religion, language, and trade moves the focus of the book to a closer examination of exchanges in the Northeast in the subsequent chapters. His role as trader gives importance to his firsthand accounts of the use and meaning of wampum, and chapter 5 details the changes in the meaning and representation of this quintessential medium of exchange in the period. Wampum raises the issue of how value is constituted and controlled in intercultural exchanges, and it is this question of control of value and meaning that is taken up in the last two chapters, dealing with missionaries and religious exchanges. The attempt on the part of the missionaries to control and authorize the meaning of what gets distributed is here presented alongside the adaptations, changes, and exchanges taking place as God's Word, in its various manifestations, was disseminated in the complex mingling of economic, cultural, and religious exchanges that constituted contact in this period.

1

Exchanging Power

ONE OF the claims I make in this book is that close attention to gifts and the rhetoric of giving in the representations of exchange works as a key to open up some of the complications in the struggle for political and cultural as well as economic power between Indians and Europeans. This is because on both sides giving was deeply implicated as an expression of power in the articulation of social relations, and when exchanges took place between the two sides they were inevitably understood and represented in these terms. In this chapter, I sketch some of the extensive debate over the significance of gifts and gift-giving, to provide a framework in which to try to understand Indian-white exchanges, and then demonstrate how this works in particular instances involving rival claims for power and sovereignty in early encounters.

First, though, I want to look at an annual American event: Thanksgiving. The name implies some relation to my theme of the gift, but I want to ask, Just what is happening at Thanksgiving? Clearly, thanks are being given. A gift is being acknowledged as coming from God, whose help allowed the Massachusetts colonists to survive. But the ingredients of the Thanksgiving dinner include an acknowledgment of the food the settlers needed to survive, the bounty of the land, which was, in the many different versions of the story, either explicitly or implicitly (i.e., through sharing knowledge of agriculture) given by Indians. The dinner, then, is a feast to give thanks, but the Indians are usually absent, and the circle of gift and countergift goes between God and the settlers in the form of their present-day representatives. Why is this? And why is the only phrase that combines Indians and giving—*Indian giver*—actually a negative one? How, indeed, might we relate these two common American terms of Indian giving and Thanksgiving?

If we look at the account of the first Puritan contact, which relates to the acquiring of food, we find some interesting parallels. According to William Bradford and Edward Winslow's account, the first encounters with the Indian cultures of New England are in fact strangely haunted and mysterious nonmeetings. After a sighting of Indians who flee into the forest, the Englishmen find signs of cultivation of corn and evidence of Indian graves. After a brief exploration of them, during which they find some arrows, they cover the graves over. As they explain, "we thought it would be odious unto them to ransack their sepulchres." Digging up a mound of freshly heaped sand covered with a kettle, they find a small basket and then another "fine great new basket, full of corn of this year, with some six and thirty goodly ears of corn, some yellow and some red, and others mixed with blue, which was a goodly sight." After being "in suspense" about what to do with it, they take the kettle and as much corn as they can carry, resolving that later "if we could find any of the people and come to parley with them, we would give them the kettle again, and satisfy them for their corn." Some days later, they return and find more buried stores of corn, as well as graves, one of which, owing to its size, they excavate in detail. They find the bones and skull of a man "with fine yellow hair still on it" embalmed in a red powder, and the remains of a child similarly preserved. From the numerous grave goods, both European (metal) and Indian (wampum) in origin, they take "sundry of the prettiest things" away with them, and cover the corpse up again, seeming to have lost the scruples expressed at their first discovery of graves.[1]

Like later commentators, they speculate on the origin and fate of the corpse, but what is relevant to present purposes is the way that the familiar trope of the abundance and plenty of the New World (as exemplified by the fertile female in van der Straet's famous image of America and by De Bry's illustrations), is here strangely transformed. In his version of this event in *Of Plymouth Plantation*, Bradford not only omits the grave-robbing episode but gives the bringing back of corn a religious gloss: "like the men from Eshcol" they "carried with them the fruits of the land and showed their brethren." The Bible reference is to Moses in Canaan, where his people gather grapes, figs, and pomegranates from the vines and trees, (Num. 13:23–26) and the effect is to efface not only the theft (or at best borrowing) of the corn but the Indians' role in its production. This plenty is the product of culture, not just of nature, but it is part of the trope of abundance to minimize Indians' role as producers and treat them as a natural hazard, like the wild animals, or at best a natural resource. (We might also note that any attempt to place all this bounty as natural has to ignore the presence in the graves of European trade goods.) In Bradford's account, even nature itself is subordinated to God as ultimate source and provider, since "the lord is never wanting unto His in their greatest needs."[2]

If we stand back from Bradford's positive and providential view, though, what we have here is a curious landscape, absent of people but containing their ambiguous traces—mounds that may be graves, may be storehouses of material plenty, or may be both. This points inescapably forward to the later activities of archeologists and treasure hunters and the arguments over the ethics of disturbing or looting ancestral sites, but what I want to concentrate on here is the absence of people in these accounts. The actual presence of the communities as well as their angry reactions to such English actions is tellingly revealed elsewhere in a reference by Thomas Morton, who describes how the Plymouth planters "defaced the monument of the ded at Pasonayessit (by taking away the herse Cloath which was two greate Beares skinnes sowed together at full lenth, and propped up over the grave of Cleatawbacks mother)" and how the "inraged" sachem denounced their actions and declared hostilities.[3]

This is not the sense of wonder or "marvelous possession" that Stephen Greenblatt finds in so many early accounts, and we have to look carefully to invest the scene with the strangeness it surely has. The Puritans' actions are the policy of *vacuum domicilium* realized in a haunting physical landscape,[4] just as powerful and effective, if not as graphic, as Cotton Mather's image of a plague-ridden land, "a meer Golgotha of unburied carcasses."[5] These Indians have only just gone or are present but hiding, out of caution about their visitors, but their trace is more usable, ideologically and practically, than they are. One last element, one more ghost, perhaps is the insistence in all the accounts that the debt incurred in taking the buried goods was intended to be, and actually was, eventually paid. Thanksgiving dinner could be thought of as this debt's being symbolically repaid, were it not for the fact that the structure of the event, with the thanks offered to God and not to the Indians, completely repeats Bradford's original substitution.

I have begun this chapter, then, with an instance not of gift-giving but of the absence of a gift—a removal, which remains more an act of theft until a return is made or thanks are given. This scene is perhaps appropriate in leaving the status of the colonists undecided as takers, traders, or thieves, as a counterpoint to Europeans' long-standing presentation of themselves as bringers of gifts, specifically, the gifts of civilization and Christianity. These were gifts so huge that they dwarfed any negative aspects that might come along with them and justified taking the bounty of the New World. So powerful and persistent has been the idea of Western civilization as the source of all that is important and valuable, and indigenous cultures as more or less needy beneficiaries, that recent emphasis on what "we" owe to Indians culturally as well as materially is felt to be claiming something new and controversial. Perhaps the most explicit general account, Jack Weatherford's book *Indian Givers*, gives a sense of the enormous changes and benefits created by what flowed from America, ranging from politics to agriculture and medicine, but it is significant that his title, in its deliberate play on an established figure of speech, reflects his awareness of reversing a commonly held belief.[6] What Weatherford does is simply to use the well-known phrase "Indian giver" literally, but to do this is to go against the grain of the phrase as generally understood in America, just as his book is designed to go against the ingrained belief that the Indians were takers. In this way, he takes the phrase back to a positive usage.

I want to look more closely at this peculiar term and what it has come to imply as a way of opening up the issues with which this chapter is concerned. *Webster's* defines an Indian giver as "one who gives something to another and then takes it back or expects an equivalent in return." The dictionary directs us to the earliest reference to this usage, in 1764 by Thomas Hutchinson, who in a footnote states, "An Indian gift is a proverbial expression, signifying a present for which an equivalent return is expected." The context of the footnote is worth following up. In describing Indian trading practices, Hutchinson comments that

R[oger] Williams compared the Quakers to them. There was no trading with them but for ready pay. He that trusted them lost his debt and his customer. The principle or persuasion that all things ought to be in common might cause hospitality, where the like was expected in return, without any great degree of virtue. Some appearances there were of compassion, gratitude and friendship, and of grief at the death or distress of their children or near relations. Some degree of these social affections is inseparable from human nature.[7]

Two different ideas coexist here. On the one hand, there is the idea of hard calculation and exact equivalence, no credit, no gifts, just narrow economic self-interest. On the other, floating in a provisional or conditional state (the whole sentence seems to revolve around "might"), is the idea of the communal, and of reciprocal and shared obligations of kinship and morality. This second idea is acknowledged grudgingly, and the passage seems to grant Indians only the normal minimal human concern for others, while implying that a communal system could give the *appearance* of more.

The passage reflects the process, exemplified in the phrase "Indian giver" itself, by which the idea of reciprocity is turned into selfishness and calculation, so that according to *Bartlett's Americanisms*, by the nineteenth century "Indian giver" was being used by schoolchildren as a taunt of meanness. It is tempting to see this transformation of complex and culturally different behavior into a demeaning and racist slur as simply and depressingly emblematic of Europeans' reductive treatment of Indians and the values of Indian cultures. This, though, would risk leaving the oppositions implicit in the Hutchinson passage, of generosity and selfishness, and gift and calculation, intact and unexamined, when it is precisely the role of these supposed oppositions in the representation of a wide range of exchanges that needs to be examined. The "Indian gift" as he characterizes it involves a misrecognition. It floats the idea of generosity only to snatch it away, and in this way it relates to the persistent coexistence in early European accounts of America of the idea of love and accord between strangers, and something much more calculating and even deceptive. The moment of giving may mask something else altogether, on either side, and the dynamic of the encounter is closer to that of the confidence trick than to that of gift-giving or trade. According to Greenblatt, the early colonists intermittently also saw their own actions as sharp practice, so we find contradictory views of the same transaction: "Where they might then have imagined mutual gift-giving, or, alternatively, a mutually satisfactory economic transaction, the Europeans instead tended to imagine an exchange of empty signs, of alluring counterfeits, for overwhelming abundance."[8]

As I shall demonstrate, though, it is not so much that market-oriented Europeans were incapable of understanding generosity as that the structure of misrecognitions goes much deeper and involves the idea of giving itself and its complex relation to power and sovereignty. Some sense of the rhetorical importance of linking giving, even more than taking, to sovereignty can be seen in the Europeans' widespread presentation of themselves at the time as the benefactors to the New World, alongside the persistent idea of the New World as a source of plenty to be exploited. This may be viewed simply as hypocrisy, a process of economic and military exploitation screened by the gift of Christianity—the Bible disguising and justifying the sword—but in preferring to deal with this contradiction as paradox and misrecognition, I aim to link it to the idea of misrecognition at the heart of the idea of the gift itself.

Both in contemporary accounts of early Indian-European encounters and in subsequent debates over the idea of the primitive and civilized, perhaps no other idea more persistently haunts the scene or is more potent than the idea of the gift. In approaching the tangled debates that have ensued over this, it might be useful initially to trace and separate out some persistent sets of oppositions.[9] At one level, there is the potent idea of the gift as a single and unilateral event, as opposed to a reciprocal exchange. How the claim of generosity and liberality operates both within and across cultures and the ideological function of this idea in all sorts of cultures need to be examined closely. At another level, there is a quite different distinction between a society in which the exchange of objects and services is organized on a reciprocal and communal basis and called "gift exchange" and one in which individual ownership, acquisition, and profit determine the exchange. This distinction is often reformulated in its starkest terms as the opposition of precapitalist or primitive economies to capitalist/commercial ones, which can be seen played out in the colonialist enterprises of Europe in the New World. As the word *precapitalist* indicates, though, there is also the idea of a historical development, so that synchronic ethnographic comparisons and contrasts are set within a diachronic account of Western development. As Marshall Sahlins has put it, "As witnesses to the colonial confrontation between the two economies, anthropologists have had the opportunity to experience the historic difference as an ethnographic event."[10] This has been one of the powerful attractions of using these other cultures as a way of discussing and analyzing Western society. Their usefulness is that they are not just "other" but also the same and can represent what the West can recognize, or misrecognize, or misremember nostalgically as its past. In some ways, this describes no more than the primitivist project in general,[11] but part of my argument is that to understand the ways in which exchange is represented, we need to be aware of the swirl and play of conflicting and contradictory views *within* the West itself, as it works these out by presenting them through an external contrast. One obvious reason for insisting on this diachronic element is to avoid applying an ahistoric model of acquisitive capitalists versus reciprocal gift exchangers to a diverse range of encounters over several dynamic centuries; another less obvious one is to draw attention to the ways in which the idea of the gift, and all it stands for in the West, itself has a history.

Deeply entangled with the debate over the gift but not identical with it is the debate over economic motivation, and whether we can or need to distinguish between societies in terms of their concepts of economic or other scales of value. Following James Carrier, I find it more useful to see the different forms of exchange as a spectrum within societies, each of which may have its own ideological codings and investments, rather than as hard-and-fast distinctions between societies.[12] This is particularly important in looking at Indian-European contacts in which the European side contained aristocratic as well as nascent market capitalist, and Catholic as well as Protestant, elements, each with different views of exchange and gift, and the Indian side too contained varying degrees of hierarchy and a wide range of productive relations. The reductive view of gift-exchanging, nonacquisitive primitives versus market-oriented Europeans needs therefore to be dismantled from both sides to see how much remains useful.

The simple opposition, from which most accounts of economic exchange start, is between a society of common ownership, with value determined only by usefulness, and a society of individual ownership, with commercial and exchange values. This is part of the larger opposition between simple or primitive societies and advanced or capitalist ones that has been elaborated in different forms since Montaigne. From its earliest manifestations, this debate represented a blend of philosophical speculations on the nature of society, drawing on Plato's commonwealth, myths of the Golden Age, and eventually Sir Thomas More's *Utopia* and Montaigne and Rousseau, and which incorporated evidence, more or less well-founded, from societies in the New World.[13] Concurrent with the idea of men living as beasts, literally from hand to mouth in a state of constant need and without society, there is the persistent image of a harmonious and natural society, in which needs are limited and therefore fulfillable. What we have in this latter scenario is an economy of abundance, not because of riches or overproduction, but because needs are naturally limited to what is freely available. This is not, then, a scarcity economics, simply because it posits a society that has no demands that cannot be met and suggests a sort of natural homeostasis.[14]

English accounts were produced within an already developed intellectual debate growing out of earlier Spanish and Portuguese voyages and the widely distributed and translated accounts of them. This material offered a whole series of vivid but often contradictory images and ideas: naked simplicity (and cannibalism) in the Caribbean and Brazil, but cities of wealth and grandeur in Mexico and Peru that had no rivals in Europe; primitive felicity and innocence, but also despotic regimes supported by human sacrifice and terror. The underlying intellectual debate through which these ideas were circulated in England and elsewhere can be seen as centering round the idea of the noble savage. This involved a philosophical exploration of European society in general, though in England this was also involved with the so-called Black Legend of Spanish brutality, which allowed the English the expression of anti-Catholic and anti-Spanish (or even, in the case of the Jesuits, anti-French) sentiment. When Shakespeare in *The Tempest* has his courtiers, newly wrecked on the island and unsure of what they will find, argue over ideas of the noble savage and primitive communism taken directly from Montaigne, he reflects the way in which a debate already developed in Europe in response to the early representations of the New World returns to be applied and misapplied in actual encounters. His courtiers take their views from prior (mis)representations rather than waiting to see what the inhabitants are actually like. In many early accounts we can sense the presence of the pre-established terms of this debate, as two brief examples illustrate.

Morton's *New English Canaan* of 1637 is in many ways a skittish and unreliable account of Indian life, influenced by the disputes with his Puritan neighbors that led to his forced removal, but his chapter "That the Salvages Live A Contented Life," which rebuts a traveler's reported surprise that the natives of New England "lived so poorly, in so rich a Country," offers a useful angle on an already well-established debate. Morton argues that in terms of availability of the real necessities, the Indians can be said to live richly, since they are not burdened by many possessions and hold most utensils and objects of use in common. Indeed, "Platoes Commonwealth is so much practiced by these people" that all things are divided and distributed.

> According to humane reason guided onely by the light of nature, these people leades the more happy and freer life, being voyde of care, which torments the mindes of so many Christians: They are not delighted in baubles, but in usefull things.

We are presented with what seems like a standard picture of primitive felicity, with objects valued for their usefulness and "superfluous commodities" dismissed. In this particular case, Morton, with a characteristic ambivalent twist, undercuts this ideal picture by imposing an unexpected skeptical and jokey conclusion, but this throwaway tone itself suggests that the arguments he presents, with their invocation of the state of nature, are well established enough to be played with.

> They may be rather accompted to live richly, wanting nothing that is needefull; and to be commended for leading a contented life, the younger being ruled by the Elder, and the Elder ruled by the Powahs, and the Powahs are ruled by the Devill, and then you may imagin what good rule is like to be amongst them.[15]

The uneasy relation here of the Christian framework to the idea of the noble savage is a particularly exposed example of a tension that appears regularly, and is handled with variable success, in accounts of Indian life. We find another standard account in Robert Beverley's report on Virginia, published in 1705. Beverley's is a positive view of primitive "felicity," in which self-sufficiency and harmony operated.

> They claim no property in Lands, but they are in Common to a whole Nation. Everyone Hunts and Fishes. Their Labour . . . is not so great, that they need quarrel for room . . . They bred no Cattle, nor had any thing

that could be call'd Riches. They valued Skins and Furs for use, and Peak
and Roenoke [wampum] for ornament.

Typical here is the absence of baneful aspects of civilized society—private property, competition, money—reminiscent of Montaigne's classic statement in "On Cannibals," itself caricatured in Gonzalo's speech in the *The Tempest*. With the advent of Europeans, though, dissatisfaction has appeared:

> The English have taken away great part of their country, and consequently made everything less plenty amongst them. They have introduc'd Drunkenness and Luxury amongst them, which have multiply'd their Wants, and put them upon desiring a thousand things they never dreamt of before.[16]

Instead of rational exchange, a mutually beneficial trade of useful objects, we have the idea here of the introduction of irrational and unnecessary "Wants" created by the English, which actually have the effect of impoverishing rather than enriching the Indians. The reference to drunkenness and luxury no doubt echoes domestic English values and the perennial warnings about lack of thrift on the part of the poor, but it also has a specific resonance in the recurrent references to the impoverishing of Indians in and through trade. The naked Indian may often be used as an image of simplicity and lack (of either the vices or the virtues, including property, of Europe), but some early accounts also give us the bizarre scene of traders creating nakedness. Jacques Cartier's first encounter involves exchanges that strip the Indians of everything. "They gave us whatsoever they had, not keeping any thing, that they were constrained to go back againe naked."[17] Gordon Sayre, in the course of an analysis that parallels mine at several points, comments on the same incident that "the Native American is first seen not naked but clothed and becomes naked only after an exchange in which he ironically removes his innocence as he removes his clothing . . . It is only after he strips the Indians that Cartier can ascribe to their nakedness a cultural absence, a space for substitution by European culture."[18]

The early colonists, too, report buying animal skins from Indian women, leaving them without clothing. The women

> sold their coats from their backs, and tied boughs about them, but with great shamefacedness, for indeed they are more modest then some of our English women are.[19]

A similar pattern appears in a description from John Josselyn. "They love alcohol dearly," he writes,

> and will part with all they have to their bare skins for it . . . Thus instead of bringing them to the knowledge of Christianitie, we have taught them to commit the beastly and crying sins of our Nation, for a little profit.[20]

We find a similar complaint in a Jesuit account:

> Drink is a demon that robs them of their reason, and so inflames their passion that, after returning from the chase richly laden with beaver skins, instead of furnishing their families with provisions, clothing and necessary supplies, they drink away the entire proceeds in one day and are forced to pass the winter in nakedness, famine and all sorts of deprivation.[21]

In these four concrete instances of literal nakedness, I have pinpointed what we can see as a much more widespread, if less literal, creation of nakedness in the form of a *lack*, created and then catered to by trade. Instead of adding something, such as education, Christianity, or civilization, the effect of contact is to reduce and create a need. The Indians are reduced by trade, and nakedness and the absences and inadequacies it implies here, are shown, as in much later theories of created Third World dependency, to be actually the product of Europe, rather than something natural that it encounters and helps to supplement.[22] (It is also interesting to see an awareness of the creation of nakedness carried out by modern governmental actions in the words of the writer Maria Campbell's grandmother, Cheechum: "When the government gives you something, they take all you have in return—your job, your dignity . . . when they are sure they have everything, they give you a blanket to cover your shame."[23])

In the development of the state of need, alcohol plays a significant role, but one that is often indeterminate in early accounts. Recognized and lamented from the beginning as destructive of Indian independence and self-respect, alcohol is seen as separate or supplementary to other exchanges, but I suggest that, like many other supplements, it is more than just an extra. A graphic illustration of this is found in Baron Lahontan's 1703 account of trade with Indians, in which he lists all the goods that are useful for trade with Indians, such as powder, kettles, and shirts, and then, set off slightly from the rest of the list, we find the phrase "Brandy goes off incomparably well." This is followed by another detailed list of the various furs and their value in French currency.

Brandy is, quite literally, incomparable here, as it stands in a direct, essential, but nonspecified relation to the objects of legitimate trade.[24]

Alcohol was seen by missionaries and many others as a cause of debt and a destroyer of that sense of rationality and frugality they were trying to develop in Indians, and in many ways we can almost see alcohol and debt as structurally related. The growing or infinite need created by alcohol is matched by a system of trade that, once established, guarantees infinite indebtedness through credit and interest. Richard White comments that "except for liquor the wants of most Indians remained inelastic," and he explicitly links alcohol and credit as ways of trying to stimulate a growth in demand. "Traders used credit as well as rum to increase Indian demand, but Indians usually treated credit as a gift."[25] On one very important level, therefore, alcohol can be seen not as an unfortunate excrescence but as a paradigm of the introduction of the market economy itself, in that it creates a new and unsatisfiable demand. Seen in this way, it is similar to drug addiction, as described by a much later American writer, William Burroughs, in representing the tyranny of supply and demand in capitalism. In an interesting phrase, alcohol was described by the interpreter and trader John Long as "the unum necessarium, without which (whatever else had been bestowed on them) I should have incurred great displeasure."[26] It might be objected that Long's account is of a later period, the end of the eighteenth century, when the controls over trade had collapsed, resulting in an unscrupulous free-for-all, but the pattern can be found earlier and elsewhere, and the more or less reluctant consensus emerged that the fur trade could not be successful without a supply of alcohol.

It is worth looking more closely at what made alcohol, in Long's phrase, the *unum necessarium*. The phrase seems to refer to the Biblical episode in which Christ distinguishes between Martha and Mary in terms of their ability to see "the one thing necessary," and I return to it more fully in my discussion of missionary enterprises in chapter 6. Here it may be just a cynical joke, but it does implicitly invoke a distinction between the sort of rational exchange implied in the reward of good works, as expected by Martha, and the unreasonable, excessive, and incalculable exchange involved in grace. Long's joke unexpectedly takes us, therefore, to the heart of the role of alcohol: it acts not just as an unfortunate addition to rational trade but as its dark alter ego, in the way that it reveals the need for excessive rather than rational behavior in the consumer—what Daniel Gookin calls its "exorbitancy."[27] It was not just that Indians wanted alcohol and could be duped when drunk, though this was a problem constantly referred to,[28] but that the demand was unlimited. According to White, for instance, alcohol was the "only commodity that the Choctaws desired not in finite amounts but in virtually infinite amounts." He refers to the traders' insistence on "introducing and maintaining the two great banes of the Indian trade—the credit system and the trade in liquor."[29]

POWERFUL THOUGH I think this analysis of the creation of needy consumers is, it runs the risk of representing the Indians entirely as acted upon rather than acting and choosing, and it is worth examining the idea of the needy or craving Indian as a recurrent theme in white accounts. John Lawson's 1709 account of his voyage to Carolina offers a way into the subject. Overall his view of the Indians is not particularly sympathetic, presenting them as greedy and moneygrubbing, but sometimes, as in the following passage, he is more reflective.

> They are a very craving People, and if a Man give them any thing of a Present, they think it obliges him to give them another; and so on, till he has given them all he has; for they have no Bounds of Satisfaction in that way; and if they give you any thing it is to receive twice the Value of it. They have no Consideration that you will want what you give them; for their way of Living is so contrary to ours, that neither we nor they can fathom one anothers Designs and Methods. They call Rum and Physick by one name, which implies that Rum makes People sick, as when they have taken any poisonous Plant; yet they cannot forebear Rum. They make Offerings of their First-Fruits, and the more serious sort of them throw into the Ashes, near the Fire, the first Bit or Spoonful of every meal they sit down to.

This passage seems to reflect genuine puzzlement. Having interpreted their craving as greed, Lawson almost comes round to hinting at a completely different attitude toward property itself with the references to waste or sacrifice of food. The reference to rum, which seems initially out of place except as illustrating their peculiarity of language, can also be seen as connected to the idea running through his observations of consumption itself. These craving people can also throw food away. These addicts to alcohol also call it poison. What makes them tick? The connection between rum and trade is made clear earlier. It is "so

much in Use with them that they will part with the dearest Thing they
have, to purchase it; and when they have got a little in their heads are
the impatientest Creatures living 'till they have enough to make 'em
quite drunk." Once the Indians are drunk, their behavior is dangerous
and self-destructive. Lawson's account is unclear, as it proceeds, about
the relation of this craving, immoderate behavior to the influence of
Europeans, in that he has direct knowledge only of those so influenced,
and must imagine what they were like before, but in his final summary
he is clear about the effect. Basically, "they are really better to us than
we are to them," in their general hospitality and generosity.

> We trade with them, it's true, but to what End? Not to show them the steps
> of Vertue, and the golden rule, to do as we would be done by. No, we have
> furnished them with the Vice of Drunkenness, which is the open Road to
> all others, and daily cheat them in everything we sell, and esteem it as a
> Gift of Christianity, not to sell to them so cheap as we do to the Christians,
> as we call ourselves.

All the terms here are about a failure of reciprocity—trade as exploitation and deception rather than exchange, gifts (alcohol, civility, and
religion) that are not gifts—and the cumulative effect is damning. His
solution continues the theme. If we "allow these savages what really
belongs to them, that is, what good Qualities and natural endowments
they possess" we can marry our strengths to theirs—quite literally by
encouraging intermarriage. This will convert more Indians than the
present means, which he describes powerfully as "a Field of Blood
and defraud."[30]

Examples of Indians represented as a "begging and insatiable set of
People"[31] could be multiplied over the centuries. At its crudest, the
image presents the craving Indian as the pathetic product of dependency, the personification of the creation of needs and demand.
Whether satisfied by charity or commerce, there is a gap to be filled,
corresponding to the trope of the poor or naked Indian. White points
out that this idea of dependency even now "looms over recent studies
of the fur trade," but he usefully analyzes the terms in which the Algonquians expressed their needs and how this related to the establishment
of social relations rather than the filling of a physical lack.

> *Besoin*, as used by the Algonquians, was not simply a statement of desire;
> the term had a particular resonance in their society because, once an appro-
> priate social relationship had been established, an assertion of need for

something could become a special claim on the thing needed. To be needy is to excite pity and thus to deserve aid. Just as in addressing manitous Algonquins sought to portray themselves as weak and miserable, so in addressing Onontio, Jesuits or traders, they usually stressed their own misery and need. The Algonquians' emphasis on exchange as a way of satisfying their *besoins*, therefore, had a meaning quite different from that expressed in the French view of commerce as a way of filling needs.[32]

Mary Black-Rogers, in a study of the later fur trade, outlines a relevant semantic field.[33] Her concern is partly with how the traders' use of the word reflects views of Indians as producers. (When they are producing only to eat, they are not producing furs. The ideal, then, is to have them needy but still above the level at which they are consuming the products they could otherwise trade.) She also describes Indian behavior in which they regularly claim to be starving and are mistrusted by whites, who see them as lying and begging, and suggests that the situation needs to be seen as more complex. In a culture in which supernatural forces are in a relation of donors to human beings and kinship relations of obligation and mutual reliance are widespread, a stance of powerlessness or neediness may have a significance different from that which it has in a society that stresses independence. Furthermore, as she shows, the terms that were often translated as pity, as in a request to have pity, which sounds like abject begging, may actually mean something closer to the bestowing of blessing. She quotes a trader who says "on his beging Me to take pitty on Him I gave him the usual Presents" and comments, "This trader got the message, whether or not he was aware of the Indian religious context—although he might have missed a more subtle point: that it could have been more a move to establish or reinforce a relationship than a request for immediate gifts."[34] Even more suggestively, she gives instances suggesting that the pose of starving and craving may sometimes have had more of the power of a greeting, even sometimes with a humorous element.[35] What all this suggests is the complexity of the craving Indian, who can range from abject and desperate to calculating and self-possessed and even to an ironic imitation of white expectations.

In an intriguing analysis of a much later encounter, Michael Taussig takes this question of ironic reversal much further. On the visit of *The Beagle* to the inhabitants of Tierra del Fuego in the nineteenth century, Charles Darwin records being worn down by the constant and clamorous din of "Yammerschooner."

Yammerschoonering, he said, meant 'Give me!'—but it is obvious from the record that 'give me' was a complex composite that did not fall neatly into British political economy, formal or informal. A composite of trade and gift, sometimes to be reciprocated, at other times not, it was all interwoven with a terrible insistence that the sailors came to define as outright theft.

As Taussig points out, though, any objects acquired were, according to Darwin, divided among the people, even if this meant tearing up garments, so that we have to see this desire to acquire as intimately related to the desire to redistribute.[36]

As REFLECTED in these various accounts, the story of the encounter of the two systems is largely figured as one of inevitable seduction, in which the primitive economy is gradually brought into a market by trade and the creation of needs, but the fundamental question of just how different societies based on gift exchange and reciprocity actually *were* from capitalist societies, based on individual ownership, contract, and money, has played an important part in the development of economic and political as well as anthropological theory.[37] The use of the gift as a key to understanding a whole complex of reciprocal relations beyond what the West would see as economic is now generally attributed to Marcel Mauss and his short but immensely influential study of 1925, *The Gift*, but this is only one of a range of texts that were demonstrating the importance of society rather than the individual, of structure rather than event, and included the work of Emile Durkheim and Bronislav Malinowski. Where Mauss has remained influential, though, is in his view of the gift in its social totality. Even within the range of primitive economies, some commentators have distinguished between Malinowski's interpretation of gift exchange, which saw the participants as what James Carrier describes as "independent calculating transactors,"[38] and Mauss's view of socially rather than individually defined values based on kin obligations and reciprocal relations. This broad distinction reflects a methodological distinction between what have come to be called formalist and substantivist approaches, the former applying a single model of economically self-interested behavior across all cultures and the latter insisting on the need for different models for different cultures. This cannot simply be reduced to neoclassical economics as a universal system versus a relativism of diverse native economic systems, and certainly not to any simple opposition of selfishness and generosity as bases of different societies. Nevertheless, the persistence of the old idea of the noble savage, combined with a renewed soul searching about civilization and its limitations, has meant that the models and alternatives apparently offered by anthropology have been given a moral dimension as a part of a larger debate about the survival of primitive cultures, and the issue of economic exchange is a key part of this. Probably the most influential writer to take up Mauss's model to develop a substantivist approach is Sahlins, who, in his *Stone Age Economics*, argues the need to see economy as "a category of culture rather than behaviour . . . not the need-serving activities of individuals, but the material life process of society."[39] Sahlins's book is a clear critique of formalist aproaches, but he is also clear about the limitations of substantivism.[40] His keen analyses of the operations of power and control and the limitations of the claims for reciprocity as a superior political model are worth following up, as they allow us to link this debate over primitive economy with the ideas of generosity and liberality as they operate in our own culture as well as cross-culturally.

Sahlins begins with the importance of a noncentralized system of production, what he calls the "domestic mode of production," and its political implications. It operates through localized and reciprocal exchanges, often seen as gifts. "Nothing within this infrastructure of production obliges the several household groups to enter into compact and cede each one some part of its autonomy. As the domestic economy is in effect the tribal economy in miniature, so politically it underwrites the condition of primitive society—society without a Sovereign." Sahlins is aware, of course, of the dangers of too simple an opposition, and in particular of accepting the claims for reciprocity at face value. Such a model of dispersed power runs up against the presence of chiefs and conventions of rank or status. This can be explained in terms of the network of distribution operating through kinship patterns: as Sahlins puts it, "Insofar as the society is socially committed to kin relationships, morally it is committed to generosity: whoever, therefore, is liberal automatically merits the general esteem." But if chiefs control the giving, their generosity is also "a manifest imposition of debt, putting the recipient in a circumspect and responsive relation to the donor." The gift is therefore always in potential conflict with the idea of reciprocity, in that the relation can hardly be reciprocal and generous at the same time and the exchange "at once equivalent and more so." Thus "the ideals of reciprocity and chiefly liberality serve as mystification of the people's dependence." Sahlins is clearly using the language of Marxist sociology here, in insisting on the mystifying power of ideology in masking rather than resolving contradictions: "The ideological ambiguity is functional. On the one hand, the ethic of chiefly generosity blesses the inequality; on the other, the ideal of reciprocity denies that it makes any difference." The implications are that "the conjunction of a norm of reciprocity with a reality of exploitation would not distinguish the primitive political economy from any other: everywhere in the world the indigenous category for exploitation is 'reciprocity.'"[41]

Where the primitive system differs from other and later systems is in its lack of state or centralized authority. Because of the noncentralized nature of gift exchange (where there is no single unit or term of equivalence), the gift

> would not organize society in a corporate sense, only in a segmentary sense. Reciprocity is a 'between' relation. It does not dissolve the separate parties within a higher unity, but on the contrary, in correlating their opposition, perpetuates it. Neither does the gift specify a third party standing over and above the separate interests of those who contract.[42]

I have quoted at length from Sahlins because he presents a detailed case for the importance and fundamental distinctiveness of the domestic mode of production, together with a keen awareness of the political implications. His skepticism about the native categories of liberality, his readiness to think in terms of false consciousness, and his privileging of use over exchange value stem from a larger Marxist-derived view to which we will return, but before we leave the general idea of the gift, it is important to indicate one other direction that discussion of it has taken. Certainly, the most influential development of Mauss's work has been to support the idea of society as a self-sustaining equilibrium in which structures and the circulation of objects and signs are the privileged means of explanation. This functionalist/structuralist model depends on the erasure of the single instance of the gift in favor of the gift exchange (i.e., structure over event), but the scandalous and excessive idea of something not reciprocated, an economy based not on equilibrium but on excess or waste, has also persisted and has recently been readdressed in ways that are relevant to my overall theme.

Put crudely, even when we have pointed out the ideological work being done by the gift, and the way it underpins temporal and political power, we still have the question of accounting for its particular power. Why do people respond to excess, waste, and sacrifice? The idea that there is a persistent and important role for an economy of excess and sacrifice is explored, using Mauss, most notably in the "heretical" work of Georges Bataille and is further developed in the work of Derrida.[43] Julian Pefanis points to the importance of these rival readings of Mauss:

> On the one side the structuralists have inferred a reciprocating, perhaps ultimately economic structure in the relations of the gift exchange . . . But on the other side of the split there is a more radical, and certainly more marginal interpretation. If the kula represents the model of the reciprocating exchange of symbols, then the potlatch is a model motivated by the unreturnable, unilateral gift, the gift of excess, a principle of agonism and the ritual *transgression* of prohibitions.[44]

Pefanis indicates here a line that stresses expenditure over exchange and leads through Bataille to Jean Baudrillard, as well as to Derrida, whose discussion of Mauss singles out the same opposition. For Derrida, Mauss pays insufficient attention to the way the gift is canceled out by exchange and ironically cannot therefore be discussed in the context of gift exchange. But even the awareness of it as gift implies the requirement of a return, so that it becomes almost a logical impossibility. "If the gift is annulled in the economic odyssey of the circle as soon as it signifies *itself as* gift," says Derrida, "there is no longer any 'logic of the gift,' and one may safely say that a consistent discourse on the gift becomes impossible; it misses its object and always speaks finally of something else."[45]

The problem, then, is not just reconciling or steering between substantivist and formalist debates but dealing with any system in a way that recognizes both the impossibility of the gift (because of the inevitable requirement of the countergift) and the reality or efficacy of belief in it within everyday practice. In one view, the gift simply disappears into the circle of social reciprocation. In the other, it is a moment of excess that appears to be disruptive rather than constitutive of social structures of reciprocity. The work of Pierre Bourdieu, who has informed a good deal of my general approach in his refusal of the usual distinctions between economic and noneconomic practices, for instance, in the idea of cultural and social as well as financial capital, is of particular relevance here, in stressing the importance of the element of time. As Bourdieu points out, a formal or structural analysis of the operations of gift and countergift closes out, in its objective model, the temporal gap between gift and countergift that allows the idea of liberality and all its concomitant associations to operate. An approach that "retrospectively projects the countergift into the project of the gift" cancels out that gap and its subjective improvisatory possibilities.

> In the same operation, it removes the conditions making possible the *institutionally organized and guaranteed misrecognition* which is the basis of gift exchange and, perhaps, of all the symbolic labour intended to transmute, by the sincere fiction of a disinterested exchange, the inevitable, and inevitably interested relations imposed by kinship, neighbourhood, or work, into elective relations of reciprocity.

The strength of Bourdieu's approach is that it is able to give due weight to the lived temporal experience of the gift without letting go of the larger structural analysis, and his warning of the pitfalls of an either-or approach is particularly relevant to the field of early Indian-white relations.

> In short, contrary to naively idyllic representations of "pre-capitalist" societies (or of the "cultural" sphere of capitalist societies), practice never ceases to conform to economic calculation even when it gives every appearance of disinterestedness by departing from the logic of interested calculation (in the narrow sense) and playing for stakes that are non-material and not easily quantified ... The only way to escape from the ethnocentric naiveties of economism, without falling into populist exaltation of the generous naivety of earlier forms of society, is to carry out in full what economism does only partially, and to extend economic calculation to *all* the goods, material and symbolic, without distinction, that present themselves as *rare* and worthy of being sought after in a particular social formation.[46]

These can range from gestures and compliments to positions of political power or the possession of knowledge, but the key thing is to recognize the "perfect interconvertibility" of economic and symbolic capital. In the interaction of different cultures, we can therefore say that all exchange, whatever else it may be, is symbolic exchange, taking place within and across multiple interlocking and sometimes conflicting value systems.

This, then, is the approach I apply to a rather disparate set of materials in other chapters, but it is important to stress here that in taking over Bourdieu's approach I do not intend to flatten out the distinctions between different sorts of societies or dismiss the importance of these perceived differences in Western intellectual debate, as it is not just at the level of "populist exaltation" of primitive generosity that such ideas have had an impact. In European accounts of Indians, we find on the one hand the enduring idea of generosity, cultures without market calculation, and on the other the idea of calculation, even coercion, that the phrase "Indian gift" reflects. (Whether Europeans themselves ever practiced the free as opposed to "Indian" gift in their dealings with Indians is quite another matter again.) The complex misrecognitions involved in Europeans' interpretation of Indian behavior can be explored in one description from the Jesuit missionary Paul Le Jeune, whose scattered comments on Indian giving in his account in the *Jesuit Relations* of 1634 are intriguing. Le Jeune observes that

> when you refuse anything to a Savage, he immediately says Khisakhitan, 'thou lovest that', sakhita, sakhita, 'Love it, Love it', as if they would say that we are attached to what we love, and that we prefer it to their friendship. (*JR* 5:171)

In a later entry he expands on this point, using the same incident:

> They are very generous among themselves and even make a show of not loving things, of not being attached to the riches of the earth, so that they may not grieve if they lose them . . . One of the greatest insults that can be offered to them is to say, 'That man likes everything, he is stingy'. If you refuse them anything here is their reproach, as I remarked last year, Khisakhitan Sakhita. 'Thou lovest that, love it as much as thou wilt'. They do not open the hand halfway when they give—I mean among themselves, for they are as ungrateful as possible towards strangers. (*JR* 6:237–9)

Le Jeune does make the crucial distinction here between reciprocal, kin-based exchange and distribution ("among themselves") and the refusal of that to strangers, but he frames it in moral terms of generosity and meanness, which cut across the distinction. Since the French are not really prepared to share everything, the Indians treat them as strangers, but Le Jeune seems unable to accept the reasonableness of that attitude.

> They are very grateful, very liberal and not in the least importunate to those of their own nation. If they conduct themselves thus toward our French, and towards other foreigners, it is because, it seems to me, that we

> do not wish to ally ourselves with them as brothers, which they would very
> much desire. But this would ruin us in three days.

Continuing a metaphor in which he had earlier described the importunate Indians as like troublesome mosquitoes, he warns, "If you carry on your affairs apart from them, despising their laws or their customs, they will drain from you, if they can, even your blood" (*JR* 6:259–61). This inability to understand the logic of the Indians' behavior allows him to make a much bigger generalization:

> A certain man said to me one day, that in his country they did not know how to conjugate the verb *do*, in the present, and still less in the past. The savages are so ignorant of this conjugation that they would not give you the value of an obole if they did not expect, so to speak, to get back a pistole; for they are ungrateful in the highest degree. (*JR* 6:257)

Assuming that the "certain man" is Indian and that *do* is the Latin verb form for 'I give', Latin is being used here by Le Jeune as a sort of lingua franca, and in the Montagnais he is presenting the idea of a society lacking not so much the word as the concept of unilateral giving. The linguistic lack is metaphorical of an actual lack (which raises the interesting prospect of Le Jeune as a proto-Whorfian). Nothing is offered unless it will bring a larger return (pistoles and oboles being French coins). What has disappeared from this generalized picture is the distinction between kin and stranger, inside and outside, made in his earlier comments, but at one level Le Jeune could be said to be correct, in that the idea of the free gift would be irrelevant. One further puzzle is his odd comment that the Indians particularly lack an understanding of the past tense of the verb *to give* ("au present, encore moins au preterit"). This suggests that he is *not* therefore really talking about the gift but about the countergift, the obligation to return, and particularly to strangers, in this case the Jesuits. In other words, Le Jeune is actually demonstrating that he himself does not understand the idea of gift other than as Indian gift, and what he is really complaining about is that the Indians fail to reciprocate. He seems at one moment to recognize the importance of kinship, and the distinction between kin and stranger, in terms of reciprocal relation, but he does not seem to understand that, having refused to enter into a kin or reciprocal relation with the Indians, the Jesuits can hardly expect to share in the distribution and circulation of goods. I have read this comment closely in order to suggest a fundamental contradiction in the European view of the gift, but it also reveals ways in which the distinction between kin and stranger could be misunderstood. In preaching a universal free gift, modeled on Christian love and sacrifice, missionaries thought they were cutting across the distinction. This message combined with a supply of gifts with no apparent demand for return may well have made it difficult for the Indians to read their behavior, and, ironically, contrary to Le Jeune, to believe that the Christians really were practicing the free gift.

One word that is puzzling in Le Jeune's account is "ungrateful" (*ingrats*) rather than "ungenerous."[47] The word "grateful" appears in my previous quotation from him, again in a surprising usage, and a little earlier we find it related to a failure on the part of the Indians to thank their gods in the appropriate way:

> What astonishes me is their ingratitude; for although they believe that the Messou has restored the world, that Nipinakhe and Pipinoukhe bring their seasons, that their Khichikouai teach them where to find Elks and Moose, and render them a thousand good offices—yet up to the present, I have not been able to learn that they render them the slightest honor. I have only observed that in their feasts, they occasionally throw a few spoonfuls of grease into the fire, pronouncing these words—'Make us find something to eat'—I believe this prayer is addressed to these Genii, to whom they present this grease as the best thing in the world. (*JR* 6:173)

The second part of this passage clearly suggests a symbolic giving of thanks, an offering back, through the animal fat, to the gods, but Le Jeune chooses to disparage this by seeing it not symbolically but quantitatively ("a few spoonfuls"). In this way he is able to misrepresent an act that seems to have all the classic ingredients of sacrificial or thanks offering, in order to disparage both their religion and their economic behavior.[48]

Le Jeune's comments could be said to reflect a deep-seated confusion between gift exchange and gift-giving. At one level, a society that uses the exchange of gifts to demonstrate social relationships of reciprocity could be said *never* to give a gift, if by "gift" we mean an isolated unilateral act for which a return is not required or expected. It is possible therefore to argue, following Jonathan Parry, that it is only with the creation of the market, and the idea of free individuals who are *not* in a relation of reciprocal obligation, that the idea of the gift can be elaborated.

> Those who make free and unconstrained contracts in the market also make free and unconstrained gifts outside it. But these gifts are defined as what market relations are not—altruistic, moral and loaded with emotion. As the economy becomes increasingly disembedded from society, as economic relations become increasingly differentiated from other types of social relationship, the transactions appropriate to each become ever more polarised in terms of their symbolism and ideology . . . I am suggesting then, that an elaborated ideology of the "pure" gift is most likely to develop in state societies with an advanced division of labour and a significant commercial sector. But what is also in my view essential to its articulation is a specific type of belief system, as is suggested by the fact that in all of the major world religions great stress is laid on the merit of gifts and alms, ideally given in secrecy and without expectations of any worldly return.[49]

Parry's argument has important ramifications across the whole range of cultural exchanges I discuss here, especially in its linking of religious and economic sensibilities. Though it does not deal exclusively with Indian giving, his overall argument provides a useful way of explaining the ambivalent and contradictory responses of Europeans, which are reflected in the phrase "Indian giver." In his view, Europeans would be right to recognize that there are no free lunches (or Thanksgiving dinners) from the Indians but would be wrong to be surprised and to expect Indians to share their ideological valorization of the free gift.

So FAR I have concentrated on giving and how to read its social significance, rather than the nature of what is being given, but since one of my major concerns in this book is the transformations of meaning and value that take place in and through exchange, it is important also to sketch here some of the issues raised by the objects of exchange themselves. This also provides another way of considering the oppositions of primitive and market economies. One way in which this opposition is reflected is in the choice between the terms used to describe the objects, namely, "goods" and "commodities." C. A. Gregory has distinguished between the neoclassical assumption of a standard economic behavior, which involves a predisposition to describe everything as "goods" and explain all behavior in the same economic terms, and a Marxist approach, which holds onto some distinctions embodied in the term "commodities." He argues that the concept of goods is "subjectivist and universal which means that the theory of goods, by definition, has no objective empirical basis for distinguishing between different economic systems. The concept 'commodity', on the other hand, presupposes . . . certain objective historical and social pre-conditions."[50]

Gregory draws on Marx's definitions to emphasize the differences between commodity and noncommodity societies and the circulation of items of value within them. Commodity exchange is "an exchange of alienable things between transactors who are in a state of reciprocal in-dependence," whereas noncommodity or gift exchange is "an exchange of inalienable things between transactors who are in a state of recipro-cal dependence." He has no difficulty relating Mauss's work on the gift to Marx, since he sees it as a logical extension. In seeing precapitalist economic structures as based on the kinship systems first explored by Lewis Henry Morgan (and built on by Marx and Engels), Mauss was able to show, acording to Gregory, that "commodity exchange estab-lishes a relationship between the objects exchanged, whereas gift ex-change establishes a relationship between the subjects. In other words commodity exchange is a price-forming process, a system of purchase and sale. Gift exchange is not."[51] Marilyn Strathern, using Gregory, also builds on this distinction between commodity and gift. Commodity ex-change "establishes a relation between the objects exchanged, whereas gift exchange establishes a relation between the exchanging subjects. In a commodity oriented economy, people thus experience their interest in commodities as a desire to appropriate goods; in a gift oriented econ-omy, the desire is to expand social relations."[52]

At the heart of Gregory's approach lies a traditional set of distinc-tions between use value and exchange value. In the classic formulations of this distinction, notably in Marx, use value functions as a privileged instance of nonalienated labor, whereas exchange value enables the pro-duction of objects that take their value as commodities from what they can be exchanged for. In this second condition there is no fixed point of value; all is relational, though the medium of exchange (money in its different forms) takes on the appearance of absolute value. Sahlins of-fers a refinement of this idea of use value. As he points out, because use was originally defined too narrowly as personal use, the idea seems to lose its relevance once it is clear that households are not self-sufficient but involved in exchange patterns. Nevertheless, the exchange, he insists, is for what the households need, and "the exchange, and the production for it, are oriented to livelihood, not to profits." He modifies the term from "production for use" to "production for use value, even through the acts of exchange, and as opposed to the quest for exchange value."[53] Here he holds onto Marx's distinction between production as a means to the end of human use and production as an end in itself, taking its value from a self-sustaining system of exchange in which human uses or values may be secondary.

The idea of use value is often traced back to Aristotle's argument in his *Politics* that every article has a potential double use, but only one is the "proper" one. Thus a shoe can be used for wearing or for exchange, but if a product designed for use becomes an object of exchange, it runs the risk of losing contact with its "proper" value and acquiring a value that is purely relational; that is, it becomes purely a medium of exchange. The next danger is that this relational value has nothing to ground it and the product begins to accrue value that is not intrinsic to it and even, as in the case of the charging of interest, multiplies in an "unnatural" way. In addition, the medium of exchange can impose a single standard of equivalence that seems to stem from the value actually in the medium. Currency can seem to have a value of its own rather than being purely an indication of value created in people's social and productive relations. As Baudrillard puts it, in Marxist theory, use value is always concrete and particular, whereas exchange value is abstract and general.

> Even if it is continually reclaimed by the process of production and exchange, use value is never truly inscribed in the field of market economy ... And within it is contained, from this standpoint the promise of a resurgence beyond the market economy, money and exchange value, in the glorious autonomy of man's simple relation to his work and his products.

Baudrillard's critique of Marx carries out a characteristic deconstructive operation of questioning the privileged status of whatever seems to be the unquestioned basis of value, the center or source that is believed to be outside the play of differences. In linguistics, questioning the privileged term led to questioning the primacy of the signified and a consequent interest in the way meaning is generated across signifiers rather than in what signifiers refer to. In a parallel operation, Baudrillard critiques the way that Marx holds onto use and labor as fixed points. This involves arguing that "use value and needs are only the effect of exchange value" rather than having a prior existence. This links Marx back to Aristotle's concern to ensure that there was always a proper use that could be contrasted with the shifting and uncertain activities of exchange.[54] It also returns us, through Aristotle, to my initial concern for metaphor, because what all these discussions of value have in common is a structure in which a proper meaning, a solid and guaranteed value, is posited, against and around which exchange can take place. In language, it is the idea of a language without metaphor, in metaphor, it is the tenor; and in economics, it is use value. Trade, money, and even writing can be seen as challenges to this proper grounded value, and even Sahlins's sophisticated account can be construed as looking for a way of avoiding the free-floating values of commodity and exchange. One reason why it is important to be clear of this investment in a fixed point of value is that the idea of a society based on a "proper" and fixed scale of value has been a constant resource in critiques of our own society, and Indian communities have been invoked as the example.

In concentrating on moments of exchange *between* cultures, we need to be aware of the danger of taking over a widespread narrative of the triumph of exchange over use value, presented as a fall from innocence or grounded values. We need to be aware of the full economies of value (which includes the discursive, religious, and cultural) on both sides as well as the new systems of value that may be emerging from the exchanges themselves, and to do so we must interrogate even the most apparently straightforward exchange, in which the scheme of value seems self-evident. Barter, for instance, is often presented as the simplest of exchanges. In many ways it is like commodity exchange, in that it seems to operate without social ties or implications, but it also precludes the idea of an explicit unit of exchange, a *numeraire* that would reduce the objects to a standard scale of value. Devoid of cultural ties and the mediating presence of money, barter is a parole without a langue, an event without a system, an idea expressed in one of the abiding images of barter: the so-called silent trade, in which each group merely leaves the object it wishes to exchange and there is no process of agreeing on a common scale of value, which brings the event close to a gift exchange but without the establishment of any relationship. (I suppose that in the Puritans' first dealings with the Indians, described at the beginning of this chapter, the absence of contact could charitably be described as one half of the silent trade, except that the Puritans left nothing in exchange—only a mental note to make a return when and if they met the Indians.) Nicholas Thomas describes the idea of barter, as used by commentators, as "a kind of origin myth":

> But what is most *telling* about the image of barter is that it does *not* speak: it is a spectacle or silent film in which we see things change hands. We have no sense of what is said or thought, and the image fades before we discover what becomes of the things, what people make of them subsequently. The objects' properties and uses thus appear to be self-evident, while participants' motives are either transparent or irrelevant.[55]

Marx, though, saw barter, with its incursion of new elements of exchange into a system of use values, as a threat, arguing that commodity exchange begins not within primitive communities, but "on their margins, on their borders, the few points where they come into contact with other communities. This is where barter begins and moves thence into the interior of the community, exerting a disintegrating influence upon it."[56] Barter might seem to be the prime occasion where common rules cannot operate, but, as Arjun Appadurai reminds us, "Wherever evidence is available, the determination of what may be bartered, where, when and by whom, as well as of what drives the demand for the goods of the 'other,' is a social affair." Rather than seeing the points of contact as lacking in sociality and rules, and therefore as minimal, it is important to look more closely at precisely these transitional points, to see objects moving in and out of barely discernible systems of meaning. And rather than trying to see whole opposed cultures, run on gift or commodity lines, it may be more useful to follow Appadurai's suggestion and see a commodity more locally as an object in a particular situation, which he defines as "the situation in which its exchangeability (past, present or future) for some other thing, is its socially relevant feature."[57] This moves away from production to the actual process of exchange and allows us to take into account the many changes that can take place in the use of the same object as it moves across cultures or the cultures change around it. As Bruce White has argued in relation to Ojibwa and Dakota use of French merchandise, "Every object has a cultural trajectory, passing successively, and sometimes simultaneously through a variety of cultural contexts."[58] Any particular exchange or transaction could then have elements of gift, commodity, or barter, and any object could be any or all of these at different times. What we would need to know in order to determine which it is, would be the set(s) of cultural rules in operation.

One recurrent theme in early accounts of the reception of Western objects is that Indians treated them as mysterious and therefore magical. This fitted into the larger pattern of credulous savages and commonsensical Europeans, of course, but rather than dismiss the idea of magical powers ascribed to objects I want to take it more seriously, in order to open up the irrational power attributed to commodities in a market economy. Europeans may have seen the commodities of trade as neutral and been amused by the Indians' wonder, but in fact these objects as commodities were already invested with social meaning, and to get a full sense of this we need to remember Marx's description of commodity fetishism. For Marx, a commodity is

> a mysterious thing, simply because in it the social character of men's labour appears to them as an objective character stamped upon the product of that labour . . . This is the reason why the products of labour become commodities, social things, whose qualities are at the same time perceptible and imperceptible by the senses.

The value that is ascribed to these objects is entirely the effect of social relations between persons, but it takes on

> the fantastic form of a relation between things. In order, therefore, to find an analogy, we must have recourse to the mist-enveloped regions of the religious world. In that world the productions of the human brain appear as independent beings endowed with life and entering into relation both with one another and the human race. So it is in the world of commodities with the products of men's hands. This I call the Fetishism which attaches itself to the products of labour, so soon as they are produced as commodities.[59]

It is only by comparing it with religion that Marx is able to throw into relief those aspects of the commodity that have been obscured by being naturalized. Similarly, it is only by contrasting our system, what he calls "this enchanted and perverted world,"[60] with a quite different one that its true nature is revealed.

> The whole mystery of commodities, all the magic and necromancy that surrounds the products of labour as long as they take the form of commodities, vanishes therefore, so soon as we come to other forms of production.[61]

It is a brilliant touch to reveal the magical nature of the West's valuation of commodities by juxtaposing them with the supposed superstition and irrationalism of primitive cultures. It is also significant that both the idea of the fetish and its development in such a way that Marx was able to adapt it were products of trade, specifically, trading relations between the Portuguese and Africans, the word stemming from the Portuguese. William Pietz describes the "intercultural spaces along the West African coast" in which Christian feudal, traditional African, and merchant capitalist mixed and it was possible "to translate and trans-value objects between radically different social systems."

> It was within this situation that there emerged a new problematic concerning the capacity of material objects to embody—simultaneously and sequentially—religious, commercial, aesthetic and sexual values. My argument, then, is that the fetish could originate only in conjunction with the emergent articulation of the commodity form that defined itself within and against the social values and religious ideologies of two radically different kinds of non-capitalist society, as they encountered each other in an ongoing cross-cultural situation.[62]

My argument is that precisely this opportunity for intercultural translation and transvaluation existed intermittently in North America and, for this reason, we need to be aware of the slipperiness of terms of value. Crucial to Marx's argument is the insistence that the value of commodities in capitalist societies is not a natural property but an ascription of value just as arbitrary and irrational as the ascription of magical properties to simple objects treated as fetishes in primitive societies. Some of this, at least, seems to have been evident to the Montagnais chief described by the Jesuit Le Jeune in his relation for 1634:

> The savages say that it [the beaver] is the animal well-beloved by the French, English and Basques—in a word, by the Europeans. I heard my host [a Montagnais chief] say one day jokingly, *Missi picoutau amiscou*, 'The beaver does everything perfectly well, it makes kettles, hatchets, swords, knives, bread; and in short it makes everything.' He was making sport of us Europeans who have such a fondness for the skin of the animal and who fight to see who will give the most to these Barbarians, to get it; they carry this to such an extent that my host said to me one day, showing me a very beautiful knife, "The English have no sense; they give us twenty knives like this for one Beaver skin." (*JR* 6:297-9)[63]

This passage has attracted a great deal of commentary, because it seems to offer evidence of an alternative and noneconomic view on the part of the Indians. This has been most contentiously argued, perhaps, by Calvin Martin, but as Ronald Trosper has suggested, Martin's acount of Indian behavior as noneconomic can actually be countered in standard economic terms. He comments approvingly that the Montagnais "described the virtues of trade and expressed his point precisely, using an economist's main variable: price."[64] For Trosper, the fact that one is a barter economy and the other has money is less important than the fact that they have agreed on one commodity as *numeraire*, or unit of account, but what he seems to ignore is the joke that the Indian can still see at this point, namely, that a medium of exchange, which the beaver seems to have become here, cannot by itself "make" anything. Only human labor can do this, and the Montagnais leader's comment fits closely with Marx's description of the role of money in capitalist society:

> Money, since it has the property of purchasing everything, of appropriating objects to itself, is therefore the object par excellence. The universal character of this property corresponds to the omnipotence of money, which is regarded as an omnipotent essence . . . money is the pander between need and object . . . but that which mediates my life, mediates also the existence of other men for me.[65]

Is the second part of the Montagnais leader's joke quite the same? He ridicules the Europeans for a false valuation of knife as against beaver, much as Europeans talked of the Indians' love of trifles and trinkets, and this could be seen as indicating his involvement not only in trade but in the logic of equivalence it established. The scene acquires poignancy when we recall the widespread awareness on the part of Europeans of the power of wampum as "the source and mother of the beaver trade" (an idea I develop in chapter 5), which would give them access to beaver because of the high regard in which Indians held it. Here we have the same ascription of energy and life to a commodity, but the joke seems to be on the Indians as well.

This raises the issue of how we compare the ascription of value to objects in different cultures. The relevance of Marx's use of the idea of fetishism is that it deliberately brings into a complex relation the realms of primitive religion and Western commerce, and he notes an instance similar in theme to the Montagnais incident: "The savages of Cuba considered gold to be the fetish of the Spaniards. So they celebrated it with a feast, danced and sang around it, and threw it into the sea to be rid of it."[66] In this apocryphal event it is not clear whether gold is seen as fetish in the savage or capitalist sense. One way of looking at it is that the Native Americans interpreted the well-documented Spanish fascination for gold as like their worship of an object having religious power—a fetish.[67] The Spanish view would be that the Indians got it wrong—they were not worshipping it for magical properties but collecting it for its economic value. It is precisely Marx's point that the two are not so very different. Michael Taussig's treatment of the responses of two modern South American peasant cultures to capitalism offers a thoroughgoing attempt to take seriously the implications of this idea of the magic of commodities. Taussig argues that "when the commodity system encroaches on a pre-capitalist social formation, the two forms of fetishism, the magic of reciprocity exchange and the magic of commodity exchange, impinge on one another and coalesce into a new form." He traces in some detail the transitional responses in which, "until the new 'rules of the game' are assimilated, the fabulations that the commodity engenders will be subject to quite different sorts of fantasy formation." He examines the development and use of the idea of the devil in a Latin American context, and in my later chapters dealing with missionaries in North America I look at some of the similar ways in which ideas and values change as they move across cultures and at the relation between the two sorts of magic Taussig identifies, tracing them back through some early conceptualizations of the idea of fetishism.

Taussig suggests that the magical properties associated with objects as they are exchanged are different from commodity fetishism, in that they are recognized as magic, whereas the insidious thing about commodity fetishism is that it presents as the natural, normal, and separate object what is in fact the product of a social relation. He refers to

the schizoid attitude with which the members of [a commodity-based] society necessarily confront the phantom objects that have been thus abstracted from social life, an attitude that shows itself to be deeply mystical. On the one hand, these abstractions are cherished as real objects akin to inert things, whereas on the other, they are thought of as animate entities with a life-force of their own akin to spirits or gods. Since these "things" have lost their original connection with social life, they appear, paradoxically, both as inert and as animate entities.

In a situation where the two systems collide, the native beliefs in magic or fetish need to be seen not as a defensive recourse to superstition but as "the creative response to an enormously deep-seated conflict between use-value and exchange-value orientations. The magic of use-value production draws out, magnifies, and counteracts the magic of exchange-value practices."[68]

Taussig's concern to demonstrate the intermeshing of value systems and to see native as well as European actions as already the product of cultural exchange is suggestive, and I develop his approach in subsequent chapters as I explore points of contact and the operations of power of all sorts. In this chapter, I have attempted to indicate the wide range of significance involved in the idea of giving and exchanging, be it in terms of the relations it establishes or confirms or the value and meaning of the objects of exchange themselves. Underlying my discussion have been the idea of power, its unequal distribution in a colonial context, and the way in which power resides in and through exchange and circulation within and between material and discursive economies. In chapter 2, this issue of power and colonialism is brought into clearer focus in relation to control over the wealth of the New World.

2

Abundance and Sovereignty

So FAR I have examined the idea of the gift and its role in the presentation and conceptualization of Indian society in Western thought as a way of opening up some of the complex issues of power involved in the act and rhetoric of giving. In this chapter, I flesh out some of these ideas by concentrating on specific exchanges and what they reflect about the struggle for power and expression of sovereignty between Europeans and Indians in early encounters. In particular, I look at the contests over who had the power to give and to take the abundance offered by the New World, as expressed in some of the contemporary discourses of encounter and exchange.

Perhaps the most widespread and persuasive framing narrative in which the European encounter with the New World is *now* seen, even by the Europeans and their descendants, is one of exploitation: Europe plundered the New World. In this narrative, what Europe gave in return was disease, alcohol, and a technology that, in destroying the original technologies, created weakness. Western civilization is thus now imaged as a virus, a gift like the blankets infested with smallpox reportedly given to Plains Indians in the nineteenth century. Earlier, though, the encounter was figured in quite different terms, as a gift that gave life—the gift of Christianity and civilization. This was a benefit so huge and indispensible that it dwarfed the negative aspects that might come with it. Either way, contact was seen not just in terms of neutral exchange, of barter or trade, but as deeply imbued with the symbolic language of power, morality, and sovereignty.

Material power and wealth may well have been the impetus behind discovery and colonization. Nevertheless it is important to allow for the power of the imagination at key points in stimulating and sustaining the enterprise,[1] and it is by looking at the whole discursive field in which accounts of discovery and encounter operate that we can best see this. This means taking more seriously than usual the metaphors and figures in which colonial relations are represented in some early texts, in order to show the importance of the overlapping of the economic, political, and spiritual realms in their full imaginative dimensions. I begin with abundance and then show how this is involved with the expression and representation of sovereignty.

Early accounts of the New World are characterized by promises of abundance, even excess, and, as Stephen Greenblatt has convincingly demonstrated, the idea of the marvelous, carrying with it an appeal to the imagination that goes beyond simple greed and acquisitiveness. At the material as well as the imaginative level, these enterprises and the texts circulated about them depended on *credit*. They needed readers to believe the accounts to be creditable and, as a consequence, to extend financial credit to support the enterprises. The speculation was financial as well as intellectual, and part of my purpose is to show the constant discursive interplay of these realms of economics and imagination. A crucial part of this complex of ideas about the abundance of the New World, though, is the complementary idea of an absence. There is the promise of a wealth of natural resources to be taken, but there is also a haunting prospect of finding nothing. The venturers thus felt a persistent need to validate the reports of plenty, to justify the credit that was being asked for, whether in the reading and crediting of the text or in the linked material investment and extension of credit in colonial enterprises.

The use of gold and the excessive desire for it as part of a critique of the evils and superfluities of society were of course well established in the Western tradition, but the discovery of huge concentrations of gold in America and its consequent influx into Europe offered a particularly clear contrast between savage and civilized in terms of simple self-sufficiency versus an unquenchable greed for wealth. As early as

Peter Martyr the evils of greed are underscored as causing the exploitation of Indians in the mines and corrupting the Europeans.

> Seized by their blind greed for gold, even those who leave Spain milder than lambs, once they have arrived there, become as ferocious as wolves ... contravening our holy laws, with no consideration for the welfare of these poor people.[2]

The metaphor of insatiable appetite is made even more explicit.

> Such is the life people lead to satisfy the sacred hunger for gold; but the richer one becomes by such work, the more does one desire to possess. The more wood is thrown on the fire, the more it crackles and spreads. The sufferer from dropsy, who thinks to appease his thirst by drinking, only excites it the more.[3]

Alarm over the way gold could operate as a false lure was part of a larger theme that condemned financial speculation as opposed to rational expectations of profit based on work. One aspect of gold that had always attracted comment was the way it concentrated value in itself, which meant that though it was a crucial part of exchange and circulation through its role in currency, it also had the tendency to cluster, to congeal, rather than flow. Martyr explicitly contrasts gold with what he sees as the ideal currency, the cocoa bean.

> O blessed money, which not only gives to the human race a useful and delightful drink, but also prevents its possessors from yielding to infernal avarice, for it cannot be piled up or hoarded for a long time.

He argues that the beans' circulating quality makes everyone in the area better off, because traders come and take the beans for goods and then use them further afield; "thus the beans circulate so easily that all the neighbouring people profit by the advantages they offer." The beans act as precious metals do elsewhere, to allow trade in foreign merchandise. "In this wise various natural products are everywhere disseminated. Such is human life, and thus must we speak." Later he refers to it as "happy" money. It is happy "because they obtain it by merely scratching the earth, and because neither the envy of the avaricious nor the terrors of war cause it to return to its subterranean hiding-place, as happens with gold and silver. This is money produced by a tree."[4]

The New World of Peru and Mexico, then, offered complicated and even contradictory examples for philosophers. On the one hand, there was the idea of an abundance that was permanent and natural and therefore needed none of the hierarchies and hoardings that followed from a scarcity economics. On the other hand, there was the concentration of gold, triggering European avarice, together with the evidence of Native American hierarchies and monarchies exceeding in extravagance and despotic power anything Europe could offer.

Even Montaigne, who is best known for invoking the example of the Tupinamba of Brazil, contrasting their simplicity (as well as their supposed cannibalism) with European civilization, uses the wealth and power of Peru and Mexico to make a point quite different from the idea of the noble savage. His essay "Of Coaches," for instance, is a complex meditation on extravagance and power, weaving its unlikely way through an account of modes of transport. It ranges across examples of extravagance and dwells on the greed for extreme riches that motivated the Spaniards in their brutal dealings in Mexico and Peru. He contrasts the Spanish greed with the way the Mexicans had accumulated gold in huge quantities. This was not money, and it did not circulate, but he is generally interested in the forms of distribution and circulation carried out within such a powerful hierarchy, and in many ways he anticipates, with characteristic skepticism, later debates over the nature of sovereignty. He analyzes the idea of the liberality and generosity of the sovereign as a confidence trick played on his subjects. Extravagant spectacles, feasts, and buildings are, for the spectators, only their own wealth displayed before them and the people should recognize that

> their eyes are feasted on what should go to feed their bellies. Liberality itself is not in its right setting in the hands of a sovereign; private individuals have more right to be liberal. For, precisely speaking, a king has nothing that is properly his own; he owes even himself to others.[5]

The power to give, which I shall argue is one of the main rhetorical expressions of sovereignty, is here subjected to a radical critique. It is shown to be based on a confidence trick, but one that is at the heart of kingship. If the power to give is really a debt, is this a reflection of the illusory power of monarchy itself?

Montaigne concludes his essay with two remarkable images. Describing the erection of the palaces of Quito and Cuzco, Montaigne refers to the way in which, in the absence of scaffolding, the earth was raised around a building during its construction and at the end removed, leaving a structure standing high on its own. Without further comment he returns, for the final image of the essay, to the gold sedan-chair with golden shafts on which the so-called King of Peru was carried. In their struggle to capture him and bring him down to the ground, the Spanish killed many of the people who were holding him aloft, but

> as many of these carriers as they killed, to bring him to earth . . . so many others strove in emulation to take the place of the dead; so that they could never bring him down, however many of his men they massacred, until a horseman seized him round the body and pulled him to the ground.[6]

What the two images have in common is the idea of the low sustaining the high, and the image of a king literally held up by the continued sacrifice of those under him resonates across political systems in general, and not just the sacrificial societies of South America. The final act of seizing the king's body itself and pulling it to the ground is a radical demystification of power based on sacrifice and tribute. And it goes even further. Montaigne opens up the relation between giving and power, one of the main themes of this book, and he does so in a way that constitutes a fundamental critique of the sources of state power. Within the larger discourse of the noble savage, he explores the extremes of hierarchy offered by the Americas as well as the idea of a society without hierarchy at all.

Perhaps the most eloquent and single-minded modern proponent of some of these ideas is Pierre Clastres, with his opposition between society and the state. Basing his arguments, like Montaigne, on South American examples, he argues for the crucial distinction between primitive societies in which power is dispersed and societies in which there is a state organization. In the first there may be leaders, but their relation to the people is recognized as obligation rather than dominance. In the second, the people have lost the power, which is exercised from the top down. Clastres has a simple way of distinguishing between these two types of society, and this is what he calls debt, or obligation. In a primitive society "the leader is in debt to society precisely because he is leader," and maintenance of the leader's indebtedness prevents the separation of power from society.

> The nature of society changes with the direction of the debt. If debt goes from the chieftainship towards society, society remains undivided, power

remains located within the homogeneous social body. If, on the contrary, debt goes from society towards the chieftainship, power has been separated from society and is concentrated in the hands of the chief, the resulting heterogeneous society is divided into the dominating and the dominated.[7]

But this is too simple. Who decides, and on what basis, which direction the debt is going in, once something is conceptualized as reciprocal? And it is precisely the circularity of the gift relation that presents the problem in distinguishing between the role of representative leaders.

Where Clastres begs the question by assuming a difference between the exercise of power, indicated by the direction of debt, Michael Taussig opens the question up by applying the terms normally used to refer to primitive societies—*magic, fetishism,* and *sacrifice*—to the modern state. In his account of the workings of a fictional state that also seems to be an amalgam of recent Latin American states, he emphasizes the circularity of what Clastres calls debt. "It's as if the state and people are bound to the immanence of an immense circle of magically reversible force," says Taussig, "in effect a never-ending exchange of some ancient gift-like force that we will call *the accursed share.*" It is not just that we cannot necessarily determine which way round the power relation is operating in acts of tribute to leaders in traditional hierarchies, but that other sorts of societies, including our own, can also be seen as founded on a paradoxical gift, a sovereign act of giving up sovereignty. This points to fundamental distinctions about the nature of society and the social contract, and returns us ultimately to Hobbes and Rousseau and the ways in which ideas of the totality and unity of the state are built on mythic foundations. According to Taussig, "This is the drama of the circulation through the metamorphosis of the gift as in the sacred covenant whereby the general will *made itself* by *giving itself* over in a superior, concentrated, violence, to found both state and society."[8] Taussig's ultimate position and strategy, which I interpret as critiquing rather than celebrating this mystical origin and unity, not only provides an initial framework in which we can see the claims for sovereignty between Europeans and Indians, but allows us to give weight to the rhetorical and psychological dimensions of these questions of representation and power.

Instead of concentrating on the legal and political powers involved in sovereignty, at this point it is worth considering the ways in which sovereign leaders have demonstrated their power and made others accept and admire it. Georges Bataille's definition, for instance, stresses not the coercive power but the power to consume without producing, which he sees as the ultimate demonstration of freedom. "What distinguishes sovereignty is the consumption of wealth, as against labor and servitude, which produce wealth without consuming it. The sovereign individual consumes and doesn't labor." This sounds like a Marxist description of surplus wealth and exploitation by expropriation, but instead of seeing it entirely negatively, Bataille looks at why it is also attractive. The most graphic expression of this consumption is expenditure, and even waste—redistribution pushed to a point beyond any functional purpose. He argues that by this means the sovereign expresses in a way that everyone can symbolically share the experience of being not a slave, not a producer for a purpose, but a free being. "Life *beyond utility* is the domain of sovereignty."[9] We need not follow through with the whole trajectory of Bataille's thought (which involves taking seriously the function of sacrifice) to be able to use this idea to see the power of the rhetoric of nobility and largesse. In this way, we can recognize the economic realities of inequality, hierarchy, and appropriation but also the psychological power of nonutility, waste, and extravagance and their symbolic and rhetorical power on both sides of the exchanges between Indians and Europeans.

The idea of sovereignty is of particular importance, then, insofar as it lies at the root of the claims to power made by each side of the encounter. At its most basic it implies a fundamental freedom and autonomy, the right to be the choosing and acting subject rather than the object of others' choices and actions. At the political level, this has involved a recognition of autonomy and independent status, and it is the relation between earlier doctrines of *vacuum domicilium* and the present legal and moral status of contemporary Indian groups and their claims to sovereignty and self-determination that make the term still an important one. At the simplest level, one can say that European kings' claims to sovereignty over other nations were based on the same ideological justifications they used to buttress claims to sovereignty within European societies. As Francis Jennings trenchantly puts it, sovereignty "had been invented to justify kings' conquests of their own peoples, [and] lent itself readily to export."[10]

The fact that the English were comparative latecomers in the New

World meant that their first encounters with the inhabitants were already overwritten for them by the Spanish actions and their textualizations. But the English venturers and writers also operated in a particular domestic political climate, and I shall begin my discussion of the role of sovereignty with a particularly rich instance of the intersection of power, gender, and empire. One of the most famous portraits of Queen Elizabeth I, the Ditchley portrait by Marcus Gheeraerts the Younger, shows her standing astride the globe. Written in Latin on the picture are three fragmentary statements describing Elizabeth, which stress a particular sort of power. They have been reconstructed and translated as "She gives and does not expect. She can, but does not take revenge. In giving back she increases." Also on the portrait are the remains of a sonnet on the sun, reflecting an established rhetorical tradition of comparisons of the monarch's power with that of the sun, as the inexhaustible source of all that is good.

The context of the portrait, and its grounding in the necessity for courtiers to recognize and celebrate the queen's power to give or withhold wealth and approval, is localized, and the part of the globe delineated under her feet is a region of England, but even so it is possible to see this as a powerful image of the imperial monarch and her power to give and control, which constitutes sovereignty. From English sovereign to imperial ruler, the rhetoric is remarkably consistent, and the idea of the nonreciprocal gift, the power to give and not receive is symbolically more potent than the power to take. Rather than seeing this idea merely as a supremely effective piece of ideological camouflage for exploitation, we might do well to ask why it is so powerful symbolically, but this takes us beyond the assumptions of an economic rationality based on quantifiable gain and loss, and eventually into ideas of expenditure, excess, and sacrifice.

Moving from the general idea of the sovereign power to give, I want now to develop some of the specific imperial contexts for this idea. Though the occasion of the portrait of Queen Elizabeth I and its message might seem to be limited to the control of the love lives of courtiers, this very aspect can be seen to be intimately connected to imperial enterprise in the figure of Sir Walter Raleigh, who provoked the queen's displeasure by having an illicit relationship with one of her ladies in waiting. The scandal was referred to by one wit as "the discoverer discovered," and Raleigh expressed his awareness of the queen's power, in terms parallel to the Latin phrases on the Ditchley portrait, in his poem "The Ocean to Cynthia."

> No other poure effectinge wo, or bliss
> Shee gave, shee tooke, shee wounded, shee appeased.[11]

Most important for my purposes, Raleigh's 1596 account of his fruitless expedition to Guiana in search of gold, *The Discoverie of the Large, Rich and Bewtiful Empyre of Guiana,* itself "discovers" for us a network of related discourses about plenty and power, closely related to the particular conditions of the queen's sovereignty. Raleigh's subordinate Laurence Keymis echoes the familiar theme of power and sovereignty in a poem prefacing his own account of the second voyage to Guiana, addressed to Elizabeth:

> Then most admired Soveraigne, let your breath
> Go foorth upon the waters, and create
> A golden world in this our yron age.

In her godlike ability to create, the queen can make a new golden age, but also, more specifically, she can sponsor their voyage in search of actual gold. Keymis's metaphorical exercises are conventional enough, but his convolutions in reconciling praise of virginity (necessary because of Elizabeth's unmarried status) and fertility and productivity point to stratagems developed in Raleigh's own text. Keymis describes Guiana as a young maid whose "rich feete are mines of golde," submitting to Elizabeth,

> our most sacred Maide: whose barrennesse
> Is the true fruite of vertue, that may get,
> Beare and bring forth anew in all perfection,
> What heretofore savage corruption held
> In barbarous Chaos; and in this affaire
> Become her father, mother, and her heire.

The deliberate play of paradox, in the collapsing of roles here, is an exercise of wit but also points to a contradiction exploited by Raleigh in his own textual navigation in the gendered discourse of New World exploitation, in which America is both a fertile woman to be possessed and a virgin (like his sovereign) to be respected and even protected from the less scrupulous attentions of the Spanish. Whereas Keymis described Guiana in graphic terms as a fertile and available female ("Whole shires of fruitfull rich grounds, lying now waste for want of people, do prostitute themeselves unto us, like a faire and beautifull woman, in the pride and floure of desired yeeres"[12]), Raleigh's approach is more complex. He is writing to Elizabeth, with whom he is in disgrace for a liaison with one of her ladies in waiting, who has become pregnant. Elizabeth is known in all the iconography and official sycophancy as the Virgin Queen, so in describing the potential of Guiana he takes a quite different tack.

> *Guiana* is a Countrey that hath yet her Maydenhead, never sackt, turned, nor wrought, the face of the earth hath not beene torne, nor the vertue and salt of the soyle spent by manurance, the graues haue not been opened for gold, the mines not broken with sledges, nor the Images puld down out of their temples. It hath neuer been entred by any armie of strength, and neuer conquered by any Christian Prince.[13]

The string of negatives here is designed to distinguish his own behavior from that of the Spanish, but the word "yet" is crucial in that the value of the virginity is in its potential to be exploited, to become productive. As Fuller has shown, Raleigh's own particular agenda requires him to present virginity positively, and he makes the connection between sexuality and material exploitation of resources in a clearly parallel set of claims.[14] He boasts that none of his company

> by violence or otherwise, ever knew any of their women, and yet we saw many hundreds, and had many in our power, and of those very yoong, and excellently favored which came among us without deceit, starke naked. Nothing got us more love among them than this usage, for I suffred not anie man to take from anie of the nations, so much as a *Pina* or a *Potato* roote, without giuing them contentment, nor any man so much as to offer to touch any of their wives or daughters; which course, so contrarie to the Spaniards (who tyrannise over them in all things) drew them to admire hir Majestie, whose commandement I told them it was.[15]

Raleigh can contrast himself with a clearly defined Spanish behavior because, like other English explorers in their accounts of discovery and colonization, he is already writing in a situation of belatedness, against the background of Spanish and Portuguese accounts; we see this clearly in the treatment of gold as a symbol of unlimited and marvelous wealth. In explaining why each expedition falls short of the marvelous discoveries in Peru and Mexico, Raleigh has two options, both feeding off the

so-called Black Legend of Spanish brutality. One option is to highlight
the cruelty and rapacity of the Spaniards, who ransacked and looted
whole cultures for gold and silver, removing what had taken many ages
to accumulate. Another is to stress the idea of a more modern and rational investment of labor to produce useful products and self-sustaining
colonies. As Fuller points out, an aspect of America's appeal besides its
excess and plenty was that it was a place where England's excesses, in
the form of idleness, could be vented and voided, and she quotes
George Chapman's description of England in "De Guiana" as "a bodie
numb'd with surfeits."[16]

One of the clearest statements of this position, which also reflects a
defensive awareness of its own lack of the "marvelous" that Stephen
Greenblatt describes as present in other earlier accounts, is to be found
in Captain John Smith's *A Map of Virginia*. Its apparently multiple authorship certainly allows for the expression of down-to-earth skepticism about the inflated hopes and styles of aristocratic adventurers expecting a quick fortune, as opposed to the real strengths of skilled
workers, but in one passage it is particularly self-reflexive about its own
status as a text of discovery.[17] The colonists' treatment of the Indians as
trading partners or rivals to be negotiated with, might, we are told,
seem to some too charitable. Others may regret that

> we washed not the ground with their blouds, nor shewed such strange in-
> ventions, in mangling, murdering, ransaking and destroying, (as did the
> Spaniards) the simple bodies of those ignorant souls.

Such people would not find the present account "delightful," since it
would not be

> stuffed with relations of heaps, and mines of gold and silver, nor such rare
> commodities as the Portugals and Spaniards found in the East and West
> Indies. The want wherof hath begot us (that were the first undertakers) no
> less scorne and contempt, then their noble conquests & valiant adventures
> (beautified with it) praise and honor.

The explanation offered is that it was simply "the Spaniards good hap"
to discover places with large populations already rich in both the means
of subsistence and accumulated precious metals and stones. The Spaniards took, therefore, "only the spoile and pillage of those countrie
people, and not the labours of their owne hands." In contrast, "we
chanced in a lande, even as God made it. Where we found only an idle,

improvident, scattered people." In such a situation, hard, unglamorous work would be necessary from any colonists "ere they can bring to perfection the commodities of the countrie." The false lure of gold was therefore destructive and distracting from the real needs of the colony.

> But the worst mischief was, our gilded refiners with their golden promises, made all men their slaves in hope of recompence, there was no talke, no hope, no worke, but dig gold, wash gold, refine gold, load gold, such a brute of gold, as one mad fellow desired to bee buried in the sandes, least they should by their art make gold of his bones.

Smith's complaint about necessary business being suspended, "to fraught such a drunken ship with so much gilded durt,"[18] is part of a general critique of the unworldly and extravagant administration of the colony by preceding presidents, in contrast to Smith's more practical approach, which is demonstrated in his commentary on his dealings with Powhatan. It is here that we see most clearly the overlapping languages of trade, exchange, and aristocratic gift-giving, and it is worth looking more closely at the language of this account, which presents a series of dialogues and tableaux in which the struggle for power is rhetorically staged.

The best-known episode of Smith's dealings with Powhatan is his rescue by Pocahontas; the part it has played in a widespread gendering of the European-Indian encounter in which America is figured as female bounty has been extensively discussed. My interest here is with Powhatan. In their lengthy negotiations with the most influential leader of the area, the colonists were often dependent on material trade with him but also at pains to assert their own and their monarch's sovereignty over him. In a curious episode, described in *A Map of Virginia*, Captain Newport attempts to crown Powhatan as a subordinate king, an enterprise described by the skeptical authors of the account as "this strange discovery, but more strange coronation."

Smith describes at some length the reception he received before the coronation from Powhatan's women (only in the second version are they described as "Pocahontas and her women"). We are told that "30 young women came naked out of the woods (only covered behind and before with a few greene leaves)." After a lengthy performance of singing and dancing from these "feindes," all wearing stag's horns, they take him to their lodging, where "no sooner was hee within the house, but all these Nimphes [the] more tormented him than ever, with crowding, and pressing and hanging vpon him, most tediously crying, loue you not me." The ensuing feast lacks for nothing, "nor any Salvage daintie their invention could devise."[19]

One may ask why the attentions of these nymphs was such a "torment." At one level, we may be seeing a continuation of Raleigh's high-minded approach, which presents the narrator as above such appeals to the flesh. At another, we have here a gift being offered which also seems to have qualities of a demand. The repeated phrase "loue you not me" (not originally in English, presumably, but problems of communication are never focused on by Smith) can be a rhetorical question or a direct one. Either way, it seems to be interpreted as a demand for reciprocity that Smith finds tedious or threatening.[20] In this way, the crowding and importuning of these erotic "feindes," with their "infernal passions," their appeal-cum-reproach about loving them, anticipates many future accounts of encounters with Indians as supplicants for gifts, as I show in chapter 4.

When this episode is viewed alongside the coronation of Powhatan, the two scenes, which occur on successive pages, offer a curious symmetry, in which gift and demand, sovereignty and subservience, are ambiguously intertwined. The scenes reflect a widespread paradox in the relation between Europeans and Indians expressed in the countless incidents of giving and receiving, which reveal in small ways the ambiguities and obfuscations of the power relations. What we have is a persistent presentation of Europeans as the givers, and a stress on the power of giving, alongside the counteridea of the New World as a bountiful, fecund place from which to take. The dissonance between these two ideas can be further explored in the account of the coronation of Powhatan. Newport's aim is to establish Powhatan, already the influential leader of his people, as both sovereign and subordinate to the English crown.

> But a fowle trouble there was to make him kneele to receaue his crowne, he neither knowing the maiestie, nor meaning of a Crowne, nor bending of the knee, indured so many perswasions, examples, and instructions, as tired them all. At last, by leaning hard on his shoulders, he a little stooped, and Newport put the Crowne on his head.[21]

The striking mixture of tribute and compulsion here is surprisingly characteristic of the maneuvers of sovereignty and power involved in the exercise of benevolent giving in an imperial and colonial context. This is a gift that is imposed rather than given, indicating not sovereignty, as the crown would suggest, but subservience. A report from the Virginia assembly in 1624 makes clear their real view of the power relations.

> We never perceaved that the natives of the Countrey did voluntarily yeeld themselves subjects to our gracious Sovraigne, nether that they took any pride in that title, nor paide at any tyme any contributione of corne for sustenation of the Colony, nor coud we at any tyme keepe them in such good respect of correspondency as we became mutually helpful each to the other but contrarily what at any [time] was done proceeded from feare and not love, and their corne procured by trade or the sworde.[22]

As for Powhatan's view, we can only speculate as to how much he understood, and whether his resistance stemmed from lack of comprehension or reluctance about what he recognized was really an act of subjection and incorporation. As Eric Cheyfitz insists, in a perceptive reading of this scene that concentrates on the issue of translation, "we can only speculate, indeed we must speculate, in order to complicate the entire problem of intercultural 'knowing' in the scenes of translation we are interpreting."[23] We can, of course, explain the logic of it from the English point of view. It was crucial to establish the Indian leaders as figures with whom a certain sort of exchange could take place, which meant giving them a recognizable status and legal standing and, in this case, formalizing Powhatan's leadership of his Algonquian Indians in the Jamestown area. Furthermore, there is a direct parallel with the policy of the time toward Ireland. Jeffrey Knapp quotes Nicholas Canny's description of the policy of confiscating the land, and then regranting it: "The essence of the scheme was that the ruling [Irish] chieftains should surrender the lands of their lordships to the king and receive them back as a fief from the crown."[24]

The language and symbolism of monarchy and nobility used in the coronation scene are a logical extension of the use of political terms from England to describe New England political systems. European terms of authority were routinely used to describe Indian leaders, so that we commonly find descriptions like "The Emperor of Virginia has sixteen Kings under his sway. He and all his vassals deal peacefully with the English."[25] More insidiously, even when native terms such as *weroance* were used, the assumptions about power and how it is supported and exercised were likely to be still in place, and perhaps still are in recent accounts. One problem is that modern discussants inevitably tend to base their analysis on early European accounts and invoke them as the authority for their analysis, rather than always problematizing their terms. According to Helen Rountree, for instance,

> Powhatan's organization was in three levels, with his viceroys being the tribes' *weroances*, and their viceroys in turn being the petty *weroances* of satellite towns. The proper term to apply to Powhatan's organization is "paramount chiefdom" rather than "empire," since Powhatan himself did not exert enough coercive force for his organization to be called a monarchical "state."[26]

Cheyfitz has disputed assumptions by Kupperman and Lurie about the monarchical nature of Powhatan society,[27] and his suspicion of the imposition of European concepts of the state, with its hierarchical systems, is instructive, but itself perhaps runs the risk of assuming too straightforward a relation between kinship and reciprocity and the exercise of power. Richard White invokes the work of Pierre Clastres to develop a distinction between a coercive model of leadership and power and a noncoercive one, which he argues was present but not discernible to early European observers.[28] However, I have already suggested in my earlier discussion of Clastres and Taussig some of the difficulties involved in deciding where power really lies.

What this little tableau of Powhatan and Newport does capture well is the mixed message being given by the Europeans. On the one hand, they recognize Powhatan's power and make him sovereign—which he already thought he was—but to do so they must first humble him, and put him below the English crown, and the element of compulsion, if comic, is entirely appropriate. In a further irony, when the crown is placed on his head, the English fire shots as a signal to their boats, but "the king start[ed] up in a horrible fear, till he saw all was well."[29] All might be well in terms of immediate danger, but from the English point of view Powhatan has now been formally fixed in a hierarchy and has *lost* sovereignty by having submitted to having it *given* to him. Within two years, Lord De La Warr is reminding him, in another complex exchange, of his coronation and the fact that his cooperation as a subject of the king is expected. In William Strachey's account, De La Warr reminds Powhatan of the English king,

> unto whom even Powhatan himself had formerly vowed not only friendship but homage, receiving from His Majesty therfor many gifts and upon

his knees a crown and scepter, with other ornaments, the symbols of civil state and Christian sovereignty, thereby obliging himself to offices of duty to His Majesty.[30]

Here, clearly demonstrated, is the symbolic importance of the physical subjection that Newport insisted on, in which "he a little stooped" has already become in De La Warr's version "upon his knees." (Powhatan, unabashed and still playing the game of status, demands a coach and three horses, as this is what he has heard the nobility have in England.)

To return to the original account of the coronation, the narrator's jaundiced stance can be explained by the overall agenda of the account, which is to contrast the extravagant and ill-judged administration of the previous presidents with that of John Smith, and it is appropriate therefore that the terms of the critique revolve around the opposition of hard-nosed self-interest and the rhetoric of benevolence and abundance. Before the coronation, Powhatan is given presents of "Bason, Ewer, Bed, Clothes, and such costly nouelties" whose efficacy Smith doubts.

They had bin much better well spared, then so ill spent: for we had his favour much better onlie for a poor peece of Copper, till this stately kinde of soliciting made him so much overvalue himself, that he respected us as nothing at all.

Powhatan's sensitivity about his status has already been evident in his comments at an earlier encounter designed to persuade him to come for his coronation.

If your king haue sent me presents, I also am a king, and this is my land, 8 daies I will stay to receaue them, your father is to come to me, not I to him, nor yet to your fort, neither will I bite at such a baite.

The gift has become, in this version, a trap with "baite," and the various descriptions of the negotiations between him and the English suggest a cat-and-mouse game between ruthlessly self-interested sides, but carried out within the language of benevolence and reciprocity. The colonists' often urgent need for corn and other staple commodities and the Indians' thwarted desire for firearms constitute the underlying agenda, but more interesting are the manueverings for position, the attempts to assert a sovereignty rather than a trading partnership, via a gift relationship. "Scorning to trade as his subjects did," Powhatan tells Captain Newport

it is not agreable with my greatnes in this pedling manner to trade for trifles; and I esteem you a great werowans. Therefore lay me down all your
commodities togither, what I like I will take; and in recompence giue you
that I thinke fitting their value.[31]

Powhatan's behavior and bearing are presented by Smith as kingly, de-
vious, or both, perhaps because these (sovereignty or market) are the
only terms in which he can conceptualize what for Powhatan may have
been, at least at certain points, an insistence on a gift relationship, in
which the equivalence of goods and getting a good bargain are less significant than the establishing of social relations. In this particular encounter, Newport, in spite of Smith's warning that Powhatan will cheat
him, attempts to "outbraue this Salvage in ostentation of greatnes, and
so to bewitch him with his bounty, so to have what he listed." Accordingly he presumably lays his goods down, only to get disappointingly
little corn in return. We then have one of the standard ingredients of
accounts of early encounters. Smith "glaunced in the eies of Powhatan
many trifles; who fixed his humour vpon a few blew beads." He plays
Powhatan along, talking up their value, so that "ere we departed, for a
pound or two of blew beads, he brought over my king for 2 or 300
bushels of corne; yet parted good friends."

The point of the story is to show Smith's skill and hardheadedness,
and it is an early instance of that paradigm of fooling the gullible savage, based on the assumption that there is a universal scale of value
including corn and blue beads, which Powhatan simply gets wrong.
What Smith also ignores is the possibility that the two transactions
were quite different in Powhatan's mind, with the first as a nontrade,
gift-giving prelude to the second, a pattern well documented elsewhere
in accounts of later fur-trading practices.[32] It may also well be the case
that Powhatan did not share Smith's easy equation of trade items. Martin Quitt points out that among the Powhatans, corn was the most pres-
tigious plant food and was raised in special fields for the paramount
chief as a highly valued form of tribute.[33]

In a description of an encounter a few months later, we see further
evidence of Smith's need to manipulate the language of gift and reciprocity to his own ends. He has to first acknowledge that Powhatan has
what he needs, rather than the other way round.

What your people had, you have engrossed, forbidding them our trade; and
nowe you thinke, by consuming the time, wee shall consume for want, not
having [the means] to fulfill your strange demandes.

In reply, Powhatan compares Smith unfavorably with Newport and, in doing so, describes not a trade relationship but a gift relationship, in which neither side disputed the value of what was given. "Captain Newport gave me swords, coppers, cloths, a bed, tooles, or what I desired; ever taking what I offered him." In contrast, from Smith he gets "nothing but what you regard not; and yet you will haue whatsoever you demand." Smith's reply also appeals to the ideal gift situation, in order to take the moral high ground, and he tries to turn a position of dependence into one of reciprocity and mutual generosity.

> Powhatan, you must knowe as I haue but one God, I honour but one king; and I live here not as your subject but as your friend to pleasure you with what I can; by the gifts you bestowe upon me, you gaine more then by trade: yet would you visite mee as I doe you, you should knowe it is not our customes to sell our curtesie as a vendible commoditie.

Interestingly, in the light of the later usage in which presidents took upon themselves the mantle of the "Great White Father in Washington," Smith invokes the language of paternity and kinship in taking up Powhatan's rebuke that though Smith pretends to defer to Newport and himself as elders, he is willful and selfish. "I call you father indeed, and as a father you shall see I will loue you: but the small care you had of such a child, caused my men perswade me to shift for my selfe."[34]

Even if Smith's narrative suggests a skepticism about the rhetoric of kingly liberality and sovereignty, another visitor to Virginia, William Strachey, was clearly fascinated by this mixture in Powhatan. While intensely aware of Powhatan's "subtile understanding and pollitique carriage," Strachey also wants to account for the source of his authority. He locates it not in brute force or material power but in something more spiritual. It might be surprising, he says, that such a

> barbarous and uncivill prince should take unto him (adorned and sett forth with no greater ornament and munificence) a forme and ostentation of such maiestie as he expresseth,

but it does succeed in striking "awe and sufficyent wonder in our people presenting themselves before him." Strachey puts this down not to charisma or personal qualities but to "the impression of the Divine nature." While careful not to endorse Powhatan's religion, Strachey wants to insist on the divine right of kings for his own domestic political reasons. Although the Indians (as other heathens forsaken by the true light) have not that porcion of the knowing blessed Christian spiritt, yet I am perswaded there is an infused kind of divinities and extraordinary (appointed that it shall be so by the King of kings) to such who are his ymedyate instruments on earth (how wretched soever otherwise under the curse of misbelief and infidelity).[35]

This brings us close to Bataille's idea that the recognition of sovereignty is, at its most fundamental level, also linked to a recognition of the sacred, an area outside the realm of utility and calculation, but it is also perhaps part of a larger fascination with the exotic and power to be found on both sides.[36]

On a more skeptical and hardheaded level, Strachey also provides us with a picture of Powhatan's political and economic power. Having listed carefully the proportions of food and skins the people had to give to Powhatan in tribute, he concludes,

and so he robbes the people in effect of all they have even to the deare's skyn wherewith they cover them from cold, in so much as they dare not dresse yt and put yt on untill he have seene yt and refused yt; for what he comaundeth they dare not disobey in the lest thinge.[37]

The determination of Algonquian leaders to control the distribution of goods was early commented on by Captain Arthur Barlowe. At a meeting with "the Kings brother" and his men, having given him some gifts,

we likewise gave somewhat to the other that sate with him on the matte; but presently he arose, and tooke all from them, and put it into his owne basket, making signes and tokens, that all things ought to be delivered unto him, and the rest were but his servants, and followers.[38]

Strachey also points to Powhatan's power to control the terms of trade and, in fact, set the price at which exchanges are made. He controls the price at which copper is traded with the English, knowing their need for corn, but then trades it at very different rates inland.

And whereas the English are now content to receave, in exchange, a few measures of corne for a great deale of that metell (valuyng it according to the extreame price yt beares with them, not to the estymacion yt has with us), Powhatan doth again vent some small quantity thereof to his neighbour nations for one hundred tyme the value, reserving, notwithstanding, for himself a plentifull quantity to leavy men withall when he shall find cause to use them against us.[39]

Strachey's ambivalent account of Powhatan can be seen as revealing not just his own confusions about the role of hierarchy and kingship (divine and/or exploitative) but a larger ambiguity about the leader's role in receiving and redistributing the wealth of the community. It can be seen, following Strachey, as an unjustified appropriation from the top, or we can stress the redistributive aspects and the relations of kinship and reciprocity that bind ruler and ruled. Is the redistribution an expression of power (a free act of largesse), or is it an expression of obligation, a demonstration of the leader's fundamental *lack* of coercive power in a reciprocal system? As I suggest in Chapter 1, the idea of the free gift can be said to rest on a fundamental moment of misrecognition in which generosity and sovereignty are enacted. This instance also perhaps demonstrates the difficulties of categorizing systems simply as hierarchical and exploitative or kinship based and reciprocal.

Another, and final, brief account of Powhatan links many of the key images and themes of this chapter. I have emphasized the importance of demonstrating the power to give and distribute as an essential attribute of sovereign leaders, but also the ambiguities of power involved in situations of gift and tribute. Powhatan, in his relation to the colonists, emerges in their accounts as effectively involved in identical stratagems of power based on aristocratic claims to sovereignty, and the language ascribed to him is identical to that of his opponents in this respect. It is therefore intriguing to have a separate account of him, admittedly still from a colonist, but presenting him in action and with his own people. In Henry Spelman's *Relation of Virgina* of 1609, we have a description of Powhatan involved in ritual behavior that presents fascinating parallels with the claims to sovereignty I earlier used Elizabeth's portrait and its message to explore. Spelman describes the regular communal planting of corn by Powhatan's people. When the king's corn is planted, though, Spelman describes a different procedure. Powhatan walks among them distributing bounty while they plant his corn, and this produces an interesting little cameo, since, as Spelman describes it, the people "goeth about the corne in maner backwardes for they going before, and the king followinge their faces are always toward the Kinge expectinge when he should fling sum beades among them which his custom is at that time." Here is the distributor of largesse, apparently in the form of a sort of wampum, dispersing his beads in a manner that is parallel to the dispersal of the seeds, and we even have the re-

verse symmetry of the act pointed out by Spelman, as the people sow
the corn "in maner backwardes." He is therefore the figure of bounty
even at the very moment the people are working to produce what will
later be his bounty to distribute to them at harvest time. (Remember
the importance of corn as special product, produced and used in tribute.) The wonderful symmetry here even extends to the parallel of
seeds and wampum as different forms of value to be distributed, which,
as I show in later chapters, is taken up metaphorically by John Eliot,
who is quick to notice that it was easier to spread the Word (referred
to regularly as "the seed") along the routes already used for the distribution of wampum. How are we to see Powhatan in this scene? As
exploitative monarch or as Clastres's noncoercive leader, locked into
kinship and reciprocal exchanges? Interestingly, Spelman mentions
that Powhatan is wearing for this event "the croune which ye Kinge of
England sent him beinge brought him by tow men, and sett upon his
heade." Spelman also tells us that the crown, together with the beades
and the bed that the King of England sent him, is "in the gods house
at Oropikes," where are kept all the king's goods and presents, together
with the remains of his ancestors, suggesting that the value being ascribed to these presents has a religious as well as a social dimension.[40]
We can say, then, that the crown has entered into a different economy,
a different circulation of values involving gods, shell beads, and rituals
that demonstrate reciprocity rather than coercion. Or we could say that
we have here most of the same ingredients as in European states, which
might lead us to question the oppositions on which so many of the
debates over primitive economy and gift-giving have been based. Either way, it is to the circulation of objects and words from the New
World, and the creation of meaning and value within and through that
circulation, that we now turn.

3

Words and Traces

THERE IS one final action by Powhatan at his coronation that remains to be commented on and serves as a bridge to the concerns of this chapter. According to Captain John Smith, at the end of the farcical ceremony, Powhatan, "remembring himselfe, to congratulate their kindnesse, he gave his old shoes and mantle to Captain Newport."[1] Old shoes and a mantle might certainly be read as a sign of kingly power to distribute, but they might also be seen as a casual, even contemptuous, appropriately secondhand return for the secondhand sovereignty offered him. For modern readers, though, the mention of Powhatan's mantle may summon an image of one of the most celebrated and beautiful objects to have been preserved from the period, which has long been known as "Powhatan's mantle." Though scholarly opinion disputes this attribution,[2] it is interesting that this (counter)gift is one of the earliest and most persistent images to survive, maintaining, through this apparently false attribution, the regal status Powhatan insisted on and gaining, as it entered the value system of the West, the status not of anonymous trade item but of specific gift. Its survival in Oxford's Ashmolean Museum today and its present status could even be seen as Powhatan's ultimate victory in the power battle: a gift that cannot be equaled or returned, the ultimate act of sovereign power. Of course, it could also be seen as yet another object brought back to Europe, an expression of the West's power to incorporate not only specific objects of the New World but also the knowledge they embodied and symbolized. The subject of this chapter is how texts incorporate and represent traces of the New World in the form of images and foreign words; but we need to see that the context is this more general bringing back of physical evidence and the processes of cultural exchange involved in such operations.

As well as the objects brought back from America that were for direct use and consumption, such as herbs, spices, foodstuffs, and precious metals, there were "curiosities" that circulated within a quite different sphere, that of the collection. Steven Mullaney describes the fashion for collecting and displaying curiosities and "strange things" in the Renaissance and contrasts the *Wunderkammern* or "wonder-cabinets," and their juxtaposition of strangenesses without an attempt at order, with the systematizations and taxonomies of the museums that replaced them; the idea of strange juxtapositions also points forward to the "ethnographic surrealism" of the twentieth century described by James Clifford.[3] Clifford deals with the surrealists' particular use of the conjunctions to be found in the jumbled and almost random collections of museums such as the Trocadero, but it could also be argued that the fascination of exotic objects is always more than a scholarly desire for ordering and collecting. We may also be reminded here of Marx's description at the beginning of *Capital* of the wealth of capitalist societies as a "monstrous collection of commodities" (*ungeheuere Warensammlung*), signaling his strategy of making strange what seemed normal and self-evident, namely, the value of commodities and the whole operation of commodity fetishism, which I describe in chapter 1.[4]

George Hamell sees a fundamental parallel between the Iroquois' adoption and adaptation of European goods, for instance, and Europeans' use of Iroquois and other objects.

> Along this shared frontier, exotic substances and objects of the mythical reality of the one culture acquired an elevated cultural efficacy within the other's mythical reality ... this process of the mundane of one mythical reality becoming the exotic of another mythical reality, assuming a disproportionate ideational efficacy within its recipient culture, was a reciprocal cultural phenomenon. How else do we explain the *Old* World ideational (religious or scientific) interest in *New* World artificialia? Twined fiber bags, quill-decorated moccasins, steatite smoking pipes, wooden ball-headed warclubs, and more, acquired and collected by European traders, travellers, scholars and kings from the northeastern New World were

placed in proud display in so-called cabinets of curiosities, the ancestors of today's great Old World ethnographical collections.[5]

It is the conjunction of the categories of the strange and marvelous with the project of categorizing and controlling knowledge that makes them so interesting and leads Denise Albanese to suggest that "rather than view the wonder-cabinet as quaint, aesthetically irrelevant, or simply estranged, it might be better to consider it as a protoinstitutional site of epistemological contestation." She uses Susan Stewart's account of souvenirs in a way particularly appropriate both to word collections and to collected objects. Souvenirs are a reminder, a metonym of something that exists but cannot be recovered in its entirety. "In fact if it could recoup the experience, it would erase its own partiality," says Stewart, "that partiality which is the very source of its power . . . the souvenir must remain impoverished and partial so that it can be supplemented by a narrative discourse, a narrative discourse which articulates the play of desire."[6]

If the cabinets can perhaps hold together the tension of system and discrete unique identity within the field of the strange or marvelous, it is with written accounts that the pressure to reprocess and recategorize elements from the New World is most powerful and influential. At the scientific and intellectual end, Margaret Hodgen suggests that whereas objects could be brought together indiscriminately in the name of the strange or exotic, the assembly of materials in written form, and particularly descriptions of manners and customs, threw up the question of organization.

> The initial problem of the collector of manners and customs thus came to be found in the realm of concepts and ideas. To assemble a collection at all, he had first to distinguish between different cultural "wholes" often called "nations" and then to analyze these into their institutional or other component parts. It was necessary for him to grasp conceptually salient themes, cultural themes, categories and structures.[7]

The increasing interest in taxonomic systems of varying levels of sophistication or accuracy and their relation to writing are explored by Michel de Certeau in his detailed analysis of the frontispiece to Joseph-François Lafitau's *Customs of the American Indians Compared with the Customs of Primitive Times* of 1724, in which he sees an allegorical representation of the writing process itself. In its profusion of disparate and exotic elements, Lafitau's frontispiece could also be fruitfully compared with Jan Kessel's earlier painting *America*, but it is the relation of the visual images or figures to the writing in Lafitau that de Certeau stresses, and he shows how the forty-one plates in the book "form an iconic discourse which traverses, from one section to another, the mass of the written discourse." Lafitau continues an "ethnological tradition" in which "from Lery or Thevet to De Bry, things seen and seeable mark off the writing, engendered by distance. White pebbles in the dark forest of the text." De Certeau focuses on how the classical and savage figures are used as part of a specific Enlightenment concern with origins and with time, and therefore the writing of history, but what is important for the present purposes is his demonstration of how visual images operate as an area of authenticity that is supplementary to the text and yet fundamental to it. "The written, therefore, refers to these 'authorities,' which have the status of *quotations*." These fragments, however, need a commentary that unites them, "a discourse where all of these primitive bursts of light are to be ordered in a 'system' . . . The law of producing a text on the site of ruins imposes itself. Henceforth, it will be necessary to create writing with the debris of the Other."[8]

De Certeau uses Lafitau to pinpoint the development of a certain sort of writing, but it is possible to see a similar impulse to order and organize in Richard Hakluyt's description of his massive enterprise of the *Principall Navigations* as a unifying of scattered elements or *disjecta membra*. As quoted by Mary Fuller, he sees it as an attempt "to bring Antiquities smothered and buried in darke silence to light"; "to gather likewise, and as it were to incorporate into one body the torne and scattered limmes of our ancient and late Navigations by Sea"; and to restore "ech particular member, before being displaced, to their true joynts and ligaments." Fuller points out that the whole to be reconstituted is not so much a body of knowledge about other cultures as something both wider and more localized. "On the one hand it seems to be the physical globe emergent to the discoverers' eyes . . . On the other hand, the body also looks something like a recomposed memory, precisely, the memory of a national(ist) history."[9]

Whatever its ultimate aim, the text can be seen as composing, systematizing, and packaging the experience of travel and discovery for consumption. Stephen Greenblatt argues that "the early discourse of the New World is among other things, a record of the colonizing of the marvelous,"[10] but the forms in which that record is kept are themselves often trying to incorporate as well as to record the marvelous, to act as trace as well as representation, and it is this unstable, complex mixture that I want to explore in some characteristic texts. Although my main focus is on the presence of actual foreign words in the text, a preliminary discussion of other unstable elements and of textual and rhetorical strategies will help to frame the discussion.

In chapter 2, I discussed the emphasis on abundance and wealth, characterized by the presence of gold in the New World, in relation to sovereignty and power, but it is worth returning briefly to Sir Walter Raleigh's *Discoverie*, to look more carefully at the rhetorical operations that are being carried out around the presence or, more important, absence of gold. Raleigh's emphasis on virginity has already been connected with Queen Elizabeth, but it is also part of an elaborate obfuscation of the fact that he did not find gold. In that sense, this is barren rather than virgin land, and he is in trouble. Raleigh's description of Guiana as a country that "hath yet her maidenhead," resonates not only with the idea of the Virgin Queen and the gendering of America whereby the failure to find gold is presented as a principled refusal literally to exploit the innocent women of the land and metaphorically to penetrate and despoil the land, but also more generally with the problem of a textual productivity based on an inevitable material absence.[11] Failing to penetrate, to find the mine or produce the actual gold, is expressed as a series of deferrals in which signs refer to other signs and gold becomes only the sign of gold.[12] This can be used as a trope of secrecy, whereby the failure to speak of something is itself presented as evidence of the authenticity of the account; for instance, in his account of Captain George Weymouth's voyage, James Rosier explains that because of the unwelcome interest of a "forrein Nation" in the location and details, he has not given full details of location. "I have likewise omitted here to adde a collection of many words in their language to the number of four or five hundred, as also the names of divers of their governours." These are "reserved for the benefit of those that shal goe in the next Voyage."[13]

Raleigh's *Discoverie*, then, is a text generated out of an absence, but it has its whole purpose in insisting that it is representing a presence, a material abundance, rather than just a textual effect, and Fuller's ac-

count of Raleigh's *Discoverie* shows how the textual operations involved
in coping with the absence of gold, precisely the thing needed to validate the voyage, reveal the larger operations in other early texts of discovery, in which the colony "will have the role of supplying raw materials, will *become* the place of the material." Furthermore they document

> a situation of enunciation in which the matter of speech, the topic, the
> referent, physically existed but was always going to be physically absent
> from the place of speaking and listening. Finally, these texts record the
> transmission from America to Europe of substantial bodies; artifacts, ani-
> mals, plants, ore—Indians. It is as if, in despair of making the New World
> present in words, language were materialized in some naive way, as a mov-
> able container faultlessly conveying meaning.[14]

If Raleigh's account was a rhetorical play of plenty and absence, his
friend Thomas Harriot's *A Briefe and True Report of the New Found Land
of Virginia*, published in 1588 and dedicated to Raleigh, is fully committed to presenting a more tangible plenty and is explicitly designed to
encourage further voyages and settlement, being addressed to "the adventurers, favorers, and wellwishers of the enterprise for the inhabiting
and planting of Virginia."[15] It is noticeable, too, that whereas Raleigh's
emphasis on gold meant that he ignored other commodities ("Where
there is store of gold, it is in effect nedeles to remember other commodities for trade"[16]), Harriot's focus is quite different, with the land
considered more for its recreational possibilities of "hunting, hawking,
fishing, fowling, and the rest." The order of the book reflects this, presenting first a

> declaration of such commodities there alreadie found or to be raised, which
> will not onely serve the ordinary turnes of you which are and shall bee the
> planters and inhabitants, but such an overplus sufficiently to bee yelded, or
> by men of skill to bee provided, as by way of trafficke and exchaunge, with
> our owne nation of England, will enrich yourselves the providers . . . which
> commodities for distinction sake I call *Merchantable*.

The plenty of the land, the "overplus," can be creamed off for trade,
and we see here how, in the terms of chapter 1, exchange value promises
to supplement and eventually supplant, use value. Harriot's remaining
two categories are commodities for sustenance and a rather vague one
of "such other commodities besides, as I am able to remember." Only
at the very end of the preface do we find a promise of "a briefe descrip-

tion of the nature and maners of the people of the countrey." In the text
he suggests that he will deal with them only as far as to demonstrate
"how that they in respect of troubling our inhabiting and planting, are
not to be feared, but that they shall have cause both to feare and love
us."[17] The Indians are presented here as marginal to the enterprise of
the book and indeed the enterprise of colonizing.

Yet Harriot's text dwells on more aspects of them than this suggests,
and the first illustrated edition of the work, issued within two years of
the first edition in four languages, and widely reprinted and adapted,
contains the De Bry engravings based on the drawings John White
made on Harriot's voyage, which bring the Indians to the fore, with
much more attention paid to their decoration, clothing, and religion
than to Virginia's "merchantable" commodities. The text is intended
as what David Quinn calls a "propagandist tract to discourage adverse
rumours about Raleigh's Virginia, and to set out the facts that would
encourage settlers to go there"[18] and specifically prioritizes the possibilities of an abundance, 'an overplus', of commodities that could en-
rich European trade and exploitation. Even in developing this quantitative inventory, the language moves toward an excess that has something
of the marvelous and sublime. For example, it is not just the fact that
the coastal area may be relatively barren but the idea of excess that
drives the rhetoric of the description of the interior, where the travelers found

> the soyle to be fatter; the trees greater and to grow thinner; the ground
> more firme and deeper mould; more and larger champions; finer grasse . . .
> more plentie of their fruites; more abondance of beaste, the more inhabited
> by people, and of greater pollicie and larger dominions.[19]

This rhetorical trope of an excess to be found just beyond where you
are standing, of El Dorado, also appears in Raleigh's *Discoverie:*

> I never saw a more beawtifull countrey, nor more lively prospectes, hils
> so raised heere and there over the vallies, the river winding into divers
> braunches, the plaines adjoyning without bush or stubble, all faire greene
> grasse, . . . the deare crossing in every path, the birds towards the evening
> singing on every tree with a thousand several tunes, cranes and herons of
> white, crimson and carnation pearching on the rivers side, the ayre fresh
> with a gentle easterly wind, and every stone that we stooped to take up,
> promised eyther golde or silver by his complexion.[20]

Even more noticeably, Harriot's text also offers a different sort of "overplus" of information about the Indians themselves. David Quinn refers to Harriot's and White's stress on Indians' leisure activities, which reflects "a refusal to be limited to a purely economic or professional view of the people," and Muriel Rukeyser, in her remarkable and imaginative account of Harriott, dwells on the presence of "delight" in his own response and in his account of the Indians' lives.[21] Even in the depiction of "Their manner of Fyshinge" the sense of abundance in the picture is foremost, and Harriot's commentary reinforces this.

> Dowbtless yt is a pleasant sighte to see the people, somtymes wadinge and goinge somtymes sailinge in those Rivers, which are shallow and not deepe, free from all care of heaping opp Riches for their posterite, content with their state, and living friendlye together of those thinges which god of his bountye hath given unto them, yet without givinge him any thankes according to his desarte. So savage is this people and deprived of the true knowledge of god.[22]

The celebratory tone is chastened by the belated reminder that these are heathens, and "ungrateful" Indians at that, recalling Paul Le Jeune's criticism in chapter 1. They enjoy the bounty but do not acknowledge it as God's gift by thanking Him. (Given the ambiguities that remain over Harriot's own possible atheism, it is perhaps equally possible to see this as rather a half-hearted dismissal.[23]) In accord with this primitive felicity, we have little sense of work or trade on the part of the Indians themselves, though in the pictures we do see fishing weirs and even the intrusion of a European trade object in the form of a doll carried by the Indian child in the picture captioned "A cheff Ladye of Pomeiooc."

Mary Campbell has pointed out that De Bry, in producing *America* from the White and Harriot materials, used none of White's watercolors of flora and fauna, even though they could have illustrated the "commodities" of America. Instead he concentrated on what she calls the ethnographic pictures, those involving Indian life, which he made slightly more European in appearance. She argues that "the result of these distortions and omissions is exoticism. The familiar features and poses of the Indian bodies set off their clothing, jewellery, weapons and so on as 'strange.'" While the difficulty of demonstrating just how the exotic was constituted or recognized in any period may create some doubt about her claims, her larger argument is that the effect of the inclusion of the pictures is to emphasize a quality already in the text, namely, a lack of narrative or historical context, creating what has since come to be called an "ethnographic present." She argues that there is an overall narrative but it is an allegorical one provided by De Bry's frontispiece of Adam and Eve, in which we have the fall in the foreground and the postlapsarian laboring in the background. Her contention, though, that these engravings "set up a parallel between colonists and colonized that portrays civilization as a cultural maturing process—a matter of historical development rather than a sign of absolute European difference" needs to be explored in light of the actual drawings and text, which give evidence of industry but also of delight.[24] Are the Indians, presented as fishing and wading, Adamic or fallen? In addition, the sheer presence of human figures surely serves more than an ethnographic or documentary purpose. Because of the absence of clothing, the human body, marked and decorated, takes center stage. There is even a picture showing "the markes of sundrye of the cheif mene of Virginia," with the markings identified as belonging to individuals, and the effect is that the personal and cultural become the "overplus," the extra, marvelous and exotic.

I return to the role of the body and its representation later in this chapter, both because of the heavy ideological investments in nakedness in any discussion of savage/civilized exchanges and because of the question of the limits of textualization and its disruptions and excesses. Ultimately, as Fuller insists, the signs of authenticity—the collection of anecdotes or actual objects or illustrations—can be understood only "as signs or metonymic figures" with no automatic route to the reality for which they stand: "We have to speak of metonymy rather than synecdoche: How do we know of what whole the object forms a part?"[25]

The fascination with the exotic often prompts a move to the pictorial, the visualization of the body, and can better be satisfied with a picture or an image. This is the point in written texts at which the language breaks down and the rhetorical disclaimer appears, gesturing toward that which it cannot describe. Thus the human body is in a similar relation to the text as the idea of the marvelous, the promise of that which lies beyond: it is supplementary to the text and yet fundamental. Since Harriot's text was first published without illustrations and there is no firm evidence that he wrote the commentaries to the pictures (though Rukeyser is not alone in assuming that they are Harriot's, "written at his freest, best, most vivid"[26]), it is difficult to talk of one authorial agenda. Rather, we have, as with many such texts, a set of ingredients whose significance may operate centrifugally, and not in any fully controlled way. In this case, the additional pictures and captions further emphasize an "overplus" that is not just economic. Creating similar problems of control and interpretation are other sorts of supplements, for example, the word list, an element peculiar to this sort of text. The early texts that record the meetings and exchanges of the two worlds also often incorporate (to invoke a fundamental trope of such early exchanges) elements of what they describe, in the form of foreign words. These words sometimes remain untranslated in the text, operating as elements of irreducible alterity and potential exoticism. Oviedo leaves the words untranslated in his *Historia* and explains his reasons very clearly.

> If some strange and barbarous words be found here, the cause is the novelty which they describe; and let no one question my good, plain language, for I was born in Madrid and raised in the royal house and have spoken with noble folk and have read somewhat. Thus let it not be suspected that I have mistaken the foreign words for my own Castilian tongue, which is held to be the best of all the vulgar languages. Whatever terms in this volume do not accord with Castilian are names or words put there to indicate those things that the Indians refer to by those names.[27]

Increasingly, though, we find separate lists of words with translations, and of course eventually dictionaries and grammars. Greenblatt has observed that in most early European accounts, "the language of the Indians is noted not in order to register cultural specificity but in order to facilitate barter, movement, and assimilation through conversion." He distinguishes explorers and traders from missionaries. "To learn a language may be a step towards mastery, but to *study* a language is to place oneself in a situation of dependency, to submit . . . This is why it is singularly appropriate that missionaries begin by learning languages, but the whole Christian ethos involves the proposition that one must submit in order to transcend, or we might say, dominate."[28] Certainly this is borne out by the fact that the serious accounts of language and the early dictionaries were produced as part of missionary projects,[29] and Greenblatt's remark is useful in pinpointing the strange mixture of the curious and the useful in many lists, even if, as I hope to show, the opposition he describes is perhaps too clear-cut and the motives more mixed.

With Roger Williams's *A Key into the Language of America* as my ultimate destination, I concentrate for the remainder of this chapter on those texts that include lists of words as supplement to an otherwise narrative or discursive structure, showing that the detectable forms of organization or structure reflect underlying agendas differing from the apparently neutral idea of the list. In particular, we can find a variety of taxonomic impulses to codify and arrange, practical agendas governing the choice of words, and a more dialogical impulse in which conversations begin to take place within the text and across the two languages. The appearance of lists of words has a close relation in its function to the lists of commodities and objects to be found in the New World (heightened by the fact that the individual words, usually nouns, appear as concrete objects in themselves). As Fuller points out, lists in general

> make a strong claim about the world by the simplicity of their form, a form which adjoins what Elaine Scarry calls "simple counting"; "Counting makes an extreme claim about its correspondence with the material realm. It asserts a one-to-one correspondence between itself and its subject matter."[30]

Word lists, as I define them, are always supplementary to something else, an account of travel or of the country itself, but, as Derrida has shown, the supplement has a more complex role in relation to the whole than it might seem. Williams's *A Key* is perhaps the first text to make the word list (as opposed to the dictionary or grammar) the main principle of organization of a whole text. Prior to him the lists operate with a variety of functions, not necessarily those given by the author. The foreign words are there sometimes as a sign of authenticity, given a meaning by the English words at their side but also operating as something foreign, both translatable and irreducibly foreign and strange. In this second aspect they operate as a curiosity just like the objects collected in the wonder-cabinets of the sixteenth and seventeenth centuries. My interest in the lists is that they are by definition points of opposition and exchange, like the accounts of first contact in Cartier and elsewhere, to which they are often attached as supplement. They demonstrate both difference and similarity, the alien but also the ability to comprehend it, and what is noticeable when we look at specific early instances is the way these different elements and intentions become confused.[31]

Probably the first and certainly the most widely circulated early list is to be found in Peter Martyr's *De Orbe Novo* of 1516, which comprises the first three "Decades" of what was later to become a much larger project.[32] His "Vocabula Barbara" is made up of parallel columns of words and phrases, with the "barbarous" side comprising a mixture of names of places and people as well as some common words. These are all matched with parallel Latin definitions or descriptions. Names of places, explained merely as "regio" or "mons," make up more than half of the five-page list, which also includes the names Cabot and Vespucci, defined as navigators, and names of plants, including exotic items like herbs and at least half a dozen names for the potato. We also find several terms translated as 'canoe' and 'gold' (or 'shining like gold') and a large number for gods or idols ('simulachri') of various sorts, including crowned idols. The preponderance of proper names over ordinary words makes this more of a glossary than a dictionary, and Martyr explains that these are words that the reader might encounter in the text (as opposed to later lists that point to experiences and uses for the words outside the text), so that the "Vocabula Barbara" refers as much to the text as to any world beyond it.

This is particularly the case with an intriguing cluster of words associated with cannibalism. On the "barbarous" side of the list we find *Antropophagi*, which is of course a Greek term, explained as 'comestores hominum'. Later in the list we have *Caribes* on the "barbarous" side explained as 'sunt antropophagi', so that *antropophagi* has switched sides. The next item in the list on the "barbarous" side is *Canibales* 'idem qui caribes'. There is a circular quality about these definitions that confirms the idea that cannibalism is always "over there" rather than actually locatable, in that the first set merely matches Greek and Latin words, rather than locating the people, and the next two repeat the same pattern in a self-feeding and, we might say, cannibalistic fashion. Thus the "Vocabula Barbara" reflects the role of the words in the original Columbus account from which it is derived, where, as Eric Cheyfitz puts it,

> the missing Arawak/Carib term that Columbus translates as *canibales* follows a particular ideological trajectory; cut off from its proper (cultural)

meaning in Native American languages, it becomes a purely political figure in European tongues, a figure that tries to erase its own rhetoricity by claiming a proper, or ethnographical, referent—the "fact" of cannibalism—which, even if it could be proved, would not justify or explain the colonial/imperial process of translation that displaces the original native term.[33]

As a set of words reflective of the idea of the barbarism of the New World, Martyr's "Vocabula Barbara" certainly contains the ingredients of the exotic and the fabulous that are to be recirculated in a self-referring and self-confirming sequence along with the corresponding visual images from De Bry.[34] Martyr, if we assume that he compiled the list,[35] gives a heady mix of exotic words. There are many place-names and words associated with gold, gilded idols, and cannibalism, but few day-to-day words. We do have words translated as 'house', 'canoe', 'serpent', and even a couple that hint at actual situations of contact (translated as the imperatives 'come' and 'take'), and the word *toatoa* translated as 'mama mama'. Perhaps the most puzzling entry in this respect is opposite the word *machabuca*, 'dicitur quid ad me'. This is intriguing because either it is not a definition at all, simply giving the word "as it was said to me" (but who is the "me," since Martyr never traveled or heard the words?), or it is the native term for *hearsay*, indicating an awareness of the mediated nature of much of the material, which would be a strange inclusion in a short vocabulary. Martyr explains in his brief introduction that for the reader's convenience, he has brought together and alphabetized the words scattered throughout the volume. He bids the reader "farewell and learn new voices / words [voces] and new names at the same time as new things to be marvelled at."

The order here is alphabetic, with proper and common nouns mixed together, but in Richard Eden's first English translation the list is severely reduced, stripped of most of the proper names and split into a glossary and a dictionary. After his list of contents, Eden (if we can attribute this organization to him, and this is always a problem) devotes a page to "the interpretacion of certeyne woordes," presumably those in the text he thinks need an explanation. Among these are words for 'continent', 'caravel', 'hemispherium', 'equinoctial', 'werst' ("an Italian mile"), 'colonie' ("an habitation"), and oddly "gatti mammoni, monkeys." He then has a section headed "The Indian language," which presents fourteen words with facing English translations. The very briefness of this list of words (only five of which are to be found in Martyr's original "Vocabula Barbara," while the rest seem to be gleaned from the text by Eden) tempts us to see it as containing some quintessential selection criteria. The full list is as follows:

> *Canoa* 'a boat or barke'
> *Caciqui* 'kynges or governours'
> *Zemes* 'an Idole'
> *Tuyra* 'the devyill'
> *Machana* 'a sworde'
> *Areitos* 'songes or balades'
> *Tona* 'the moon'
> *Tonatico* 'the sun'
> *Quines* 'prestes'
> *chiuy* 'a man'
> *Ira* 'a woman'
> *Boa* 'a house'
> *Cauni* 'gold'
> *Mayani* 'nothing &c'[36]

This is a fascinating set, presenting basic words but reflecting concerns of power and religion (king, devil, priest, sword) and the new and exotic (canoe, song). It concludes with the stark opposition haunting the dreams of investors and adventurers, around which Raleigh and others constructed their later accounts: gold and nothing. This is a trenchant illustration of Greenblatt's description of the European discursive economy as it encountered America with "its paradoxical yoking of empty and full, worthless and valuable, counterfeit and real."[37]

Eden's introduction to another very early travel account also plays on this sense of the text as a scene of the marvelous, giving traces or promises of an even more marvelous reality.

> I hadde entended here (well beeloved Reader,) to have spoken somewhat of such straunge thynges and Monsters, whereof mencion is made in thys Booke, to thende that suche as by the narownes of thyr understandinge are not of capacitie to conceave the causes and natures of thynges, myght partly have been satissfyed wyth some sensyble reasons, But beynge at thys tyme otherwise hyndered, it shal suffice al good and honest wittes, that whatoever the Lorde hath pleased, that hath he doen in heaven and earth, and in the Sea and in all depe places.

He ends with a quotation from Eccles. 1, "The eye is not satisfyed with syght, & the eare is not filed with hearinge," which gestures toward a wonder greater than the senses can apprehend, though what he is offering is exotic and sensational rather than the transcendent experience the Biblical invocation suggests.[38]

The only complete modern English translation from the Latin of *De Orbe Novo* omits Martyr's list without comment, and Eden's short list is likewise generally ignored, yet these lists have a revealing and complex relation to the texts they supplement. Other early lists have equally mixed agendas and organizational principles. Alonso de Ercilla y Zuniga's long epic poem *La Araucana* of 1590, for instance, includes a small glossary of Indian words, which appear in the main text untranslated, because of their common use, together with place-names and names of leaders. These words consist in their entirety of three words for tribute and taxation and one for 'el demonio, por el qual juran quando quieren obligarse infaliblemente, a cumplir lo que prometen'.[39]

So far the word lists could be said to point back toward the text, where they first appear, rather than to the original experiences and cultures to which the text refers. They act as an explanation or an aid to reading rather than an aid actually to encountering another culture, and it could be argued that this internally self-referential role remains important for the word list even when it is played down in favor of other, more utilitarian claims. The most explicit—indeed perhaps the only explicit—recognition of the multiple roles the word list plays and the keenest sense of an intended audience is to be found in William Wood's 1634 *New England's Prospect*. Prefacing a couple pages of common Indian words, listed alphabetically with English equivalents alongside, he explains,

> Because many have desired to heare some of the Natives Language, I have here inserted a small *Nomenclator, with the Names of their chiefe Kings, Rivers, Moneths, and dayes, whereby such as have in-sight into the Tongues,* may know to what language it is most inclining; and such as desire it as an unknown language onely, may reape *delight, if they can get no profit.*[40]

This is designed for consumption by either the scholar of languages, who can look for resemblances, as with the widespread interest in Hebrew connections, or the armchair traveler, to whom he refers on the title page, when he writes of enriching the knowledge of "the mind-travelling reader" as well as the future voyager.

A much more characteristic utilitarian justification, though, is implicit in Jacques Cartier's accounts of his two early voyages, an extract from which I present in the Introduction. Greenblatt has pinpointed the conjunctions of religious, linguistic, and economic in Cartier and the "blank refusal of logical connectives characteristic of much early travel writing,"[41] but he does not discuss the word lists that supplement the account of each voyage. At the end of the first account, the words appear in matching columns, Indian and English, but in no apparent order, and they are an intriguing mix: words translated as 'God', 'sun', 'heaven', 'day', 'night', 'head', 'throat', and 'nose', and also the vocabulary of exchange and trade in words for 'hatchet', 'brass', 'red cloth', 'knife', and 'gold'. In the second account the list is not much longer, considering the much more complex dealings that had been taking place and the fact that they had with them the two native interpreters whom they had taken back to Europe after the first voyage, but it does show clear signs of organization. First there are the numbers one to ten and then "the names of the chiefest partes of man, and other wordes necessary to be known." The twenty-two words for the parts of the body end with those for 'a man's member' and 'a woman's member', and the general words include some conversational phrases ('give me supper', 'come and speake with me', let's goe to bedde', and 'give me a hatchet').[42] This move into phrases and sentences also reflects the fact that the most basic lists involve nouns, single objects, almost like concrete unrelated things brought back. Verbs, on the other hand, imply actions, situations, and ultimately therefore some sort of interaction and dialogue, but before looking at this development it is worth looking further at some of the forms of organization and what they imply.

In *The Historie of Travaile into Virginia Britannia*, William Strachey includes a list of about eight hundred diverse words, variously described in the different manuscripts as "for the better enabling of such who shalbe thither ymployed" and "by which, such who shall be Imployed thether may know the readyer how to confer, and how to truck and Trade with the People."[43] The list is organized alphabetically from *Ahone* 'God' to *Zanckone* 'to sneeze' but, confusingly, with some English words also listed within the alphabetical sequence. The alphabetical order seems partly to dictate things (why the word for 'sneeze', except that it starts with a z?), and even in the most basic list other agendas shape the organization, so that sometimes basic grammar on the Latin model is incorporated, as in the conjugations of verbs. Captain John Smith prefaces his *Map of Virginia* with a few pages of words and their English equivalents, "because many doe desire to knowe the maner of their language." As well as the basic numbers we have a list of objects, all nouns and tending to reflect the experience of trade and contact (skins, copper, shoes, and guns), though with a strange and presumably humorous insertion of the word for cuckold—what Karen Robertson describes as "one fissure of curiosity about patriarchal sexual arrangements intersecting the material." At the end are a couple of whole sentences in the form of questions that reflect pointedly the agenda and anxieties of each side and are left unanswered, as parts of a dialogue that are not joined: If the Europeans were concerned with survival—'I am verie hungrie, what shall I eate?' the Indians may have seen a different threat—'In how many daies will there come hether any more English ships?.' The list ends with the most developed statement, 'Bid Pokahontas bring hither two little Baskets, and I will give her white beads to make her a chaine'. In this sentence we have the conjunction of all the elements of trade, but, as Jeffrey Knapp notes, relating this passage to the larger question of Smith's relation to Pocahontas, its "change in tone and temporal inconsequence make it sound like a dreamy afterthought, connected to the previous dialogue [which Knapp argues is all about the English food supply] only through information the text has yet to provide, and then still detached by Smith's evocation of merely 'little' food baskets."[44]

Here the list is rounded off with an exchange, involving characters who are later mythologically linked to the whole idea of Indian-white relations, but in other cases the closure insisted on by the organization of the word list is of a different kind. In the brief "Dictionary of the Huron Language" that Gabriel Sagard appends to his *Le Grand Voyage du Pays des Hurons* of 1632 and describes as "necessaire a ceux qui n'ont a l'intelligence d'icelle, & ont a traiter avec les sauvages du pays," the words are arranged alphabetically by the French words (though sometimes in broad categories, such as "animaux"). At the end of the list, though, we find not a French word but *Yoscaha*, the Huron word for 'the Creator', which allows Sagard to end his dictionary with a sort of catechism of phrases in which the Creator is the Christian God. Sagard is in fact explicit from the outset that the encounter with new experiences should not challenge his established views. He contrasts his own journey with that of Apollonius of Tyre, who expected to learn and find better societies. Rather ominously for any reader expecting an objective or responsive approach to the Indians, he assures us that

> I for my part have never had so crazed a longing to acquire knowledge by travel, for I was brought up in the school of God, under the rule and discipline of the Seraphic Order of St Francis, wherein is taught the sound knowledge of the saints, apart from which all that is learnt is but the vain trifling of curiosity.

He already has the framework with which to judge all that happens to him and all that he sees, and he actually describes it in terms of a visual frame or "fix."

> You shall see as in a perspective picture, richly engraved, the wretchedness of human nature, tainted at the source, deprived of the training of the faith, destitute of morality.[45]

With its structure manipulated to end with God and a Christian sentiment, the word list reflects precisely this perspective,[46] and a Christian resolution similar to Sagard's, though it points to an absence, is to be found in Charles de Rochefort's account, which includes a "Vocabulaire Caraibe" of a dozen pages, arranged in subject headings, including family terms and parts of the body. The last section is "choses spirituelles, ou de Religion," with a few Carib terms for "spirit," but then de Rochefort adds at the end, "Invocation, priere, ceremonie, adoration. Ils ne savent ce que c'est."[47]

One of the inherent possibilities of the word list, especially as it begins to incorporate sentences or phrases as grammatical examples and variations, is dialogue. The religious forms of this dialogue are examined in succeeding chapters, so I limit my examples here to one particular but influential aspect of the dialogue, which was to be important in Enlightenment debates over the noble savage. Jean de Lery's word list, included in his *History of A Voyage to the Land of Brazil* of 1578, is perhaps the first to develop, through grammatical exercises and variations, into an exchange of views as well as words. Chapter 20, which concludes de Lery's actual stay in Brazil and is in the form of a "colloquy" in both French and Tupi, is described by de Certeau as providing "a code for linguistic transformation," which can then demonstrate the homogeneity underlying the diversity that has been surveyed in the previous detailed descriptions of exotic flora and fauna. "It allows unity

to be restored by folding upon one another all the heterogeneous peel-
ings that cover an identity of substance." This is not the same, though,
as reducing difference to a common original. It is a conversion of one
thing into another but differs from religious conversion in not privileging any side. As de Certeau puts it, "it replaces the being-there of a
beginning with a transformation which unravels on the surface of languages, which makes a single meaning pass from tongue to tongue."
The colloquy is a demonstration of translation via a dialogue in which,
as the grammatical systematization and exercises take over, the characters fade from the scene. This means that the fictions of difference and
differentiated identity give way to the play of transformation and an
underlying common identity, but it also means that the Indian's speech
becomes effaced as our sense of just who is speaking begins to falter.
In one way, then, what we have here in dramatic form is—depending
on one's view of humanist universalism—either the emergence of a
common humanity out of a dialogue of difference or the subsuming of
Indian identity under an Enlightenment conception of a common
humanity.[48]

This concern to locate underlying universals often uses the idea of
the naked body, in contradistinction to the changing externals of
clothes. It is perhaps a similar impulse in word lists, which from the
beginning included sets of words, either randomly or arranged as a specific group, for the parts of the body. This also relates closely to the
way the human body is presented and used in early texts of contact and
discovery, through the theme of covering and discovering or revealing.
As we saw with Cartier, one of the earliest groupings was parts of the
body, and it is worth considering what this might imply. Perhaps the
earliest and most interesting instance is to be found in de Lery, where,
after the colloquy he gives in both languages a list of the parts of the
body, followed by three terms in Tupinamba only. These he describes
as "Names of parts of the body that it is not decent to name" (in the
original the phrase is "Noms de parties du corps qui ne sont honnestes
a nommer," and in De Bry's edition in part 3 of *America*, it is "nomina
partium corporis pudendarum"). And yet, of course, he gives the Tupinamba names. What does it mean to write down a word which is too
obscene to be translated? What purpose is it serving? Given de Lery's
overall rather positive view of the Indians, we could say that this was
the linguistic parallel to their innocent nakedness described earlier in

the chapter. The words, like the parts of the body, are shameful only to those who have postlapsarian shame. Interestingly, Janet Whatley's recent edition provides a footnote to tell us that they are the words for "the male member, the visible female parts and the internal female parts," which language would certainly seem to indicate no disappearance of the sort of linguistic decorum or prudery that led scholars to translate offensive passages from Indian and other texts not into English but into Latin.[49]

We find something similar to de Lery, though with a stronger moral opprobrium, in Louis Hennepin's *New Discovery* of 1698. In a chapter titled "What Salvages are cloathed and what not," Hennepin describes the Indians of the South (as distinct from those of the North, who "have always gone Cloath'd even before they had any Commerce with the Europeans") as apparently without shame about their nakedness, "but they rather seem to glory in it. When they talk amongst themselves, they often make use of the Word *Tchetanga*, which is obscene." Alexander Whitaker in 1613 also aligns language and clothing in an intriguing way.

> They live naked in bodie, as if their shame of their sinne deserved no covering. Their names are as naked as their bodie: they esteeme it a vertue to lie, deceive and steale as their master the divell teacheth them.[50]

If the names are "naked," this would suggest a lack of the sort of civilized decorum or euphemism that we see in Hennepin and de Lery, and perhaps an account of Indians as noble savages would present it in this way, but instead Whitaker immediately goes in the opposite direction in his next sentence, with a description of language used dishonestly (lying and deceiving), suggesting the complex connotations of nakedness, which he is apparently unable to control or use consistently, and which I develop more fully in my discussion of Roger Williams in chapter 4.

I have been concentrating on the parts of the body because of the body's important role in the larger discursive terms of similarity and difference that underlie texts of contact and discovery. The body is where we all are the same, and at the same time it is the most charged area where difference (sexual, racial, and cultural) is played out. That this enterprise of comparison was not just a one-way street is revealed in an account from the end of the sixteenth century of Indians' language learning. A visitor to Dominica describes the Indians'

> great desire to learn the English tongue; for some of them will point to most parts of his body, and having told the name of it in the language of Dominica, he would not rest till he were told the name of it in English, which having once told he would repeate till he could either name it right, or at least till he thought it was right and so commonly it should be.[51]

The "naming of parts" therefore can be seen as an attempt at equivalence and communication, but in the texts that are produced from these encounters in Europe there is often an attempt to order what is potentially exorbitant, that is, to control the exchange. The obscene, in the sense of what is not concealed but should be, keeps intruding, not from outside but from within the European system itself as a product of its rules and concealments, and I want to pursue this further by returning to the role of the savage body in de Lery.

De Lery's account appeared after Harriot's, to form part of the third volume of De Bry's *America*, but preceding this edition by ten years the original edition of his *History of a New Voyage to the Land of Brazil* included a small number of highly influential pictures of the Tupinamba Indians. In addition to the visual representation of the Indian body, though, de Lery provides a particularly full and self-conscious verbal account, which is worth consideration. Although in many ways the details he gives in his overall account of the Tupinamba, most infamously their cannibalism, are alienating, there is also a complicating sense of the vitality and hospitality of the Tupinamba culture. Whether we want to see this as just his firsthand experience transcending the Christian framework or as a different set of templates via sixteenth-century humanism and even Rabelaisian sources, as Whatley suggests, we do have a more self-consciously shifting perspective. In his first chapter, "Of the Natural Qualities, Strength, Stature, Nudity, Disposition and Ornamentation of the Body of the Brazilian Savages," after quite a detailed account he offers a sort of summary by the device of offering the reader a succession of verbal pictures (the first backed up by an actual illustration). Now that he has given us the information, it is up to us:

> If you would picture to yourself a savage according to this description, you may imagine in the first place a naked man, well formed and proportioned in all his limbs.

He then details the addition of paint and ornaments, so that "you will see him as he usually is in his country." But de Lery then gives several more versions. For the second "contemplation," we are to remove all the "flourishes" and cover him with feathers. For the third, we are to imagine him in full ceremonial regalia, when we might say he is in "full Papal splendour," and for the fourth, to leave him half-dressed and give him European breeches and jacket with different-colored sleeves, presumably like a harlequin. Then, "you will judge that he no longer needs anything but a fool's bauble." Finally, we are to give him the rattles and equipment to see him as he looks when he dances and performs. What is intriguing about this is the sense of presenting a changing figure for our entertainment, who is dressed and undressed like a puppet, or perhaps a doll in a collection, going from noble savage to object of ridicule in European clothes. Lery's final valediction seems poised between irony (in the mocking word "magnificence") and approval of their relish for life: "Now let us leave a little to one side our Tupinamba in all their magnificence, frolicking and enjoying the good times that they know so well how to have."[52]

When he turns to the Indian women, he describes their painting and bodily ornamentation but stresses as "doubly strange and marvellous" that they categorically refused to wear clothes. Even those who were captives of the Europeans and were forced "by great strokes of the whip" to clothe themselves would not be content "unless, before going to bed they could promenade naked all around the island." Whatley describes this as a "rather troubling" passage that "compels us to take measure of the assumptions that separate us from Lery." It is certainly difficult to be sure of the tone, both here and in de Lery's next paragraph, when he ends his description emphasizing nakedness. "So, without any epilogue here, let the reader, by this narration, contemplate them as he will." If one assumes a gendered reader here, it is certainly possible to detect a wink and a nudge, but at the end of the chapter de Lery is categorical that "this crude nakedness in such a woman is much less alluring than one might expect." It is not that their natural beauty is less than the Europeans—far from it—but that "the elaborate attire, paint, wigs, curled hair, great ruffs, farthingales, robes upon robes" of European women are the cause of "more ills" in the form of wantonness than are the savage women. If "decorum" allowed, he would "give reasons so evident that no-one could deny them." This technique of indicating that something is not said, pointing to the absence, surrounds the representations of sexuality and relates to the recognition of the eroticism of concealment over disclosure, in which the "robes upon robes" are more erotic than the naked body. This is a tricky area for de Lery, and he then has to dissociate himself from any idea that nakedness is acceptable. The Biblical reference to Adam and Eve's shame means that we should reject nakedness as "against the law of nature," which particular law "is by no means observed among our poor Americans." He does not follow up any of the implications of this, for instance, in the direction of the Indians being prelapsarian, settling for using them as an attack on the superfluities and hypocrisies of Europe, but the idea of an innocent nakedness does resonate here.[53]

De Certeau's reading of de Lery emphasizes the savage body as an aspect of the textualization of such encounters. "What travel literature really fabricates is the primitive as a *body of pleasure* . . . Such eroticizing of the other's body—of the primitive nudity and the primitive voice— goes hand in hand with the formation of an ethics of production." His argument is based on a fundamental distinction between voice and writing, which he aligns with a set of nature/culture oppositions. He traces in de Lery the ways in which the physical presence of sound, voice, and body operates in spite of the production of an objectifying knowledge through writing, or rather is produced by it as a remainder, a leftover. "This waste product of constructive thinking—its fallout and its repressed—will finally become the other." He shows how for de Lery the memories of the physical sounds themselves, the voices and songs, escape the scriptural economy and signify that "other economy" of pleasure and excess that "the economy of production had to repress in order to be founded as such." Having established this model of repression and desire, de Certeau is able to connect voice and body with other excluded and subversive phenomena, such as witchcraft, cannibalism, and woman herself. "The native world, like the diabolical cosmos, becomes Woman. It is declined in the feminine gender." The very inclusiveness of this model of exclusion and repression, which makes such connections possible, also creates its own problems in assuming that all texts are the same. Nevertheless de Certeau's insistence on the integral relation of what is outside of the text is useful as a way of approaching early texts of encounter and their supplements.[54]

De Lery's text, like Harriot's, presents fascinating, unstable combinations of materials. Visual images, foreign words, and foreign bodies are more or less incorporated or assimilated into the discursive patterns of the text. I began this chapter with the exchange of an object, Powhatan's mantle, and its symbolic domestication, but what these texts reveal is the complexities of translating and transforming signs, as reflected in what might at first appear to be the peripheral element of word lists. In chapter 4, I turn to the most complex example of the form, to show in detail how a reading of Roger Williams's *Key into the Language of America* opens up the interlocking discourses of his particular time and place.

4

Roger Williams's Key into America

ROGER WILLIAMS is probably best known today for his distinctive role in early American history as the champion of religious and civil freedoms for the new colonists, a man whose opposition to the Puritans' theocratic ambitions led to his exile to Rhode Island, where he lived in proximity to the Indians of the region. In this chapter, I concentrate on one remarkable product of that exile, his book *A Key into the Language of America, or An Help to the Language of the Natives in that part of America called New England*.[1] Williams's peculiar position between white and Indian societies makes him a useful and intriguing figure. A shrewd trader who was also fully committed to religious conversion and the values of Christianity and civilization, Williams had a thoroughly unsentimental but unusually well-informed view of the Narragansetts and other local Indian people. He was regularly occupied as translator and mediator between Indians and whites, and *A Key* embodies this experience and accumulated knowledge to form perhaps the most complex account of contact produced in early New England. For the present purposes, it serves as a unique key into the complex of ideas and activities represented as translation, exchange, and conversion between Indians and whites in early contacts.

A Key was written literally between Europe and America, according to Williams, on his sea voyage back to visit England, and was designed for the information and use of the English. As such it can be seen as intermediate between the tradition of voyages and visits to the New

World, written retrospectively from Europe, and a classic American text of foundation, John Winthrop's *Modell of Christian Charity*, written on the way *to* America. The explicit intention was to aid practical communication with Indians as well as giving information about them, and the emphasis is on the activities of conversion and (less discussed by later commentators) trade. It is therefore, perhaps more than any other work of the time, set firmly and consciously within the overlapping terms of exchange, conversion, and translation.

Williams's metaphor of a key is worth pursuing, as he himself does in his preface:

> I present you with a *Key;* I have not heard of the like, yet framed, since it pleased God to bring that mighty *Continent* of *America* to light . . . This *Key*, respects the *Native Language* of it, and happily may unlocke some *Rarities* concerning the *Natives* themselves, not yet discovered. (83)

The key can unlock knowledge that is imaged as treasures ("some *Rarities*") he has himself acquired ("so dearly bought in some few yeares hardship and charges among the *Barbarians*"). Rather than "bury those Materialls in my Grave at land or Sea," he offers them for the pleasure and profit of his readers. This way of describing locked rarities and treasures suggests a connection with the fashion, discussed in Chapter 3 and by this point on the wane, for collecting and displaying curiosities and "strange things." Williams's key can be both a literal key to a secret cabinet and a key in the sense of an organizing principle, since his collection is organized, like the early word lists and the cabinets of early science, both to display the element of curiosity or strangeness and to remove it by translating and explaining it. Cotton Mather describes Williams's book as a "little relation with observations, wherein he *spiritualises* the curiosities with two and thirty chapters, whereof he entertains his reader."[2] For Mather, the spiritualizing presumably refers to the impulse, best seen in the poems that close each section, to place the Indians in a larger Christian frame, but Williams's book is not ultimately limited by the Christian perpective applied so rigorously by Gabriel Sagard, as described in chapter 3.

The knowledge Williams offers is valuable, and can be put to use: "A little Key may open a Box, where lies a bunch of Keys" (83). The image of keys opening up access to other keys suggests a branching and proliferation, but the idea of locked secrets, of privileged and limited

points of access, also suggests a hermetic element, the need for interpretation and control over meaning, which looks forward to the concerns of recent critiques of ethnographic and other representations of
different cultures[3] as well as back to the widespread Renaissance fascination with secret keys, codes, and ciphers. (It is an intriguing irony
that some documents left by Thomas Harriot were believed for many
years to be in code but were in fact his notes on the Algonquian language.[4])

Williams's image of opening up and multiplying access through the
ability to communicate is applicable both to commerce and to proselytizing. Martin Luther's description of the importance of language is notable for the proliferation of similar metaphors:

> Languages . . . are the ark, or the secret repositories, which preserve this
> noble treasure locked up in it. They are the cups, in which we receive and
> carry round the health-giving drink. They are the cells ever ready from
> which the worthy preacher brings forth the Gospel bread. And, as the sa-
> cred writings themselves indicate, they are the baskets in which the loaves
> and fragments remaining are placed, so that they may not perish.[5]

Williams's key is different from any other "yet framed, since it pleased
God to bring that mighty *Continent* of *America* to light." Bringing to
light implies both a revealing, or dis-covering, of knowledge and an
exposure to the light of Christianity, and the two are inseparable in
Williams's rationale.

With the Narragansett language one is able to "converse with thousands" and spread "civilitie" and Christianity, because, as he says in two
further changes of metaphor, "one Candle will light ten thousand, and
it may please God to bless a little Leaven to season the mightie Lump
of those Peoples and territories" (84). The idea of proliferation and
dissemination, here expressed through keys, candles, and yeast, is more
often expressed as the seed and the Word, with their clear biblical over-
tones,[6] but it is the overlap of the commercial and the religious as well
as the linguistic that interests me. Knowledge, here, is the power to
open up a treasure in the form of resources as well as souls for conversion. But in a maneuver to be repeated in later centuries in the pro-
cessing of information about others in museums, ethnographies, and
official reports, the representation and what it stands for become inextricably connected, and power over one becomes power over the other.

This is reflected in the congruence of Williams's language in the opening address to his readership of "Friends and Country-men in old and new England." He explains that in writing the book, "I drew the Materialls in a rude lumpe at sea, as a private helpe to my owne memorie" (84). These materials are presumably linguistic, and they are to be "cast" or shaped into this key, but a page later he also talks of "the mightie lump of those Peoples and Territories" so that the place and peoples themselves are also seen as inchoate. Knowledge, like the light of God, strikes order into chaos, and the organized "key" of language can help organize the more general "lump" to which it gives access.

The book is organized around topics such as salutation, hunting, nakedness, seasons, and trading, and each chapter contains a list of phrases in both languages in the form of what Williams calls an "implicit dialogue," giving characteristic phrases and brief verbal questions and answers. Williams adds introductory and running "Observations," and then rounds off each chapter with a poem embodying a Christian moral. The editors of the latest scholarly edition, Teunissen and Hinz, describe the three-part structure as modeled on the contemporary use of emblems, as in the work of Francis Quarles, in which we have a symbolic engraving, here replaced by the list of words themselves; a moral epigram; and then an explicatory poem. However, in Williams's text the separate parts keep escaping from their role, and in combination they make the work complex and unsettling in ways I cannot recognize in Quarles.[7] In Gordon Brotherston's view, the concluding poems "round off and hence insulate each chapter topic in itself, with an appropriate touch of Christian piety,"[8] and in many cases the poems do act to seal off the disturbing oppositions within a larger whole of Christianity, but in some cases the words themselves carry an instability that is not entirely contained.

The particular form in which the "rude lump" of Indian language itself is cast within each chapter is worth closer examination. The alternation of sections of comment, headed "Observation," with bilingual lists of words and phrases allows for an intriguingly random effect, in which the chapter progresses by a process akin to word association. If we read the lists of words and phrases horizontally, there is a strict correspondence. Indian word is matched with English word—or so we assume, but since we cannot make anything of the Indian words or fit them into any linguistic framework (and nor could the original readership envisaged by Williams), they really operate as a guarantee, a *sign* of knowledge and authority that guarantees the observations. Narragansett is not now spoken, and the scholarly material on it is to some extent dependent on Williams's book as a source of information, so it is difficult to find a position outside Williams's own work from which to judge his linguistic competence. Ives Goddard's summary, though, suggests its limitations. "He shows an extensive knowledge of vocabulary and a fair control of the basic grammar, but his idiomatic usage breaks down outside the commonest everyday expressions, as when he tries to write dialogues on Christian doctrine."[9] Eric Cheyfitz has alerted us to the long-standing ideological investment in underplaying and effacing the real problems of communication across languages and exaggerating linguistic competence, and this suggests the need for caution in following up the claims Williams and others made for his book.

What is fascinating about Williams's book is the relation between the words, in their two opposing columns, and the commentaries and poems, and the ways in which this leads us into questions of exchange of all sorts. John Canup's discussion of the layout of the vocabulary sections of *A Key* concentrates on the gap between the two lists of words (this sense of the division between the words is strengthened when we look at the original edition, which has the two sides separated by a black vertical line that is omitted in the Teunissen and Hinz edition). As he sees it, Williams's book, far from offering access, could have the effect of confirming to contemporaries the sheer alienness of the Algonquian language. "The spaces between the two columns of words could thus perform the distancing function of the cultural barrier the English sought to maintain between themselves and the native people."[10]

Canup does also argue, though, that "the ground between is a place of meeting, a linguistic neutral zone in which meanings can converge and blend." For him, Williams's "implicit dialogue" is "an exercise in linguistic and cultural counterpoint,"[11] but it is not clear exactly how this linguistic neutral zone might work in the text and how the physical gap between languages turns into a dialogue. The complexity of the form, combined with the exceptionally detailed and often sympathetic understanding of Indian life Williams reveals, might lead us to take this idea of an implicit dialogue a little further, but any suggestion of a Bakhtinian dialogizing or relativizing of the dominant language or values just by the inclusion of foreign words and the semidramatic presentation of Indian speech needs to be treated with caution. If we try to read across the page from Narragansett to English, we are bounced back off the Indian word increasingly quickly, so that we end up reading vertically down the English side, rather than operating in any linguistic middle ground. This gives the possibility for the Anglophone who reads down rather than across to form almost random metonymic connections and thereby to unravel the thematic unity of the topic and the closure of the moral expressed in the concluding poem.[12] The effect is a swirl of repetition and variation that moves us in seemingly random directions, which Williams's "Observation" sections follow up. In my reading of *A Key*, I have chosen to give full weight to the effects created by the conjunctions resulting from this particular form and to read it as a product, like a poem, of the imagination as well as the antiquarian or linguistic faculties and therefore capable of reflecting and revealing the "rude lump" that is the unconscious or involuntary aspect of the work. In other words, I read it as a key to unlock a further box.

In a penetrating analysis of *A Key*, Eric Wertheimer presents Williams as seeing in the dialogue of languages the way to harmonize the religious claims of Calvinism with the civil state of America. He argues, "It is the visible and vocal Indian of Williams' poetry who facilitated that dialogue."[13] This is perhaps overstating the case for dialogue, but there are places where Williams, for the purposes of his own argument against the authorities, does use the Indian words effectively. For instance, in the chapter "Of discourse and News" he pauses at the word for 'if he say true', and gives a pointed anecdote about Canonicus, the Narragansett leader who, he says, often repeated this word.

> *Wunnaumwayean, Englishman;* if the *Englishman* speake true, if he meane truly' . . . I replied, that he had no cause (as I hoped) to question *Englishmans, Wunnaumwauonck*, that is faithfulnesse. . . . He took a stick and broke it into ten pieces and related ten instances (laying down a sticke to every instance) which gave him cause thus to feare and say; I satisfied him in some presently, and presented the rest to the Governours of the English, who, I hope, will be far from giving just cause to have *Barbarians* to question their *Wunnaumwauonck*, or faithfulnesse. (136–7)

Williams's insistent use of the word *Wunnaumwauonck* in conjunction with *Barbarians* suggests an ironic and skeptical view of the English authorities, and to the extent that he uses the Indian position to do so, he puts the Indian into dialogical relation to the English. The use of the word is also part of Williams's own agenda, however, his long-standing dispute with the authorities, which involved his defense of Indian ownership of land as well as his better-known defense of liberty of conscience and opposition to church authority in state affairs.[14] In contrast, when he turns to religion, a subject on which he sees no room for dialogue beyond Christianity, we find a monologic chapter, with few Indian words included and more than usually intrusive sections of authoritative, even dogmatic, commentary.

The conjunction in Williams's text of Indian and English languages and cultures, in his chosen form, allows for a complex exploration of some of the fundamental oppositions within which Europeans thought about civilization and savagery, and I shall focus my exploration of how this works in Williams around one theme: nakedness and clothing. First, though, it is important to understand the importance of Williams's relation to his own society and the extent to which his discussion of Indians is also already inscribed within religious debates. *A Key* needs to be seen in the context of Williams's arguments with other factions within the Christian church and the reason for his trip back to England, which was to secure a charter for what was to become Rhode Island. The tangible evidence in the text of his lengthy engagement with Indians and knowledge of them can be seen as a deliberate demonstration of the colonial ability to comprehend and to represent, in texts and in discourses of knowledge and regulation, and therefore a bid for recognition of this colonial authority by the crown.[15] The book therefore needs to be seen in relation to Williams's other polemical writing, in particular "Christenings Make Not Christians: Or A Briefe Discourse concerning that name *Heathen* commonly given to the INDIANS," written at the same time.[16] For Williams it is partly a question of demonstrating the qualities and possibilities of the Indians as worthy beneficiaries of the gospel, and therefore justifying his enterprise, and partly a matter of using them within a larger argument about who exactly has the right to take to themselves the position of being the saved or favored people of God. Because of his own marginality, he is at pains to question the idea of a centrality, a position from which everything else can be seen and named as "other." Thus *A Key* and "Christenings" contain some decentering and unsettling challenges not only to Puritan authority but also implicitly to ethnocentrism.

Williams's position on the margins, and its usefulness to the authorities, is something he felt keenly, as is reflected in a letter he wrote to the General Court of Massachusetts Bay in 1656, in which he points out with some irony that they have found it quite useful to have someone between them and the Indians.

> We have bene esteemed by some of you as your thornie hedge on this side of you: If so, yet an hedge to be maintained; If as out sentinells, yet not to be discouraged.[17]

The implicit reference is to the idea of the church as an enclosed garden, taken from the Song of Solomon ("a garden inclosed is my sister, my spouse").[18]

The underlying argument is over the dominion of the church authorities in the New World and whether Williams was an irresponsible Separatist or a defender of the true church, and goes back to his exclusion from Massachusetts some years before. However, the terms in which this argument is couched are relevant to my discussion. Williams exhaustively exploits the ambiguities in the position of the Massachusetts authorities through typological analysis,[19] and the reason why a typological argument could be so powerful and far-reaching for Williams lay in the fact that the Puritans had already extensively used Biblical parallels to describe and justify their own enterprise in America. Just as God had made a Covenant with the Jews, so the settlers in New England were under a special dispensation as His holy people. Following from this, the magistrates and authorities of the new society, like the Jewish rulers, had both civil and spiritual authority. As John Cotton puts it,

> Though the nations now have not that typical holiness which the nation of Israel had, yet all the churches of the saints have as much truth and reality of holiness as Israel had. And therefore what holy care of religion lay upon the kings of Israel in the Old Testament, the same lieth now upon the Christian kings in the New Testament, to protect the same in their churches.[20]

Williams disagreed. While Israel could be seen as the type of an antitype that was later to appear in the New Testament, that antitype could be only the *spiritual* version of Israel. The Jews, as God's chosen people, did embody in their state the civil and spiritual combined, and since the coming of Christ the status of God's chosen people had indeed moved to Christians—but it was wrong to assume that this meant any particular society that merely *claimed* to be Christian. On the contrary, since the Christian antitype of the type of Israel was a spiritual and not a physical entity, no actual society could claim the special status of chosen people that would justify them in a theocratic rule.[21]

Williams focuses his argument on the question of names. Taking the basic opposition of *Jew* and *Gentile* to represent the chosen and the others, he subjects these names and a cluster of others, including *heathen*, to a series of transformations. He points out that the word heathen

> signifieth no more then *Nations* or *Gentiles;* so do our Translations from the Hebrew . . . and the Greek . . . in the old and New Testament promiscuously render these words *Gentiles, Nations, Heathens.*

The Jews, being then "the onely People and Nation of God," saw all other people, those with stately cities as well as those who went naked, as "Ethnicke, Gentiles, Heathen, or the Nations of the world." After Christ's coming, the Christians became chosen, and Jews joined the other Gentiles as nations outside the pale. Williams's inquiry into labels also extends, of course, to the word *Christian* itself. If only those who actually follow Christ's precepts can be called Christians, what does that make of all the other so-called Christians who fail to meet this criterion?

> This is the CHRISSION WORLD, or Christendome, in which respect men stand upon their tearmes of *high opposition* between the CHRISTIAN and the TURKE . . . between the CHRISTIANS of this Christian WORLD and the JEW, and the CHRISTIAN and the HEATHEN, that is the naked *American.* But since *Without* is turned to be *Within,* the WORLD turned CHRISTIAN, and atheittle [the little?] *flocke* of JESUS CHRIST hath marvellously increased in such wonderful conversions, let me be bold to aske what is Christ? What are the Christians?

His answer excludes most who call themselves such, and in his attack on "high opposition" there is not only a reproof against Christian pride but a certain relish in overturning categories as in itself a radical Christian act. The reference to the outside becoming inside, for instance, is to Paul's remarks on the church at Corinth and the distinction between Christians and others in 1 Cor. 5:10–13. Characteristically, Williams rhetorically invokes an absolute, the idea of a true Christian, in order to relativize and criticize worldly claims and categories. In terms of Indians, this has the effect of making them not so different from the

self-styled Christians, but more specifically, it also serves to problematize the idea of conversion. If Christianity is so elusive, conversion
must not be taken lightly, and he distinguishes his own cautious practice from the "Antichristian conversions" achieved by coercion or attention only to superficialities, an issue I return to in chapter 7.[22]

In *A Key*, Williams is concerned with the question of difference between Christians and others, and how it was recognized and named,
and is at pains to give both the names Indians gave themselves and
those the English gave them. Though the Indians had no name "to
difference themselves from strangers for they knew none," they now,
hearing the English use it, "will call themselves Indians in opposition
to English" (85). This multiplicity of names, and the conventional
rather than essential nature of them, echoes his questionings in "Christenings." He is in fact constantly playing with such words, partly because of his typological readings and partly to destabilize the terms of
his own society, as, for instance, in his preface when he expresses the
confidence that

> that Father of Spirits, who was graciously pleased to perswade Japhet (the
> Gentiles) to dwell in the Tents of Shem (the Jews) will in his holy season
> . . . perswade, these Gentiles of America to partake of the mercies of Eu-
> rope. (85)[23]

At the end of the chapter "Of their Religion," he talks of the way
the "wandring Generations of Adams lost posteritie" have "lost the true
and living God" and created their own "false and fainted Gods," (199),
but a poem that rounds off the chapter performs an operation that is
typical of the strategy of the book as a whole. Like the other poems, it
begins with a twofold division, this time of two sorts of men who will
stand "before the burning ire" of God, but these turn out not to be
simply Christian and heathen. A further division of true and false muddies the distinction in a way that echoes his linguistic distinctions in
"Christenings."

> If woe to Indians, Where shall Turk,
> Where shall appear the Jew?
> O, where shall stand the Christian false?
> O blessed then the True. (200)

This way of introducing a binary division that fails to survive the description is very noticeable where certain fundamental oppositions—Indian and English, naked and clothed, savage and civilized, Christian and heathen—are themselves the object of inquiry rather than being the frame in which the discussion takes place. It could be argued that this is not fundamentally relativizing, since they are all subjected to an absolute standard or opposition of Christian truth and falsehood, so it is hardly a truly deconstructive enterprise. Keith Staveley, for instance, argues that "like most Puritans, Williams' thought was grounded in stark antithetical contrasts . . . His originality lay in his sharpenings of such antitheses, his application of them in unexpected directions."[24] Thus he could critique the Puritans in their own terms but never, for instance, break through the oppositions separating Indians and Europeans sufficient to bring to the surface the relativizing implications of the observations of the Narragansetts contained within *A Key*. Even if this is true at the larger level, at the local level this method does allow for a good deal of local slippage, in which the antitheses struggle to stay in place, and I want to examine these slippages as they take us deeper into the complexities of exchange and transformation than the broad oppositions with which Williams is explicitly working.

We see the technique in operation right from the beginning of the first chapter, titled "Salutation."

> The Natives are of two sorts, (as the English are). Some more Rude and Clownish, who are not so apt to Salute, but upon Salutation resalute lovingly. Others, and the generall, are sober and grave, and yet chearful in a mean, and as ready to begin a Salutation as to Resalute, which yet the English generally begin, out of desire to Civilize them.
> What cheare Netop? is the generall salutation of all English toward them, Netop is friend.
> Netompauog   Friends
> They are exceedingly delighted with Salutations in their own Language. (93)

The first bold classificatory statement is dissipated by qualifications ("as," "but," and a bracket). Beginning with the basic contact between Indians and English, we see a complex range of relations into which the words and phrases that follow must be put. The first Indian word we are given is that for 'friends', in a greeting, a point of contact, but

before we reach it we are given oppositions and distinctions that revolve around the ideas of civility. This, though, has a structure similar
to that of reciprocity described in Paul Le Jeune's description, in that
saluting and resaluting correspond to giving and returning.

A characteristic Williams binary also begins one of the most complex explorations of the similarities and differences between "barbarian" and civilized, in the chapter titled "Of their nakednesse and clothing," which I want to look at in detail.

> They have a two-fold nakednesse: First, ordinary and constant when al-
> though they have a Beasts skin, or an English mantle on, yet that covers
> ordinarily but their hindparts and all their foreparts from top to toe, (excep
> their secret parts, covered with a little Apron, after the pattern of their and
> our first Parents) I say all else open and naked . . . Their second nakednesse
> is when their men often abroad, and both men and women within doores,
> leave off their beast skin, or English cloth and so (excepting their little
> Apron) are wholly naked; yet but few of the women but will keepe their skin
> or cloth though loose) or near them ready to gather it up about them. (185)

The first thing to say, of course, is that neither of these is a state of
nakedness, in the sense of complete nudity, as we would use the word
today, and the word *nakedness* was fairly generally used to imply a relative absence of clothes or a simplicity of dress.[25] Instead of talking
about degrees of clothedness or opposing clothed to naked, Williams
begins with nakedness and then produces such a series of qualifications
and exceptions ("although," "yet," and "except") that he has to emphasize his point and repeat himself by the end of the sentence ("I say all
else"). The other qualification referring to "their and our first Parents,"
aligning the Indians with "us" as children of Adam, also muddies the
water; interestingly, according to Teunissen and Hinz, this phrase was
omitted, together with material critical of white behavior, when the
prose sections were reprinted by the Massachusetts Historical Society
at the end of the nineteenth century (24).

In the poem that concludes this chapter, Christ is imaged as offering
the necessary clothing for the soul.

> Israell was naked, wearing Clothes!
> The best-clad English-man,
> Not cloth'd with Christ, more naked is:
> Then Naked Indian. (188)

The play of terms here is designed to relativize the absolute opposition of physical nakedness versus clothing by invoking the "clothing" of Grace offered by Christ, and we find a similar opposition in the poem that concludes the chapter "Of Their Paintings," which discusses how the Indians decorated their clothes and bodies. The poem begins

> Truth is a Native, naked Beauty; but
> Lying Inventions are but Indian Paints,
> Disembling hearts their Beautie's but a Lye,
> Truth is the proper Beauty of Gods Saints. (281)

In this striking opening, Williams first seems to privilege Indian ("Native, naked") over civilized and then qualifies this by associating falseness with Indian paints. Another reversal occurs in the second verse, in which Williams describes Indian hair and painted faces as "fowle" but then sees "such Haire, such Face" when it is found in Israel or England as "more fowle" (281). In the final verse, nakedness is again privileged in the invocation of the purification of "Christs washing flames of fire" and being washed in "Repentance Teares," and Teunissen and Hinz argue that the paradox of the stanza "lies in the association of truth with both the native and the saint" (64).

In early accounts of Indians, nakedness was commonly used as shorthand for all sorts of other lacks or deficiencies said to characterize savagery, and we find a classic example of this in Williams.

> They have no *Clothes, Bookes*, nor *Letters*, and conceive their *Fathers* never had; and therefore they are easily perswaded that the *God* that made *English* men is a greater *God*, because Hee hath so richly endowed the *English* above *themselves*. (85)

The association of writing with civilization and ultimately Christianity has been well documented; here I need only note the assumptions, first, that the painting and various mnemonic systems to which he refers do not add up to anything equivalent to writing and, second, that the Indians see the absence of writing as a lack.[26]

In "Christenings," we find another variation on the naked/clothed opposition in relation to conversion. Rejecting the idea of a merely superficial change, Williams images it in a set of dramatic contrasts of death and life:

> *America* (as *Europe* and all nations) lyes dead in sin and trespasses: It is not a suite of crimson Satten will make a dead man live, take off and change

his crimson into white he is dead still, off with that, and shift him into cloth
of gold, and from that to cloth of diamonds, he is but a dead man still: For
it is not a forme, nor the change of one forme into another, a finer, and a
finer . . . that makes a man a convert.

The association of spiritual death, hypocrisy, and empty wealth in the
striking image of the corpse clothed in gold is used to make a point
about false conversion, but it is made to apply not only to Indians but
to all those already professing Christianity. If forms can change and
deceive, if hypocrites "may but glister and be no solid gold,"[27] the question of any fixed or proper value is thrown into doubt, and the naked
Indian is seen to be a more complicated idea than at first appears. In
this way, Williams uses the Indians in dialogical and critical engagement with Massachusetts Bay and his various rivals within a series of
terms that he shuffles in unstable oppositions. Thus, natural is inferior
to civilized but can be used against false civilization, as in the use of
naked or in the last verse of the chapter on government. When Indians
hear of the "horrid filths" practiced by Christians, their response is

> We weare no Cloaths, have many Gods,
> And yet our sinnes are lesse:
> You are barbarians, Pagans wild,
> Your Land's the Wildernesse. (204)

One of the other powerful and persistent images of the people of
the New World was of monsters, misshapen creatures half-man and
half-beast, and it is interesting to see Williams explicitly invoke this
idea but turn it against what he saw as a European perversion, namely,
priestly celibacy. When Indians hear that there are men who practice
this, "They aske if such doe goe in Cloaths," that is, if they are civilized.
When they hear that they are "richly clad / know God, yet practice so,"
they can only see them as "Beasts not men,"

> Or men have mixt with Beasts and so,
> Brought forth that monstrous Race. (209)

Here we have the ultimate breakdown and mingling of oppositions and
categories, but in a monstrous form that is European and not of exotic origin.

There is another form of connection with animals via nakedness
and skin that is worth pursuing at some length. The long list of terms

for clothing that occupies the middle of the chapter "Of their naked-nesse and clothing" works against Williams's initial assertion of the Indi-ans' nakedness, demonstrating once again the actual presence of Indian clothing as opposed to the symbolic importance of the idea of naked-ness. As is not uncommon, too, Williams's apparently random juxtapo-sition of phrases seems to resonate with his discussion in uncontrolled ways.

Nippoaskenitch	I am rob'd of my coat
Nippoaskenitch ewo	He takes away my coat
Acoh	Their Deere skin
Tummockquashunck	A Beavers coat
Nkequashunck	An Otters coat.
Mohewonck	A Rakoone-skin coat
Natoquashunck	A Wolves-skin coat (185–6)

The list goes on through coats made of turkey feathers ("as velvet with us") to English coats, shoes, and so on, but what is striking is the way his opening term echoes what he himself is doing in describing the Indians as naked. He is, after all, robbing them of their clothes in in-sisting on their nakedness, and the clash of meanings within "rob'd" of *robbed* and *robed* for a modern reader again points to the ambivalence of the whole section. Furthermore, as we go down the list, the odd-ness of the phrasing intrudes into our consciousness. He writes "Their [presumably the Indians'] Deere skin," but "A Beavers coat," which is strangely dislocating in suggesting either the skin of a beaver or, more surreally, a beaver wearing a coat, but not primarily and immediately a person wearing a coat made of beaver. While it may be objected that I am pushing the connotations of the words and punctuation here further than is normal, I do so deliberately, to bring out what is a real instability in the terms Williams uses. At the heart of this instability is the idea of an animal skin, which is both clothing and a sign of barbarism, or ani-mality, a clothedness that is simultaneously like nakedness, as in the description of Indian nakedness that he gives immediately after the list I have quoted from

Within their skin or coat they creepe contentedly, by day or night, in house, or in the woods, and sleep soundly counting it as a felicitie, (as in-deed an earthly one it is; *Intra pelliculum quen, que tenere suam,* That every man be content with his skin. (186)

Williams even puns deliberately on the idea of skin as implying both nakedness and clothing. His (mis)quotation from Martial confirms the pun, in that Martial also exploits both meanings in his epigram, in telling the cobbler to "keep yourself now in your own little skin" (*Epigrams* 3:16). It is ironic that when worn by Indians, the animal skins are associated with barbarism and proximity to animality, but when traded they become the very mark of civilization and refinement. This reversal is given concrete form in the literal reversal of the skin, with Indians wearing the fur inside and Europeans wearing it outside. In this way, the European becomes, at his or her most civilized and refined, most like that image of the hairy monster, the wild man with whom early Indians were persistently associated. That Williams was potentially quite capable of recognizing these ironies is demonstrated in a remarkable later passage about trade networks.

He begins by praising the infinite wisdom of God, who has made Europe so much more "advanced" than America that "there is not a sorry Howe, Hatchet, Knife, nor a rag of cloth in all America, but what comes over the dreadfull Atlantick Ocean from Europe" (166). He follows this with a balancing statement, which is an exhortation to further commercial exploitation and a reminder of the value of the fur trade in New England, but his image is a powerful and evocative one:

> and yet that *Europe* be not proud, nor *America* discouraged. What treasures are hid in some parts of *America*, and in our *New English* parts, how have foule hands (in smoakie houses) the first handling of those Furres which are after worne upon the hands of Queens and heads of Princes? (166)

What seems at first to be a promotional reminder of the possibilities of exploitation takes on, via a conventional enough attack on the vanities of Europe, a sense almost of wonder at the process by which goods are transformed into commodities. (It is worth remembering that the various sumptuary laws had long restricted the wearing of certain furs to levels on the social hierarchy, so that Williams's rhetoric of lowest to highest here is concretely based.[28]) It is almost as if Williams here glimpses the vast process of trade and its relativizing capacities, the sublime of commodity fetishism in which the processes of production, the "foule hands" and smoke, are effaced. (The fact that some furs gained value if worn first by Indians with the fur on the inside, because of the softening processes of sweat and grease and the removal of long hairs, underscores the real material connections between each contrasting end of the process of trade and exchange.[29])

Using the idea of skin as both a key symbol, via nakedness, in the discursive economy of civilization and savagery and an actual object of exchange between the two sides of that ideological divide, as I am doing here, alerts us to the importance of the economic even where it is not obvious. The Puritans' routing of Thomas Morton's settlement at Mare Mount, or Merry Mount, has been presented, most famously by Nathaniel Hawthorne, as a clash of cultures, "jollity and gloom contending for an empire,"[30] with the cutting down of the maypole signifying the Puritan mistrust of pleasure and imposition of law. A more complex and ambiguous position emerges from Morton's report of the infamous revels at Mare Mount, where, in the last verse of their drinking song we have

> Give to the Nymphe thats free from scorne,
> No Irish; stuff nor Scotch overworne,
> Lasses in beaver coats come away
> Yee shall be welcome to us night and day.

Morton follows this with comments that seem designed to excuse or play down the young men's interest in the fur-clad "lasses," who I assume are Indian, describing it as "this harmeles mirth made by younger men (that lived in hope to have wifes brought over to them)."[31] Even so, the idea of the lasses in beaver coats seems to confirm all of the Separatists' fears (they "much distasted" the song, he tells us) in raising the prospect of the overturning of a number of different but interlocking hierarchies. If beaver was valuable and therefore worn by the rich, the idea of lasses in beaver coats raises a rather wonderful image of sexual freedom cutting across the remaining vestiges of sumptuary regulations, so that fur operates as both natural and exotic and exclusive, the very stuff of later fetishism.[32] What is significant here, and usually overlooked in the more literary treatments of this episode, is the fact that Merry Mount was above all a trading post and Morton made a successful living unscrupulously trading precisely those objects that were outside the range of Puritan trade, namely, alcohol and guns. Both in their different ways undermined the Puritans' relation to the

Indians as controlled consumers, and when Morton returned after being deported to England, the Puritans confiscated his goods and burned down his trading house.[33]

Like Morton, Williams was a trader and in a marginalized relation to the Puritan authorities, though of course the differences between them are considerable. Owning and running a trading post for fifteen years, Williams was in a position to appreciate the crucial interrelation of linguistic, religious, and economic exchanges, and his book has important sections on trade, debt, and money that are often overlooked in critical accounts concentrating on language and culture.[34] His letters are packed with references to financial as well as political dealings with specific Indians, and it was his close daily dealings with them that gave him a key role as political broker and intermediary. It not surprising therefore that in keeping with the purpose of *A Key* to aid Europeans' contact with Indians, Williams is at pains to give a full account of trade and money. In some ways his treatment of the Indians and trade is one of the least relativizing or self-reflexive sections of the book, in that much of his terminology assumes a fit between Indian and European economic practices.[35] The Indians are seen as skilled, even ruthless traders, with the same agenda as whites, and his word lists have plenty of terms of dispute and mistrust. The chapter that follows those on coin and trading is "On debts and trusting," and it has even more terms of suspicion and distrust.

Relations, as presented here, are narrowly economic, and while Williams's overall view of the Indians assumes the possibility of rational and honorable agreement, there is also another register of language, ascribing base motives to them simply because of their savage state, in his remark that "tis true there is no feare of God before their eye, and all the Cords that ever bound the Barbarous to Forreiners were made of Selfe and Covetuousness."[36] In the chapter "Of their Trading," he describes a performance of the "begging Indian" that we have already examined in chapter 1 and he is quite clear about its calculating character:

> They will often confesse for their own ends, that the English are richer and wiser and valianter then themselves; yet it is for their owne ends, and therefore they adde *Nanoue*, give me this or that, a disease which they are generally infected with: some more ingenuous, scorne it; but I have often seene

an *Indian* with great quantities of money about him, beg a Knife of an English man, who happily hath never a peny of money. (164)

The surprising juxtaposition of the greedy, calculating Indian and the
carefree, gullible Englishman is modified if we remember that the word
happily here has the sense of "haply," but even so we have a clear sense
of the Indians as calculators rather than ingenuous givers. Williams's
word lists reflect the hard bargaining and mistrust rather than concord,
and the chapter's concluding poem describes the Indians fearful of deception and bereavement at the hands of the English, and "shie / Of
strangers, fearful to be catcht / by fraud deceipt, or lie" (167). Williams
uses the word *Nanoue* here and translates it 'give me this or that', but
elsewhere, in the course of an attack on John Cotton, he uses and translates it quite differently.

> The *Indians* of this *Countrie* have a Way calld *Nanowwe*, or *Giving* their
> Commodities *freely*, by which they get better *bargaines*, then if they stood
> stiffly on their *Tearmes* of *Anaqusbento*, or *Trading*; And when not *satisfied* to
> the *utmost* they *grudge, revile*, &c.

Here *Nanoue* means giving, though in a manipulative way that will ensure return, and Williams's unease with the term seems similar to Darwin's description of the term *Yammerschooner*, as discussed in chapter 1.
Williams describes the process as *"Deceitfulnesse of Heart*,"[37] but this
strongly reductive assumption that the sole motive is maximization of
gain may be explained partly by his larger agenda here and his animus
against Cotton He is criticizing the pressure the Massachusetts authorities put on the people to pay their ministers and argues that the pressure is no less oppressive or real for being a moral pressure, working
on shame, rather than law. He explicitly compares this with the Indian
approach here and thereby concisely deconstructs exactly the appeal to
aristocratic reciprocity I have discussed in earlier chapters.

Such instances, while raising some questions about Williams's linguistic objectivity, do reflect a keen awareness on Williams's part of the
complex agendas involved in exchanges of all sorts between Indians and
Europeans, and it is worth looking more carefully at the full context
in which he and his contemporaries were able to conceptualize their
economic dealings with the Indians. One of the most significant issues
is the relation beween sacred and secular in relation to the realm of the

economic. Keith Staveley has pointed out that with his "particular and peculiar version of Protestant biblical typology, Williams placed himself at the cutting edge of the processes of secularization that were going forward in the seventeenth century." The importance and consequences of such a change, whereby the realm of the sacred is in effect restricted and reduced by having its purity protected, are clearly seen in the realm of economic thought. As Benjamin Nelson has shown, the division between Jew and Gentile entailed a distinction between a kin group or closed community and strangers or foreigners. From this distinction various economic rules and restrictions followed. Building on Max Weber's analysis of the relation of Protestantism to the development of capitalism, Nelson focuses on the move from a brother / stranger opposition to a universal view in which everyone is to be dealt with in the same way, which had the dual effects of reducing exclusive obligations to members of kin and tribe and increasing obligations to strangers. "Medieval Christianity, aspiring to universalism, rejected the Deuteronomic distinction against the alien as anachronistic and obnoxious, and proposed to transcend the morality of clan by joining the 'other' to the 'brother,'" says Nelson. "In modern capitalism all are 'brothers' in being equally 'others.'" If the Puritans were really claiming special status as chosen people, a great deal, economically, could follow for people determined to read the Bible literally and typologically. Although the Puritans apparently were never so committed to the Covenant parallels with the Jews that they followed the prohibitions over usury, they did use the argument the other way around, to deny the special rights of Indians to exclusive rights over their land and property.[38]

The effect of the discovery and settlement of the New World was both to unsettle the sense of what was domestic or "proper" and what foreign and to increase the ideological weighting of these terms because of the need to justify the expropriation of Indian land. For the Puritans, it was possible to generalize the diasporic nature of their own experiences into a view of the world that can sometimes sound curiously modern. In their writings we trace their concern to establish the "proper" in situations with no clear guidelines. For Robert Cushman, for instance, the emigration to America can be justified by the absence, in the modern world, of those reserved lands decreed by God, as in the Bible. There is no longer any land or possession now, like unto the possession which the Jews had in Canaan, being legally holy and appropriated unto a holy people, the seed of Abraham, in which they dealt securely, and had their days prolonged, it being by an immediate voice said, that he (the Lord) gave it them as a land of rest after their weary travels, and a type of eternal rest in heaven. But now there is no land of that sanctimony, no land so appropriated, none typical . . . But now we are all, in all places, strangers and pilgrims, travellers and sojourners, most properly, having no dwelling but in this earthen tabernacle; our dwelling is but a wandering, and our abiding but as a fleeting, and in a word our home is nowhere but in the heavens.

They are "most properly" without any possession "appropriated" for them, so they must work things out for themselves, guided not by direct revelation ("an immediate voice") but by careful interpretation of the Scriptures. Whereas in earlier times God instructed men by "predictions, dreams, visions and certain illuminations," now the Scriptures, "reasonably and rightly understood and applied must be the voice and the word that must call us."[39] The substitution of the printed word and the need for interpretation to supplement the immediacy of the voice is one way Christians were able to distinguish their own religion from that of the heathens, but it also points to a potential tension; that the primitive religion has much more in common with the bases of the Old Testament than is always comfortable. The stress on the written word perhaps also increases the importance of producing written gospels in Indian languages, as well as the larger cultural investment in writing as an integral part of civilization.

For Cushman, the absence of revelation meant a stress on rational procedures and agreements: "now, as natural, civil and religious bands tie men, so they must be bound, and as good reasons for things terrene and heavenly appear, so they must be led."[40] If no people or nation is like the Jews, with their own proper land, this includes the Indians, who likewise have no special claim on the land, especially since they scarcely use it, and his justification for occupation rehearses many of the *vacuum domicilium* arguments about empty or improperly used land and sovereignty repeated over the centuries.

Williams's attack on the Puritans as chosen people is a defense not only of his own defection and religious liberty, but of Indians' rights to their own land. His objection to the Puritan claim to jurisdiction over Indian land was one of his earliest and most consistent disagreements

with them, but he also on many occasions had to justify his own possession of Indian land and his means of acquiring it. In general, as revealed
in his descriptions of trading and economic transactions, he sees the
Indians as sophisticated traders with the same sense of market as himself. That is, they are strangers with whom one deals fairly, as in the
modern way. But when he talks about his own acquisition of land in
Rhode Island, later to be contested as part of the power struggles of
the new colony, he is at pains to claim a different sort of legitimacy. He
does this, significantly, not by demonstrating a commercial contract or
evidence of purchase, but by invoking the bonds of friendship and the
gift as the origin and foundation of the relationship. In his testimony
of June 18, 1682, he declares that

> were it not for the favor God gave me with Canonicus, none of these parts,
> no, not Rhode Island, had been parchased or obtained, for I never got any
> thing out of Canonicus but by gift.

Clearly, "by gift" means as a gift, but the other suggestion contained
within the phrase is that it is by means of a (prior) gift, and this reveals
the underlying stress on the idea of reciprocity. In describing to Winthrop the means by which several islands were acquired, Williams insists that

> neither of them were sold properly, for a thousand fathom would not have
> bought either, by strangers. The truth is, not a penny was demanded for
> either, and what was paid was only gratuity, though I chose, for better as-
> surance and form, to call it sale.

This is a consistent claim of Williams, as in his written statement to
the General Court of Commissioners of Providence Plantations in
1658, where he insists on a relationship prior, both temporally and
morally, to any that can be limited to legal niceties. His metaphors reflect this:

> Yet, since there is so much sound and noyse of Purchase and Purchasers, I
> judge it not unseasonable to declare the Rise and bottom of the planting
> of Rode Iland in the fountaine of it. It was not price nor Money that could
> have purchased Rode Iland. Rode Iland was obtained by Love: by that Love
> and Favour wch that honble [honorable] Gentleman Sir Hen. Vane and my
> selfe had with that great Sachim Miantunnomu about that Leauge, wch I
> had procured betweene the Massachuset English etc and the Narrigansets
> in the Pequot War.[41]

As John Garrett says, "He wanted to emphasise, later, that this was the true formulation of proprietary right for himself or those who came later. Legally he was unrealistic; but the quality of the original agreements, love, was precious to him." We might want to see his language in the broader context of the tension between gift and trade, but in Williams the element of personal regard is more consistent and more substantiated by his own very direct dealings with Indians than in many other more formal expressions. When he describes the circumstances of the establishment of his trading post, the distinction between the different forms of exchange is clear. This is no doubt partly because of the problematic legal status of the exchanges in the light of later wranglings, but I suggest that it also reveals a real tension between different forms of economic relation.

> Caunounicus laid me out Ground for a trading howse at Nahigonset with his owne hand but he never traded with me, but had freely what he desird Goods Mony etc. so that tis simple to imagine that many hundrets excused me to the last of that mans breath whom (dying) sent for me and desired to be buried in my cloth of Free gift and so he was.[42]

In spite of his hardheaded attitude and his general cynicism about the motives of both sides,[43] Williams here invokes a position above the calculations of trade. The trading and economic calculation in which he was occupied for so many years are framed here by an inaugural act, a gift of land, that is characterized as the opposite of trade and by a closure, the death of Canonicus, and the "cloth of free gift" that constitutes his winding sheet. In ending with this final clothing of Canonicus by Williams, I want to echo not only the gift of Powhatan's mantle, but the larger theme of Indian nakedness and neediness explored in chapter 1.

5

Wampum

Roger Williams's vision of a network of demand and desire linking "foule hands" and princes through the circulation of furs demonstrates a striking awareness of expanding worldwide markets, but it would be misleading to suggest that he was the only one at the time aware of such connections. As I show in chapter 6, the relation between religion and economics was something of which both sides were keenly aware. In a remarkable letter to Richard Baxter in 1669, John Eliot makes an unusually explicit connection between his own missionary enterprises and the network of distribution in a larger economy. He justifies the use of the particular Indian language he is learning, Massachusett, by linking it with trading networks and the distribution of wampum. "By an eminent providence of God," he says, the range of the language is very wide, because

> the Narraganset Bay is the principal if not the only place in all this country where that shellfish is found, of which shell they make their jewels and money of great valew, and the royal ornaments—of use and valew as far as Mexico, as may be gathered from Peter Martyr, the Spanyard, his trade.

This makes the area the center of a huge trade network, making their villages "places of great resort from all parts and their language desirable—also since the English came to these parts, these places are much resorted to."[1] They use native trade networks that have become further developed since European contact.

Eliot's claims for the wide acceptability of Massachusett as an Algonquian language can be seen as part of his overall project to promote the work of translating the Bible, later to be superseded by a change of policy by the New England Company.[2] Nevertheless, his awareness of routes by which trade, information, and cultural values can pass is striking, and in a letter to the Commissioners of the New England Company he complains of the negative uses of trade connections.

> I greatly wish that such as travaile and set up houses of trading among them [the Indians under Uncas], might be such as had an heart also to teach them; and not to corrupt them by setting strong liquors in such plenty as to cause drunkennesse, with other examples of vanity and sinne Satan endeavours to underwork us by. Had we a magazine of goods to supply the Indians needs, and were fit places restrained and confined unto such as would chiefly regard the instruction of them in the word of the Lord, much good might be done.[3]

Thus those propagating religion and trade were involved in and aware of the same networks of distribution and dependency and control, a goods-and-gospel operation designed to convert Indians into Christian consumers, and Williams's *A Key into the Language of America*, as the product of his twin activities of missionary and trader, can be seen in the context of that larger project of exploitation and control. Recent analyses have shown such an expansion to be part of a larger process of pulling the Indians into a peripheral relation to a more extensive world market system. Lynn Ceci argues that wampum was a crucial element in the conversion of New England into a peripheral resource through its ability to facilitate the fur trade along pre-existing trade routes, and Williams himself comments on the way that the Indians "bring downe all their sorts of Furs, which they take in the countrey, both to the Indians and to the English for this Indian money" (208). Ceci outlines the process whereby "the Northeast and its natives who hunted, prepared and offered skins to Europeans gradually evolved from a zone external to the world-system to a periphery within."[4] Her use here of the concept of a world system from Immanuel Wallerstein, in which a core uses and exploits a periphery, allows her to identify a process by which Indian societies are moved from outside the orbit of Europe into a trading relationship that makes them dependent and exploitable.[5]

The Dutch and English early recognized the crucial importance of wampum and the preeminence it gave to those who could produce it.

Foremost among these groups were the Narragansetts, with whom Williams primarily traded, and the development of a new trade dynamic, with the introduction of European goods, further increased their importance. In 1634 William Wood explicitly describes the Narragansetts as the richest and most industrious people in the area, "being the store-house of all such kind of wild merchandise as is amongst them." They are "the most curious minters of their wampompeag and mowhacheis," supplying their neighbors in most directions. In addition, they successfully act as middlemen in the fur trade, bringing furs down to Narragansett Bay and "returning back loaded with English commodities, of which they make a double profit, by selling them to more remote Indians." This occupation may have brought the scorn of the neighboring Pequots, who described them as "women-like men" because of their unwillingness to "expose themselves to the uncertain events of war," preferring "rather to grow rich by industry than famous by deeds of chevalry."[6] Nevertheless, they occupied a crucial position in what William Turnbaugh describes as a classic triangular trade

> First, inexpensive goods from Europe were exchanged for wampum produced primarily by the Narragansett; then, this wampum was transported inland and exchanged for furs; which, finally, were returned to Europe to be sold at great profit . . . As the "minters" of the wampum and as primary recipients of European goods they controlled two of the three classes of commodities.[7]

Furthermore, the increased production of wampum, aided by the introduction of European tools, meant that the Narragansetts became major producers of a commodity that was itself taking on a different and more strictly monetary value than its precontact uses.

Kevin McBride demonstrates that the Dutch, French, and English, vying for the fur trade, recognized that wampum was "the source and mother of the fur trade," and that Dutch strategy was to divert English attention to trade in northern New England, even supplying them with the wampum to do it, "because the seeking after wampum by them is prejudicial, inasmuch as they would, by doing so, discover the trade in furs; which if they were to find out, it would be a great trouble for us to maintain."[8] The English defeat of the Pequots in 1637, together with the large tributes in wampum they exacted from Pequots and neighboring tribes alike, established their trade supremacy—it also underscored the crucial importance of wampum. As Ceci points out, this involved not only producing a vastly greater quantity of beads, but gaining control over wampum from the Indians, and she sees the exacting of tributes of specific quantities of wampum from Indian communities as a way of gaining control and attaining "a partial underwriting of New England colonization costs by the conquered natives." The millions of beads produced by the conquered Algonquians went to pay for furs from the Iroquois, who were still relatively independent, being still "at the edge of the periphery." As the coastal Indians of the Northeast had to produce more and more wampum, they became fixed in residence at the coast, had less time to produce their own basic necessities, and so became increasingly dependent on European trade goods. As Ceci puts it, they became "laborers who could never quite satisfy their creditors."[9]

Eliot's awareness of wampum's importance as a means and object of trade and exchange is echoed continually by later traders, who realize its significance in helping them to develop the fur trade. In the words of a later commentator, it was "the magnet which drew the beaver out of the interior forests." Thomas Morton is explicit about the ultimate use of wampum: "We have used to sell them our commodities for this Wampampeak, because we know, we can have beaver againe of them for it; and these beads are currant in all the parts of New England, from one end of the Coast to the other." William Bradford's account of the increasing use of wampum supports the idea of its importance. For the struggling Puritans, "that which turned most to their profit in time, was an entrance into the trade of wampumpeag." By introducing it to the Indians inland, the Puritans were able actually to create a market and a demand, since, once the Indians were acquainted with it, they "could scarce ever get enough for them, for many years together."[10]

So far in this chapter I have been trying to demonstrate the accuracy of Williams's awareness of the network of trade involving fur and other commodities, particularly wampum, to which he devotes a chapter of *A Key*. In adopting the large-scale analysis of world systems, though, there is a danger, as critics of the approach have pointed out, of assuming that the Indians are passive recipients of Western ideas and markets or that they do not have their own agendas which allow them to use as well as be used. Ceci's argument seems to entail an initial distinction, perhaps intrinsic to the world system approach between primitive and market economies, which means insisting on a clear change of function for wampum. She maintains, "Clearly, the function of wampum among northeastern natives had shifted from giftgiving and reciprocal exchange to a more capitalistic market exchange which in turn, engendered intertribal competition and conflict."[11] It is this assumption, though, that needs to be explored through a closer examination of the multiple functions and representations of wampum itself, since changes in its function and significance offer a good instance of the difficulties in assessing the ideas of value across different cultures.

It is now generally agreed that the impact of European metal tools, particularly awls, allowed for an expansion in the amount of wampum and a change from discoid to tubular beads, so that the widespread use of wampum in large quantities as either a medium of exchange or a ceremonial item in the form of belts can be seen as an effect of contact. While archeological and ethnographic evidence does demonstrate the existence of trade networks involving worked shells, which indicates that they were considered valuable, it would be dangerous to see post-contact wampum uses as identical with earlier practices or beliefs. It is also useful to distinguish broadly between the use of wampum in strings or even as individual beads (as it is described, for instance, in early accounts of the Narragansett) as a sort of currency and its use in belts, as in the elaborate ceremonial use among the Iroquois. It is in this later form, the result of an increase in production generated by European technology, that wampum is now best known, and Daniel Richter points to the irony in which "that quintessentially Iroquois cultural artefact, the elaborate ceremonial wampum belt composed of thousands of beads, could be created only as a result of extensive trade with Europeans and other natives."[12]

Clearly, at different times and in different places wampum operated as currency, ceremonial gift, decoration, and form of writing or mnemonic system. While it is important to recognize and pinpoint these categories and the differences between them, it is also part of my purpose to insist on the instability of these distinctions and the importance of wampum in revealing the difficulty of identifying criteria of value in exchange. In a cross-cultural encounter there is always the problem of reading the signs and, in particular, knowing whether you are looking at the medium or the message. Wampum is especially interesting because its complex role as treasure in itself but also a medium—as money or message—continually creates problems of interpretation. In the rest of this chapter, I examine the immediate context for Williams's and Eliot's observations and the crucial role of wampum at the time; I then broaden the analysis to the wider significance of wampum and the ways it has been represented, at the time and since, to show it as a prime example of a hybrid object both in origin and in its multiple and undecidable uses.

Most detailed studies of early New England economic policies and thought ignore the role of wampum,[13] but the Europeans of the time quickly became aware of its importance to the Indians and its potential value and relevance to themselves. We need, though, to look carefully at what sort of value they recognized. They saw in wampum primarily its exchange value, that is, its value as it manifested itself to them in their exchanges and barters with Indians, and therefore they equated it with the monetary values of their own society. Once they recognized it as a commodity of that sort, they started producing it themselves.

There is an early and intriguing reference to the English manufacture of "beades," presumably from shells, in the Virginia Company's records of 1621.

> The makinge of beades is one of Capt Norton's cheife employmentes wch being the mony you trade with the natives we would by no meanes have through to much abundance vilified or the Virginians at all pirmitted to see or understand the manufacture of them. Wee therefore pray you to consider seriously what proportion of beads can be vented and their worth not abated.[14]

The suggestion is that the use of metal tools to make wampum gives the English an advantage they do not wish to share with the Indians, and the immediate awareness of the dangers of overproduction and inflation suggests that they saw wampum as directly comparable with European currency. Although the English are here trying to enter the system of currency without changing or devaluing it, the whole larger effect of the introduction of metal awls and European demands did massively change the amount and functions of wampum. One crucial question is whether the previously mixed functions of wampum were reduced to a single European measure of value. The earliest record of wampum being used with a European quantifiable value is dated 1622 and reports a Pequot chief being held to ransom for wampum. "He paid one hundred and forty fathoms of *Zeewan*, which consists of small beads they manufacture themselves, and which they value as jewels." It is not clear whether the measurement by fathoms is taking over a native practice here, but the value of wampum soon became linked explicitly to European currency values. Van den Bogart seems to assume a convertible value in 1634 when he reports that the Mohawk "sold each salmon for one guilder or two hands of sewant." In a description of a trading meeting a month later, though, another function for wampum is clear when he reports that "the Indians hung up a belt of sewant and some other strung sewant that the chief had brought back from the French Indians as a token of peace that the French Indians were free to come among them." Because of the shortage of English specie, a recurrent colonial problem, wampum was for fifteen years full legal tender and was used for smaller sums long after that, operating at a rate of exchange (which to the Indians' confusion and annoyance fluctuated according to the price of beaver in London) against sterling and at a fixed rate between white and blue wampum. (There is even a suggestion that the blue was an imitation of blue trade beads.) By 1662, the Rhode Island Court had decided that as wampum had fallen to such a low rate, "it cannot but be judged that it is but a commodity, and that it is unreasonable that it should be forced upon any man," thus changing its status.[15]

With its status as currency comes a concomitant concern with the idea of a genuine article rather than an adulterated or counterfeited one. This raises an interesting question about whether Indians and Europeans were looking for the same things. There are references to the shrewdness of the Indians in passing on inferior beads and then refusing to take them back later, but this does raise the question of what would make wampum invalid or counterfeit. The Massachusetts Bay Colony Court in 1648 decreed that "all passable or payable peage henceforth shall be intire, without breaches, both the white & black, without deforming spots." Richard LeBaron Bowen, from whom this quotation is taken, has no problem in asserting that "the Indians were the first counterfeiters in Rhode Island,"[16] but even in the court's decree there is confusion about whether wampum gains its value as a commodity or a unit of currency. What is the difference between a counterfeit as opposed to a badly made string of wampum? Morton sees the English as producing the inferior product.

Though they have tried, yet none hath ever, as yet, attained to any perfection in the composure of them, but that the Salvages have found a great difference to be in the one and the other; and have knowne the counterfett beads from those of their owne making, and have, and doe slight them.[17]

Similarly, John Josselyn's description of 1674 clears the Indians of counterfeiting: "there are two sorts, blew Beads and white Beads, the first is their Gold, the last their Silver, these they work out of certain shells so cunningly that neither *Jew* nor Devil can counterfeit, they dril them and string them, and make many curious works with them to adorn the persons of their *Sagamours* and principal men and young women."[18]

Williams presents wampum as a direct equivalent of English money, referring to it as "coin," and there is no question, as he presents it, of wampum being involved in any other scale of value, ceremonial or aesthetic. Only in the concluding poem of the chapter titled "Of Their Coyne" does he raise the issue of the relativity of the value of money, and here it is contrasted with God's grace, which represents the only source of real value, but the stress on the idea of localized value and the arbitrary nature of money is clear.

> The *Indians* prize not *English* gold,
> Nor *English Indians* shell:
> Each in his place will passe for ought,
> What ere men buy or sell. (214)

Not only is gold worthless compared with God's worth, but it is also intrinsically no more valuable than wampum. "Each in his place will passe." In a higher realm, though, to which Indians and English all "passe" this sort of value counts for nothing.

> Where shels nor finest gold's worth ought,
> Where nought's worth ought but Grace. (214)

The punning insistence here on "ought" as meaning anything or nothing ("ought" being the word for the symbol *O*) underlines Williams's point of contrast: money, being able to be anything, is actually nothing, having only an arbitrary and conditional value, unlike the eternal, fixed value underwritten, as it were, by God. This is a classic instance of Williams's technique of radical deconstruction of fixed oppositions and values, enabled and underpinned by an appeal to a fixed point outside and more fundamental than the play of opposition and signification, namely, God.

Real value is not recognized even by those who have had the opportunity to see it.

> This Coyne [God] the *Indians* know not of,
> Who knowes how soon they may?
> The English knowing, prize it not,
> But fling't like dross away. (214)

Eliot adopts the same metaphor when he compares superficial conversions to Christianity with counterfeit or worthless currency, in a description of the "art of coyning Christians or putting Christs name and image upon copper mettle,"[19] which I discuss more fully in the next chapter, but here perhaps Williams also allows us to sense something of the practical and immediate power of the image in a colony where shortage of specie entailed the adoption of other "primitive" forms of currency.

Given the Europeans' tendency to assume that value could only be like that represented in Europe by money, or gold and silver, it is difficult to discern whether a changing attitude on the part of Indians is being described, which would accord with Ceci's view. Bradford's comment is tantalizingly vague: "And strange it was to see the great alteration it made in a few years among the Indians themselves." Because of its rarity, he notes, previously it was only "the sachems and some special persons that wore a little of it for ornament." Clearly here it has value, as it is owned only by powerful people, but presumably not exchange value. Kathleen Bragdon uses Bradford's observation to illustrate the possibility that wampum "formed part of a 'separate sphere' of exchange, involving only wampum and other symbolically charged goods, a sphere in which only sachems could participate." Support for this may be found in the phrasing of Daniel Gookin's account:

> With this wompompeague they pay tribute, redeem captives, satisfy for murders and other wrongs, purchase peace with their potent neighbours, as occasion requires; in a word, it answers all occasions with them, as gold and silver doth with us. They delight much in having and using knives, combs, scissors, hatchets, hoes, guns, needles awls, looking-glasses, and such like necessaries, which they purchase of the English and Dutch with their peague, and then sell them their peltry for their wompompeague.[20]

What is being pinpointed here is the importance to the Europeans of having wampum in order to buy furs, but what is not so clear is whether there is a distinction implicit in different sorts of transactions. Why, for instance, did they not simply exchange European goods for furs? Is there an implication of gift-giving in some exchanges and not others, or, as is seen elsewhere, a gift exchange as preliminary to trade? It might be overreading this particular passage to try to perceive distinctions, but given the complex role of wampum it is worth being aware, at least, of Bragdon's suggestion of separate spheres.

Apart from the written record, there is, of course, the archeological record, which has produced some particularly relevant findings and discussions. The presence of grave goods of European origin and the recirculation and transformation of objects and practices have been extensively discussed in relation to ritual objects as they cross cultures, and there are also some suggestive findings on wampum. Concentrating on the Narragansett, Patricia Rubertone, noting the punitive demand on the part of the colonial government for tribute payments of huge quantities of wampum, argues that this would represent a relationship very different from the traditional payment of wampum as tribute to sachems. Instead of a voluntary act, in which "wampum's value was more symbolic than monetary" and related to a complex pattern of redistribution, the colonists, by demanding tribute, "divested it of the quality of a voluntary offering, and transformed it into a tactic aimed at enforcing submission to colonial authority." Given this demand, she attributes particular significance to the presence of relatively large amounts of wampum recovered from a burial ground, which, she argues,

> reveal that wampum was being taken out of circulation by placing it in the graves of the dead. Interestingly, the wampum occurred not as caches of loose beads, but were incorporated into single and multiple strands, or woven into intricately patterned bands, that were distributed among only a few graves.

The suggestion is that this implies a clear ritual consumption, which in the context of the colonial demand represents "an unwritten statement of political resistance" upholding Narragansett tribal authority and tradition.[21] Rubertone and others have argued that the persistence and even intensification of Indian mortuary practices in the seventeenth century indicate some of the ways in which Indians, rather than merely assimilating European influences and goods, were incorporating them into new social practices and values.[22]

One of the recurrent difficulties is in pinpointing wampum's subtly changing status, and a discussion of a contemporary shell currency raises interesting questions about just what wampum may have represented at particular points to Indians. Deborah Gewertz and Frederick Errington describe how the attempt to export shell currency from East New Britain in Papua New Guinea to a German museum in 1991 was blocked as a cultural threat and point out the irony of something that is meant to be transferable becoming in this case inalienable. In this society, however, even though Australian and indigenous shell money both circulated as interchangeable currency, they had subtly but significantly different status, as this incident reveals. Carrying an additional level of value that other currency did not have, shell money was an embodiment of cultural heritage, but it was also an interchangeable currency at the crossover point between cultures. It could represent not just pure value (and therefore be pure medium) but something specifically cultural, too. "Because shell money had been both means and marker of intercultural negotiation, it had acquired a particularly salient representational value."[23] The authors refer to the parallel recent arguments over cultural property in North America involving bones, but the more intriguing parallel with wampum is not made. Perhaps we can be no more than speculative, but we know that, as in the Papuan case, indigenous and introduced currency was used concurrently and interchangeably, and we know that wampum had supplementary representational significance. Given the colonial as opposed to postcolonial conditions obtaining at the time, perhaps the opportunity of sustaining cultural values through its circulation disappeared and moved to other spheres. Nevertheless, an awareness of the East New Britain situation may help to make us more aware of the many levels of representation and exchange involved.

In dealing with wampum, it is important to remember that it was only one of the objects of value being traded. Early trade was as likely to be for objects of spiritual value as to be for practical objects, given the material self-sufficiency of the Indian groups. Richter, for instance, talking of the Iroquois, connects such objects with the idea of gifts from the gods to be acquired from under the earth or the sea.

Particularly prized as gifts from great sources of power were chunks or worked plates of copper originating in the great Lakes region, beads made from seashells from the Atlantic coast, and exotic stones or volcanic materials from any distant locale ... Small-scale long-distance trade supplied many of these vital, spiritually powerful goods.

He even makes the point that those neighboring peoples with which the Iroquois maintained peaceful relations in precontact times all "sat astride routes to the sources of exotic commodities associated with spiritual power that were not available in the homelands of the Five Nations."[24]

One of the recurrent functions of wampum commented on by Europeans, which overlaps with its status as money just as gold does in Europe, is as ornament. For instance, although Williams identifies it as coin, he also describes how the men, women, and children wear it on their necks and wrists. "Yea the Princes make rich Caps and Aprons (or small breeches) of these Beads thus curiously strung into many formes and figures" (157).[25] There is plenty of evidence for this, and King Philip's wearing of wampum, for instance, is commented on in several places.[26] The king had a coat "made all of wampampeag," and the dual role of wampum as quantifiable and distributable wealth as well as decoration is indicated in the comment that when Philip is short of money, he cuts the coat to pieces "and distributes it plentifully among the Nipmoog sachems and others, as well to the eastward as southward, and all round about."[27] In one account we also find an interesting instance of European coin's being taken over and used in the same way as wampum, as decoration and display of wealth. Mary White Rowlandson's description of her captor is a hostile one, ridiculing his and his wife's vanity:

> he had his silver buttons, his white stockings, his garters were hung round with shillings, and he had girdles of wampum upon his head and shoulders.

Later, when drunk, he pursues one of his wives, "with his money jingling round his knees."[28] Rowlandson's Puritan agenda is to the fore here, with vanity, lust, and drunkenness her targets for scorn, but, as Mitchell Breitwieser has shown, she is involved in a series of complex economic exchanges with her captors. He argues that her particular situation and traumatized state of grief have made her resistant to any view or appreciation of "the symbolic armature of Indian exchange" so that she operates at a purely instrumental and practical level, "neither absorbing nor disputing, she leaves their spirituality alone, trades knitting for food."[29]

While the interpretation of function is always a problem, it is complicated by the commentators' own confusions over how money functions even in their own system. For John Lawson, writing in 1709, the "general and current species of all the Indians in Carolina and I believe all over the Continent" was Peak and Roanoak, "that which at New York they call Wampum and have used it as current Money among the Inhabitants for a great many Years." Though he recognizes it as a medium of exchange, he is also aware of the work it takes to create it. An Englishman "could not afford to make so much of the Wampum for five or ten times the Value." Only because the Indians "never value their time" can they make it so cheaply. As a manufactured item, it seems to be valued against some standard other than itself, as a commodity. At the same time, Lawson stresses its almost magical power as a medium and repository of value.

> This is the Money with which you may buy Skins, Furs, Slaves, or any thing the Indians have; it being the Mammon (as our money is to us) that entices and persuades them to do anything and part with every thing that they possess, except their children for slaves. As for their wives, they are often sold and their daughters violated for it. With this they buy off murders; and whatsoever a man can do that is ill, this Wampum will quit him of.[30]

This description may remind us of Marx's depiction of money as a universal pander, in which he is himself following other writers, including Shakespeare, in seeing the frightening power of money to act as universal solvent of all other categories of value. Nevertheless, it is worth looking more closely at what Lawson is describing. The presence of exchanges of wampum at both the trade of material objects and at marriages and condolences leads him to assume that the same activity of buying is taking place, but it is precisely the character of wampum to perform different functions, in accompanying, solemnizing, or symbolizing an exchange or encounter, with reciprocal implications that might be invisible to the outsider. For instance, in a detailed description of a healing ceremony, Lawson mentions that the shaman or "conjure" holds a "String of Roenoak," which is the same as a "String of small Beads," but which is what he has previously called money.[31] The use of dowries as payment and present would be the most widely recognized example, but in another context George Snyderman warns us, for instance, of the danger of assuming that the use of wampum belts farther north to recover prisoners was just a payment of a ransom, "for the wampum was not given in payment for the release of the captive. Rather it signified the tribe's acceptance of its responsibility to keep its warriors from seeking vengeance."[32]

Robert Beverley, writing in 1705 about the Indians of Virginia, is perhaps more inclined to stress their innocence in their "simple state of nature" before European intrusion. He explicitly defends them against charges of prostitution such as that made by Lawson, finding no evidence that the young women "prostitute their bodies for Wampom, Peak, Runtees, Beads and other such fineries." It is rather that their "harmless freedom" of manner is misinterpreted by cynical Europeans. Similarly, Europeans have corrupted a primitive society of simple plenty and created a society of needs and dissatisfaction. This has been achieved in two ways: by actually depriving them of a large part of their land, creating inevitable shortages of necessary things, and by introducing false needs. "They have introduc'd Drunkenness and Luxury amongst them, which have multiply'd their Wants, and put them upon desiring a thousand things they never dreamt of before." Whereas Lawson sees wampum as an aboriginal equivalent of European money, Beverley, in line with his primitivism, makes a clear distinction between its use before and after European contact. They held land in common, bred no catttle "nor had any thing that could be call'd Riches. They valued Skins and Furs for use, and Peak and Roenoke for ornament." The difficulties Beverley has in dealing with the idea of wealth are shown, though, in the next chapter, called "Of the Treasure and Riches of the Indians." Again he tells us they had nothing that counted as riches, but this time he adds,

> except Peak, Roenoke and such like trifles made out of the Cunk shell. These past with them instead of Gold and Silver, and serv'd them both for Money and Ornament. It was the English alone that taught them first to put a value on their Skins and Furs, and to make a Trade of them.[33]

Use, ornament, and money are in an unstable relation, and this is then connected in an unexplained way with furs and the ascription of an exchange value rather than a use value to them.

These bewildering shifts in terms can also be seen in Father Joseph

Lafitau's account of 1724. He begins by describing wampum as a form of record keeping, if not writing: "All matters of business are treated by strings and belts of wampum which replace memoranda, writs and contracts." As he goes on, though, he moves into describing it as money. Although their trade is still "as it was at its origin" (i.e., universally), merely barter of goods, wampum "may be looked upon as a kind of money." He explains it in confusing terms, however. "It is their jewellery, their precious stones. They count every bead and for them it takes the place of all their wealth." "Takes the place of" here is an interesting phrase in that it suggests that wampum is not itself the wealth, but can represent it. Money can take the place of wealth, but jewelery *is* wealth. This representative function is important to pin down, because it also connects with the ceremonial use of wampum in belts for what Lafitau calls "affairs of state." In his next section, headed "The Bank or Public Treasury," he describes wampum belts kept in the place of contracts and public records, in the absence of written records.[34] Here then we find a complete confusion of ceremonial belts and beads as measurable currency and public record, and while this may be accounted for by Lafitau's generalizing, it does point to a persistent confusion about value in such a cross-cultural situation.

THE USE of wampum as a form of record or representation is well documented from formal assemblies and treaty signings with whites, but the exact mix of functions, as with Lafitau, is difficult to be sure of. After describing the belts of wampum, which he calls "coliers," Baron Lahontan remarks,

> Without the Intervention of these *Coliers*, there's no business to be negotiated with the Savages for being altogether unacquainted with Writing, they make use of them for Contracts and Obligations. Sometimes they keep for an Age the *Coliers* that they have receiv'd from their Neighbours, and in regard that every *Colier* has its own peculiar *Mark*, they learn from the old Persons, the Circumstances of the Time and Place in which they were deliver'd; but after that Age is over, they are made use for new Treaties.[35]

The colier, or belt, is therefore an intermediary, an object of value in exchange and *by* exchange, and also a mnemonic record. It can also be completely transformed, literally broken up and reassembled to mean something else, as the individual elements are recombined.

In its public symbolic role, the wampum belt as described by Lahontan has a great deal in common with another staple of diplomatic
exchanges and negotiations, the calumet, or ceremonial pipe. Like
wampum, the calumet took its significance from the interchanges it was
involved with. The ceremony of smoking the pipe, according to Richard White, "formed a part of a conscious framework for peace, alliance,
exchange, and free movement" and "created a fictive kinship relation
between the person offering the pipe and the person specifically hon-
ored by the calumet."[36] The act of giving locks the recipient into an
activity that demonstrates friendship, and Lahontan's account includes
a perfectly symmetrical visual representation of the moment of meeting
and negotiation.

In the drawing included in Lahontan's book we have Governor La
Barre, in front of his camp, flanked by two interpreters and the French
officers. Facing him is the Iroquois leader, named here as "The Gran-
gula," who is backed up by his "retinue, set squat upon their tails."
Lined up along one side are La Barre's militia and regular troops, and
on the other are the huts of the Iroquois. Between the two leaders,
though, and larger in scale than either of them, are "the calumet of
peace" and "the porcelain colier." Here we have, set out most explicitly,
the elements of communication, and in the background and surrounding the meeting there is the presence of force and the danger of armed
confrontation. The importance of the linguistic exchange is emphasized by the presence of the interpreters, but the center of the scene,
literally in the middle ground between the two sides are the two symbolic objects on which success will depend.

By the time of Lahontan, Europeans well understood the importance of such exchanges, but much earlier we find in the *Jesuit Relations*
an account of the use of wampum in which a number of functions are
described, which are typically difficult to disentangle. Christianized Indians, we are told, make

> a little present every Sunday to the Virgin, each one giving a Porcelain
> bead for each rosary recited during the week. The number of these
> beads,—which are the pearls of the country,—runs sometimes as high as
> seven or eight hundred; and their devotion has prompted them to make
> collars of these in the style of embroidery,—in which, interweaving beads
> of violet and white porcelain, they write what they wish to say in honour

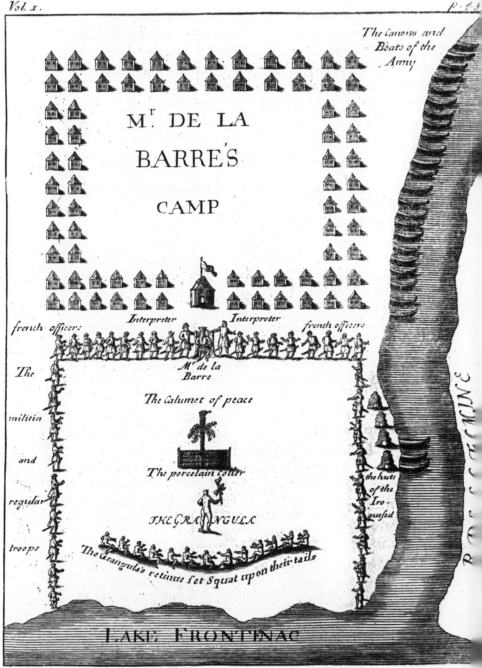

Drawing from Baron Lahontan, *New Voyages to North America.*
Courtesy the John Carter Brown Library at Brown University.

of the Virgin. They have formed a kind of public treasury, made up from their poverty,—I mean from their little presents,—which with a piety truly admirable, they use in helping the poor.[37]

Here we have beads operating initially in association with rosaries (which, as we shall see later, were often reported as being split up and used as secular beads or worn as a necklace); then becoming a writing medium, presumably here in French alphabetic writing, as in the famous wampum belt sent to Chartres; but then retaining their economic value as a treasury, convertible into basic necessities of food and clothing.

When an Iroquois leader says that the belt he hands over preserves his words, or when the Jesuit Rasles says, "The custom of these Tribes when they write to another Tribe is to send a collar or broad belt upon which they make many figures with porcelain beads of different colors" (*JR* 67:187), we seem to be dealing with something that, though not writing as we know it, fulfills many of its public functions. What is significant, though, is the relation between the valuable and the representative, because there is an interesting overlap of terms. When messages are sent, and speeches are made, they are accompanied by the transfer of wampum, which is referred to in *Jesuit Relations* as "presents." Of course, this word can apply to things other than wampum, which can create ambiguities, but in the accounts of formal speeches the use is so formalized that wampum is clearly indicated. In the earliest recorded treaty, which also happens to be one of the fullest, the Iroquois display on a cord between two poles "the words that they were to bring us,—that is to say, the presents they wished to make us, which consisted of seventeeen collars of porcelain beads, a portion of which were on their bodies" (*JR* 27:253).[38] Records of speeches often refer to each part of the message as a present, and speeches not accompanied by wampum are not even counted as such. In a later part of the same account, this is spelled out.

> It is needless for me to repeat so often that words of importance in this country are presents. Suffice it to say that, as he who harangued gave no presents, he spoke in these terms: "I have no voice; do not listen to me. I speak not; I hold in my hand only a paddle to bring you back a Frenchman in whose mouth is the message from all our country." (*JR* 27:281)

On the basis of this it would be easy to see wampum operating as a sort of official seal cum mnemonic, giving communal authority to individual authorities, and we can refer to the myths of the origin of wampum, as in the Deganawidah epic, in which wampum shells "become words and lift away the darkness."[39] Interestingly, however, even here there is a suggestion of monetary value, in that presents seem to have had measurable exchange value, at least in some circumstances. According to Frank Speck, a present meant at least seven hundred wampum beads. Furthermore, the presents sealing the words can apparently be items other than wampum, so the question of value cannot be separated into ceremonial and practical. Louis Hennepin underscores the importance of wampum but lists other commodities alongside when he stresses their persuasive importance: "For the best Reasons in the World are not listened to amongst them, unless they are enforc'd with presents." In an account of a meeting between the French and the Iroquois, he describes the usual presents of furs and collars of porcelain, commenting, "In a word, there were no Speeches nor Answers made but by Presents which pass'd for words in their Harangues." So widespread was the association of words and gifts that according to Cornelius Jaenen, the distribution of presents "was popularly referred to as 'speaking with the hand' or 'making words.'"[40]

Given these ambiguities, we should not assume that the well-known statement from Jerome Lalemant on the importance of gifts indicates a gift-giving economy of the sort discussed by Marcel Mauss and others.

> Presents among these peoples despatch all the affairs of the country. They dry up tears, they appease anger, they deliver prisoners, and revive the dead ... One hardly ever speaks or answers except by presents. That is why, in the harangues, a present passes for a word. (*JR* 22:291)

On the next page, though, the example given of a present is three porcelain collars, that is, wampum belts. What is being referred to here, primarily if not exclusively, is wampum, and the difficulty is in knowing how often the word "presents" implies the same formal and functional properties. Lafitau, for instance, while describing the belts as presents is also aware of the medium itself, and his description of reciprocity reveals a scarcity element.

> Their wampum would soon be exhausted if it did not circulate; but in almost all affairs, whether internal or external, the laws demand that an answer be made word for word, that is, for a belt another is given, of almost

the same value, some difference being observed, nevertheless, of a greater
or lesser number of beads, since these must be proportionate to the rank
of the persons or nations with whom business is being transacted.[41]

The variation in numbers here certainly suggests something more like
a payment of at least a quantifiable gift than a message or word.

For each Indian group, the particular overlap of functions was presumably complex but consistent and may have changed over time.
Richter describes, for instance, the Iroquois association of words and
presents as in wampum. "In both internal politics and external diplomacy, gifts symbolized a close relationship between a leader's roles as a
speaker of words, a representative of his kin and followers, and a provider and distributor of economic resources." This balance was undermined not only by the introduction of more quantitative uses of wampum but by the sheer dominance of white authorities, who eventually
had the power to make its symbolic role irrelevant. Snyderman cites an
example from Sir William Johnson's papers of a white official who refuses a gift of skins, telling the Iroquois Indians to "take them away &
purchase a Blanket or two with the traders," and a gift of wampum "telling them it cost money at the same time I told them I had confidence
in them." This rational and apparently benevolent approach both reduces all items to their monetary value and underscores the Indians'
inferior status and dependency. In denying the Indians' power to give,
this official echoes the motto on Queen Elizabeth's portrait, discussed
in chapter 1, as well as undermines the whole symbolic role of wampum.[42]

For outside observers, one or another function of wampum was
chosen as the source or explanation of its value, and this tendency has
persisted with later commentators and historians. W. H. Holmes, for
instance, writing about shell decorations in 1883, recognizes their use
as money ("they formed a natural currency, their universal employment
for purposes of ornament giving them a fixed and uniform value"), but
his assumptions about the noneconomic nature of primitive life lead
him to insist that "on the part of the open-handed savages they were
probably valued more as personal ornaments than as a means of gratify-
ing avaricious propensities." Perhaps the most revealing of later accounts is William Weeden's *Indian Money as a Factor in New England
Civilization*. Written in 1884, the book embodies an evolutionist view
of Indians as representing an early stage of social development, giving

way before "the inevitable conflict between races in different stages of civilization." In Weeden's account, wampum is taken up by the new communities because of a shortage of currency and is dropped as the settlers assume economic power and control of the resources on which the value of wampum was based, reducing it to a commodity rather than a currency. "The relegation of his precious toil-worn beads to the rank of common commodities marks the decline of the savage in New England life."[43]

Weeden's view of wampum is confusing and confused, but it is worth pursuing a bit further. He seems to argue that its value resided not in its intrinsic worth or arbitrary exchange value but in its tie to beaver, which was the real object of value. To be a currency, an object must have an "essence of exchange, a force within itself which could compel not only that particular exchange, but any exchange at the will of the owner." A modern reader could argue that confidence, convention, or an agreed arbitrary designation can make up that "force," but Weeden is still thinking in terms of an equivalent to the gold standard. "This exchangeable quality was contributed by furs and especially by beaver. The colonist desired corn and venison but all the world desired beaver. Wampum was the magnet which drew the beaver out of the interior forests." This ascription of a magical power or essence recurs around money or any object of value, as I note in the discussion of fetishism in chapter 1, and Weeden is clearly intrigued by the role wampum plays, even locating rather accurately many of its ingredients in an intriguing description. "This curious article, half natural, half artificial, getting its value from labor on the one hand and the desires fomented by the rude civilization of the barbarians on the other, played back and forth between the greedy Indian and the poor colonists for a long period."[44]

Leaving aside the prejudices that make the colonists appear the victims of barbarian greed, the foregoing passage is unusually useful in pointing to some of the sources of confusion and fascination around the question of value and what creates it. As in Williams's negotiations between ideas of civilization and savagery, the oppositions in this passage fail to hold up, or at least the second set of oppositions is difficult to map onto the first. Shell as natural is opposed to worked object as artificial, but then we are told that its value comes from labor and from fomented desires. If the opposition was just desire versus labor, we could think of this as natural versus artificial, but the word "fomented" suggests a reverse of this. This desire seems to go beyond use and to be one created by an artificial system of supply and demand, but what is striking is that Weeden wants to ascribe this artificial consumer demand to Indians and their greed, and not to Europeans' introduction of trade and the logic and demands of a market economy. This explains his otherwise puzzling and contradictory idea of the "rude civilization of the barbarians." He needs to make the Indians "artificial" enough to have consumer demands, but still savage, allowing him to ignore the fact that the escalation of trade and the use of wampum exclusively as a medium of exchange, as the universal pander of Lawson's description, is an effect of bringing Indians into European markets and economic networks. An added level of ethnocentrism is Weeden's assumptions about gender roles. Wampum's role as ornament and its "elegance" suggests a female activity, but it was "so highly prized and became so dignified by use in adorning the highest personages that we may with reason imagine the braves themselves lending their doughty hands to bring out these works of art from Neptune's raw material." Bragdon notes that in fact both sexes made it, but among the people of southern New England, "beads had their greatest significance when woven into belts, which was apparently the work of women." Natalie Zemon Davis also points out the irony that among the Iroquois farther north, the women strung the wampum that was the material and symbolic basis of the celebrated male oratory of diplomacy and power.[45]

Weeden distinguishes between objects for use and those for exchange, suggesting that wampum is both, but he deals with the actual uses of wampum in ways that problematize the very opposition of use and exchange. Wampum's use as decoration "like the gold and silver jewellery of our day" is closely linked to its exchange value (though Weeden's own refusal to accept this as the source of value of gold and jewels in his own society might make this difficult for him to pursue), and its other use as a medium of communication similarly takes us back into the realm of exchange and representation, but his way of presenting this use emphasizes wampum's fixedness and concreteness. As a mnemonic, embodying and preserving the speakers' words, "it gave the words the weight of hard physical facts and made the expression an emblem of great force and significance."[46]

This emphasis on the concrete chimes with the prevailing association of Indian languages with both concreteness and figurativeness, via the idea of the poetic nature of primitive languages, and it allows Weeden to connect the representational and currency aspects of wampum, as indicative of a transitional evolutionary stage. "Wampum marks the passage of ideas into symbols. The belt is arrested literature,"[47] or a "germ" of the developed capacity for abstraction and thought of civilized society.

I have dealt with Weeden at some length because his views not only reflect those of his particular period, but point to some of the problematic distinctions that continue to haunt later commentators. As late as 1924, Edwin Stanley Welles rhetorically makes wampum represent the Indians themselves. Once so plentiful, the beads are now "mere scattered fragments of what once existed." To "some thoughtful Indians" the reduction of value of beads to the purely economic must have seemed "debasing," prefiguring "the extinction of their race . . . But let us remember that, while they were thus hastening that end for themselves, they were materially contributing toward laying the foundations of this nation."[48]

More substantially, Snyderman, in his wide-ranging survey of the uses of wampum, is at pains to show the symbolic functions of wampum that may have been obscured by a monetarist view. His thoroughly substantivist view stresses the need to be aware of the social and symbolic resonances of different occasions of exchange,[49] but this leads him to insist on the nonmonetary aspects of early uses of wampum. "There is no evidence that the Indian ever needed, wanted or used a medium of exchange prior to the arrival of White man."[50] His need to make a clear contrast between the Europeans' market economy and the Indians' reciprocal and barter-based economy entails him invoking a distinctive Indian worldview, and he insists on the ability of Indians to think and act symbolically. Because they understand that material objects only stand for spiritual or communally agreed values, they are able to substitute other objects, which then function in the same way. Thus, when wampum is unavailable, a stick or another object can be recognized as a substitute. Snyderman also stresses metaphor, and although his explanation for its prevalence is conventional (the Indians lived close to nature and therefore drew from it for figures to express spiritual meanings), we can link it with the idea of substitution and transformation to produce a view of Indian society as involved in symbolic exchange that is more fundamental than Snyderman's model.

James Bradley develops this suggestively in relation to the Onondaga and the Iroquois Confederacy. Detailing the pre-existing trade networks and the postcontact changes in them, he draws on George Hamell's view of trade objects as offering various forms of "power," which word he uses "as a shorthand for the complex set of relationships that defined how and why Onondaga valued certain substances." This includes ideas of value, wealth, and well-being associated with, for instance, shell and native copper, but the idea of power allows him "to emphasise the ideological rather than the materialistic importance of the substances." He also draws on studies of later revitalization movements centered around the idea of "cargo," in which European manufactured goods play a crucial role as offering not a change to the new world of which they are a part, but a spiritual power "to communicate with ancestors, power to regenerate, power to create a better life." His suggestion of this as a framework for looking at the expansionism of the Iroquois is beyond my scope here, but it is interesting that the central symbolic expression of the unity of the confederacy, the covenant chain, was regularly "brightened" by the exchange of wampum, which by this time had certainly become, in its manufacture and use, what he calls "an acculturative product, a blending of traditional native and novel European conceptions." As one of the first "cross-cultural hybrids," it served "not only as currency but as the emblem of Iroquois diplomacy."[51]

Another way of focusing this is to return to the relation between wampum as message and wampum as medium. Michael Foster has suggested that the exchange of wampum belts by the Iroquois is really about the act of communication itself as much as any particular message; in terms of communication theory, it is the channel as much as the message. He also points to some of the recurrent motifs on the belts and images used to describe the meetings at which exchanges took place. "The metaphors of the fire, the path and the chain reveal a set toward the alliance which recognizes a degree of entropy in the system." The covenant chain has been widely recognized as an important symbolic expression of real political and economic relationships between the Iroquois and the English (and before them the Dutch). The idea of a rope mooring the visitor's ships eventually became imaged as an iron chain linking the two parties, and then a silver one. This chain was regularly "brightened," or had the rust removed, by the exchange of presents, and in this way the existence of the chain was both proclaimed and actually demonstrated in that the exchange of presents literally linked the parties, locked them into reciprocal relations like links of a chain. In the same way, the wampum that so often was exchanged and used to commemorate and record the event, was both performative as well as referential. William Johnson's care to invoke these images in speeches to the Indians reflects their importance.

> Upon our first acquaintance we shook hands and finding we should be useful to one another, entered into a covenant of Brotherly love and mutual friendship. And tho' we were at first only tied together by a Rope, yet lest this Rope should grow Rotten and break, we tied ourselves together by an iron Chain—lest time and accident might rust and destroy this Chain of iron we afterwards made one of Silver . . . You well know also that from the beginning to this time we have almost every year strengthened and brightened this Covenant Chain in the most publick and solemn manner.[52]

Still, the idea of the chain that binds is a distinctly ambiguous one, suggesting restraint as well as unity, and debt and demand as well as support. As Francis Jennings has pointed out, the views of it on each side may have been quite different, with the English seeing the covenant chain as a set of subsidiary connections under a general British sovereignty, whereas for the Indians, "although each tribe had an English colonial protector, the Chain had been the Indians' protection against the protectors." He suggests that the view of the chain has been based on "assumptions of European sovereignty which mask both the chain's formal structure and its historic functions,"[53] not allowing for a more sophisticated anthropological awareness of the possible forms of sovereignty. Crucially, the chain stretched beyond the two parties who were renewing their alliance, to other tribes in the chain. The gifts exchanged would travel in trade networks, and with exchange along the chain went also the possibilities of transformation of function and form.

6

The Gift of Religion

THE SUBJECT of the next two chapters is religion, and particularly conversion in all its forms. I examine the way religious encounters and exchanges are represented by Europeans; their attempts to control the process of exchange; and, in chapter 7 particularly, some of the ways in which the exchanges go beyond that control. As I show in chapters 1 and 2, for Europeans coming to America, whether for trade or religion, the terms of exchange are imbued with the language of giving and benevolence. This is especially complex in the case of religious exchanges, where we have a mingling of economic and spiritual metaphors. In addition, the various Christian denominations themselves have different emphases. I argue in this chapter that in order fully to understand the missionary enterprise, we need to recognize the actual and rhetorical importance of the idea of unilateral giving and excess, and even of the extravagant and exorbitant. One reason for this is simply that Christianity as missionaries were presenting it to the Indians in the seventeenth and early eighteenth centuries in North America contained both an ideal of excess and sacrifice and a contradictory model of ascetic and rational self-control. The coexistence of these elements meant that missionaries were in fact operating within two sorts of economy—possessive individualism *and* sacrifice and excess. This put them in a complex relation both to the people they were trying to convert and to their own culture.

The Indians were supposedly double beneficiaries, being given material as well as spiritual improvement, and it is the relation between these two realms, and in particular the interchangeability of the metaphors used to discuss them, which I explore next. I look at the idea of the incommensurable and unreturnable gift in relation to the whole complex of cultural exchanges actually taking place and in relation to Christian theology. There are, of course, major differences between Puritans, Jesuits, and the ministers of the Great Awakening in doctrine and economic and political relation to the specific Indian groups. For example, the increased emphasis placed by many eighteenth-century preachers on the power and efficacy of feeling meant that the idea of excess may have been more to the fore. There are also many continuities, though, and by concentrating in this chapter on Protestant missionaries, and eventually on the writings of just one figure, David Brainerd, I demonstrate some of the complexity of what is being given and taken. In chapter 7, I broaden the picture to include the many other exchanges within which Christian conversion is taking place and is itself being converted.

From the beginning the economic and spiritual are intertwined, as are civilization and conversion, and this can be seen in the early promotional literature. In English accounts of America, the spiritual benefits and justifications are stressed, but they are given little real attention, reflecting the low priority that missionary work had. There is a consistent pattern in which a symmetry and balance are asserted, but the terms of the equation are always shifting. In the earliest discussions, the spiritual benefit is mentioned first, as if to give it greatest importance, and thereafter is ignored. For example, in his "Discourse of Western Planting" of 1584, Richard Hakluyt devotes his opening chapter to the prospects for spreading the gospel and then leaves the subject completely. The original title, too, is specific about the material benefits to England: "A particuler discourse concerninge the great necessitie and manifolde comodyties that are like to growe to this Realm of England by the Western discoveries lately attempted, written in the year 1584." In an invocation to be repeated much later by the Massachusetts Bay Company, Hakluyt cites Acts 16:9 in which Paul has a vision of a man from Macedonia asking him to "Come into Macedonia and help us."[1] So, he says "the people of America crye oute unto us their nexte neighboures to come and helpe them." To the people who open their coffers to "the furtherance of this most godly enterprise, God shall open the bottomless treasures of his riches, and fill them with aboundance of his hidden blessings."[2]

Here we have the characteristic rhetorical balance. Those who offer economic gifts to sponsor spiritual help to the Indians will be given spiritual returns, and, in a recurrent gesture in this sort of writing, there is an indirect reference in the phrase "bottomless treasures" to Paul's statement in *Eph.* 3:8: "Unto me, who am less than the least of all saints, is this grace given, that I should preach among the Gentiles the unsearchable riches of Christ." After striking this initial spiritual note, the rest of the discourse is remorselessly focused on material advantages.

Richard Hakluyt the Elder's more trenchant summary of the purposes of a proposed early voyage to Virginia similarly puts Christianity first and moves quickly on:

The ends of this voyage are these:

1) To plant Christian religion
2) To trafficke
3) To conquer
Or, to doe all three.

He questions how far each can be done independently of the others and admits that "to plant Christian religion without conquest, will bee hard," but in spite of putting this first on his list he otherwise ignores it and concentrates on the requirements for trade, where his assessments of what is required are particularly penetrating.

If the people [of Virginia] be content to live naked, and to content themselves with few things of meere necessity, then trafficke is not. So then in vaine seemeth our voyage unless this nature may be altered, as by conquest and other good meanes it may be, but not on a sudden . . . If the people in the Inland be clothed, and desire to live in the abundance of all such things as Europe doth, and have at home all the same in plentie, yet we can not have trafficke with them, by meane they want not any thing that we can yeeld them.[3]

The two states that would prevent trade would be (a) living naked and not wanting or needing to be different and (b) being fully clothed and equivalent to the Europeans and therefore not needing anything. The ideal state therefore is to be naked and wanting in all senses, and we see clearly here the use of nakedness as a synecdoche for a larger lack, as discussed in chapter 1. This lack is both spiritual and material, but the same prerequisite is that the Indians must be constituted as wanting, even if their "nature" must be changed.

In *Nova Britannia: Offering Most Excellent Fruites by Planting in Virginia*, printed in 1609, Robert Johnson insists that

> Our intrusion into their possessions shall tend to their great good, and no way to their hurt, unlesse as unbridled beastes, they procure it to themselves . . . First in regard of God the Creator and of Jesus Christ their Redeemer if they beleeve in him: And secondly, in respect of earthly blessings, whereof they have now no comfortable use, but in breastly brutish manner.

He then focuses, though, on the trade-off between material and spiritual for the benefit of his English investors. He stresses the need to invigorate England economically and spiritually and sees Virginia as the answer, but his language is carefully poised between an appeal to material profit, likely to tempt an investor, and a loftier ideal. The new country is described as bountiful and productive, but Johnson has to warn against false and easy expectations, lest "that bitter root of greedy gaine be not so settled in our harts, that beeing in a golden dreame, if it fall not out presently to our expectations, we slinke away with discontent." The "golden dreame" seems to hark back to the less worthy ambitions of the Spanish further south, and even perhaps the tortuous textual operations of Sir Walter Raleigh (discussed in chapter 2), and Johnson is insistent that material gain should not be uppermost in the thoughts of the investors. He uses the Biblical injunction "Cast thy bread upon the waters: for after many days thou shalt finde it" (Eccles. 11:1) to imply material return, but in God's own good time ("after many days").[4]

Alexander Whitaker's *Good Newes From Virginia* of 1613 takes a similar tack in a more generalized religious appeal sent to "the Counsell and Company of Virginia, resident in England." Whitaker describes it in his dedication as a "few lines of exhortation, to encourage the noble spirits of so many honorable Adventurers." Beginning with an attack on the vanity of riches, he too uses Eccles. 11:1 as starting point. "The sentence is rhetoricall, full of figures, and needs some explaining." Riches are superfluous and "nakednesse is the riches of Nature." The bread of the text is our possessions, but also "all those things by which we may relieve the necessities of our neighbours," and "liberalitie" is "a liberall giving away of such things as we do possesse." But we must give, send out, in the right spirit. In contrast, "some of our Adventurers in *London* have been most miserable, covetous men, sold over to Usury, Extortion and Oppression." Only halfway through the text does he first mention Virginia as "fit subject for the exercise of your liberalitie," and he urges his readers to "let the miserable condition of these naked slaves of the divell move you to compassion toward them."[5]

Whitaker wants the adventurers of Virginia to cast more bread, but he has to be careful, given his audience, not to emphasize the unconditional gift too much, and he rounds up a clutch of quotations that involve the certainty of a return on the gift, not immediately but eventually. ("Be not over hastie with God.") The husbandman does not expect immediate crops, and even "the base affections of the Usurer will not looke for the overplus of encrease, until the covenanted time of his loane be expired." This fits Whitaker's practical end and can be contrasted with the more overt language of sacrifice used by some later missionaries. As Whitaker says, God would have us "to tast of some temporall blesings besides," and he ends with mentioning "a few commodities" that might soon be obtained from Virginia.[6]

A similar twofold appeal is made by John Eliot, who holds out the promise of translating the material into the spiritual but, in doing so, still manages to express the spiritual itself in quantitative and financial terms.

> *Come forth, ye Masters of money*, part with your Gold to promote the Gospel. Let the gift of God in temporal things make way, for the Indians receipt of spirituals ... If you give anything into *banke*, Christ will keep *account* thereof, and reward it. You hear of what things are necessary in order to the advancement of that one *thing necessary.*[7]

Interestingly, though, his final reference to the one thing necessary points us to a crucial distinction between grace and good works, through the story of Mary and Martha, which could serve to undercut such a quantitative and calculating approach and has already cropped up in my discussion of alcohol in chapter 1. The reference is to Luke 10:42, in which Christ distinguishes between Martha, who has been working hard at serving and supplying the necessities, and Mary, who has not but who has been able to make an immediate emotional response and thereby react with the one thing that is necessary, against which no amount of good works can be weighed. The two realms are incommensurable, just as a gift cannot be measured in the economic terms of a market exchange.

This balancing act between the dream of excess and abundance and the hard economics of investment, combined with the language of Christianity, creates constant shifts and checks in the argument. In some cases, for instance, in George Herbert's poem "The Church Militant" of 1633, it also makes for an unsettling critique of civilization.

> Religion stands on tiptoe in our land,
> Ready to pass to the American strand,
> . . . .
>
> My God, thou dost prepare for them a way,
> By carrying first their gold from them away,
> For gold and grace did never yet agree;
> Religion always sides with poverty.
> We think we rob them but we think amiss;
> We are more poor—they are more rich.
> By this thou wilt revenge their quarrel, making grace
> To pay our debts, and leave our ancient place,
> To give to them, while that which now their nation
> But lends to us shall be our desolation.[8]

In the manner of Roger Williams in the poems with which he rounds out the chapters of *A Key into the Language of America* Herbert uses the oppositions and paradoxes inherent in Christian devotional writing to mount a social critique. He shows the incompatibility of wealth and grace, whereas the promoters of voyages are trying to suggest that profit can sit comfortably with virtue.

A particularly clear instance of the dual project of mutual economic and spiritual benefit is seen in the pamphlet attributed to Cotton Mather and published in 1707, whose full title best describes its purpose: *Another Tongue brought in to Confess the Great SAVIOUR of the World, or Some Communications of Christianity, Put into a Tongue used among the Iroquois Indians in America. And Put into the Hands of the English and the Dutch traders: To accommodate the Great Intention of Communicating the Christian Religion, unto the savages, among whom they may find anything of this Language to be Intelligible.* The text offers some basic Christian precepts in Iroquois, Latin, English, and Dutch, and it is certainly difficult to imagine quite how it would be used by fur traders, but its introductory letter reveals its desire to make the economic and the spiritual complementary.

> You are now earnestly Sollicited, *That* you who are Traders for *Bever-Skins*, would be as Instrumental as you can to Convey the *Garment* of *Righteousness* and *Salvation* among the Naked Salvages; That while you seek to Enrich your selves by Trading with the wretched Salvages, You may try to *Administer unto them in Spiritual things* and to communicate the *Unsearchable Riches of CHRIST unto them.*[9]

Here we find a familiar symmetry being developed. The colonists take beaver skins for clothing and decoration, but they give garments of a different sort. As well as enriching themselves financially, they are to give unsearchable riches (again echoing Ephesians) of a different sort to the Indians.[10] A more cynical view of the intertwining of trade and conversion is taken by a disenchanted French interpreter in an argument with the Jesuit Jean de Brebeuf, recounted by Samuel de Champlain. To Brebeuf's insistence that "It was nothing but a pure desire to promote the glory of God and effect the conversion of the savages in these parts that has brought us here to brave all the perils and dangers," the scornful interpreter Michel retorts, "Yes, yes, to convert the savages! Say rather, to convert the beavers."[11]

In likening the conversion of skins into commodities to the conversion of souls, Michel is suggesting an ulterior motive of the Jesuits, and he is not the only one to draw this parallel. An Algonquian Indian is reported by Jerome Lalemant as expressing God's grace in the same metaphor: "Grace is like a beautiful robe of beaver fur, with which God our Father clothes the souls of his good children." Lalemant reports the remark at some length to demonstrate the reasoning powers of this "Christian savage," but in its use of the trope of the naked Indian in need of clothing it could also be said to show, as James Ronda suggests, a partial synthesis of Christian and native elements.[12] The beaver was already an important element in Huron and Algonquian traditional religion, but equally relevant is the fact that the Indian expresses the idea of value through an object he knows white people valued immensely. In other words, the beaver robe here could be signifying value in either or both value systems.

While the official aim of the Puritans was to convert the Indians, their slowness in mounting any missionary activity eventually became glaring enough, both to them and to their supporters in England, that action was necessary. Eliot's activities, celebrated in a series of publications now known as the "Eliot Tracts" and aimed at English financial backers, were crucial in giving spiritual legitimacy to their economic and diplomatic activities, though even he, the celebrated "Apostle to the Indians" took a long time to find his vocation.[13] Crucial to Eliot's enterprise were his pioneering work as translator of religious texts into Massachusett and the setting up of what came to be known as "Praying Towns," reflecting the Puritan belief that full conversion of Indians required both full understanding of the tenets of religious faith and a way of life likely to embody and encourage them. The self had to be reconstructed along Puritan lines, and this involved all aspects of life, including the secular, so that, as Cotton Mather later put it, Eliot had "a double work incumbent upon him; he was to make men of them, e'er he could hope to see them *saints;* they must be *civilized* e'er they could be *christianized.*"[14] An adequate account of the Praying Indians is beyond my scope here, but it is important to note the limitations in practice of the idea of benevolence and the apparent gift of civility, in that Indians were not accepted as equals or embraced within the Christian communities, but kept apart. Furthermore, as I show in chapter 7, the Indians' redistribution of the things they did acquire also had the effect of maintaining their relations with the larger non-Christian Indian community and its values.

Eliot contrasts his own measured approach to conversion with that of the Roman Catholics, who, he claims, allowed baptism after the learning of "a short answer or two to some Popish questions." By this means, or "if we would hire them to it by giving them coates and shirts," he, too, could have had spectacular success.

> If wee would force them to baptisme (as the Spaniards do about Cusco, Peru, and Mexico, having learnt them a short answer or two to some Popish questions) . . . we could have gathered many hundreds, yea thousands it may bee by this time, into the name of the Churches; but wee have not learnt as yet that art of coyning Christians, or putting Christs name and image upon copper mettle.

His resort to a metaphor of currency is appropriate in its invocation of a circulation of signs, but signs whose value is ultimately based on something—here it is gold—that guarantees and authorizes them. The idea of coining contains not just the idea of too easy a production, but also the idea of counterfeiting, as we can see in his use of it to distinguish beween genuine and superficial conversions. The problem is that conversion itself raises the prospect of counterfeiting, of false values masquerading as true, a prospect profoundly threatening to a Puritan community that wishes to protect its claim to the true faith but is involved in powerful internal dissensions as well as threats from outside, whether Catholic or Indian. Describing a sincere question asked by one of the Indian converts, Eliot insists that it "could not be learned from the English, nor did it seem a coyned feigned thing, but a reall matter gathered from the experience of his own heart, and from an inward observation of himself."[15] What is interesting, in light of his monetary metaphor of "coyning," is the link he explicitly makes between the circulation of the Word in Massachusett and the circulation of Indian currency in the letter to Richard Baxter discussed at the beginning of chapter 5.

Eliot believed that in the larger scheme of things, Indians, as "lost and scattered Israelites," would be gathered together as part of an overall unification, and he regularly cites Isa. 66:18 in support, as in his prefatory citation to *The Indian Grammar Begun:* "It shall come that I will gather all nations and tongues, and they shall come and see my glory." In a reference to Ezek. 3:9–10 that Mather mentions him using as a sermon,[16] Eliot describes the Indians as lost people, "dry and scattered bones, if any be in the world; and the work of God upon all such dry bones I beleeve will be in many things *Symmetrical.*" Nevertheless, until that day, the more limited task is to be one of converting by more mundane means: "but the work of the day is to civilise them, and it will be very chargable [expensive]."[17] This idea of the scattering of nations and the ultimate need to unify them relates closely to the idea of the gift of tongues, which holds out the idea of a transcendence of the division and confusion of languages since Babel.[18] Hakluyt, as early as 1584, is clear about the need first to "learne the language of the people nere adjoyninge (the gifte of tongues beinge nowe taken awaye)" and so gradually to "distill into their purged myndes the swete and lively liquor of the gospell."[19] Here the gift of tongues, as reflecting an essential spirit that transcends or underlies all language, is consigned to the past, but the relevant passages from Acts and Corinthians are reinterpreted by the later missionaries as justifying the work of translation and the hitherto potentially blasphemous idea of putting the Word of God into unworthy and primitive languages. Running through the whole venture, though, is the tension between expressing the Word as an unchanging essence and the risks of adaptation and distortion involved in translation.

Vincente Rafael, writing about the translation into the vernacular (in this case, Tagalog) from Latin, the language of imperial and religious authority in the Philippines, identifies these two contrary directions.

> Just as the significance of Christ's death and resurrection can be communicated only if it is ritually repeated, and thus its reality deferred, translation leads to conversion at the same time that it promotes the promise of a fully transparent language ruling over linguistic diversity. And the power of that promise qua promise is based precisely on its ability to point to another place and another time that frames as it regulates the multiplication of translations and the repetitions of rituals inherent in conversion.

On the one hand, there is the idea that the Word of God, as pure and direct, is without need of mediation, a gift like the Pentecostal gift of tongues to be passed on in a language beyond languages. On the other hand, there is the sheer complexity and diversity of the vernacular, the metonymic slippage and substitution that can confound such a project. The linguistic work of creating grammars and lexicons is part of the refashioning of the vernacular into the Word, "a gift to be circulated, and an instrument for the insertion of its speakers into a spiralling network of obligations with the Father." Translating into the vernacular, though, begins a process of circulation and transformation that is not necessarily controllable in this way, for in setting languages in motion, translation can "cast intentions adrift, now laying, now subverting the ideological grounds of colonial hegemony."[20]

In addition to translations, Eliot produced *The Logick Primer. Some Logical Notions to initiate the INDIANS in the knowledge of the Rule of reason; and to know how to make use thereof, specially for the Instruction of such as are Teachers among them.* It is described as "Composed by J.E for the use of the Praying Indians" and consists of a series of exercises in logic, or the analytic divisions necessary to begin logical thinking, beginning with oppositions and leading to basic syllogisms. As he says at the beginning in the truncated English interlinear that accompanies the Massachusett, the premise is that "Logick the Rule, whereby every thing every Speech is composed analysed, or opened to be known." What exactly the Indians would make of this highly technical approach is difficult to imagine, but Eliot's intention is clear on the title page. "The use of this Iron Key is to open the rich treasury of the Holy scriptures."[21] The plain iron that leads to (golden) riches could also imply the power of the printing process itself, but of course a key, as we have seen with Roger Williams, both opens up and, in organizing and systematizing, locks into place.[22]

The purpose is to "reduce" the Indians to rules and, in a larger sense, to civility. The opening of the riches is also the locking into place of a fixed means of thinking and of interpreting the Scriptures, and the complex relation between education itself as opening up (as in leading out) and locking up (as in indoctrination) is brought out in the importance he attaches to the question-and-answer sessions with his audience. The idea of a dialogue may contain within it the idea of a two-way process with possibilities of change and learning on each side, but this is not the way Eliot sees it or uses it. In his writing, and particularly the *Indian Dialogues*, we get set-piece exchanges rather than true interchanges, but his exercise of linguistic and interpretive as well as political authority is only occasionally thrown into clear relief. In one instance, for example, we learn how a famous "powah" or shaman had told people

> that there was a certain little hummingbird that did come and peck at him when he did aught that was wrong, and sing sweetly to him when he did a good thing or spake the right words; which coming to Mr Eliot's ear he made him confess, in the presence of the congregation, that he did only mean, by the figure of the bird, the sense he had of right and wrong in his own mind.

Eliot controls who has the proper meaning ("he did only mean"). It is interesting to note, though, that this "powah" continues to be seen as difficult. We are told that he was "exceeding cunning, and did often ask questions to be answered touching the creation of the Devil and the fall of man."[23]

In one of his letters, Eliot ends with "a few questions which they have propounded." These are mainly doctrinal: "How must I wait on God?" and "Do all evil thoughts come from the Devill, and all good ones from God? When all the world shall be burnt up, what shall be in the roome of it?" Some, though, have a surreal quality. "Why must we be like Salt?" He feels that these are the "best" questions he has been asked, and "best" here clearly means giving the strongest indication of progress toward thinking in Christian categories and a Christian framework.[24] In Eliot's letters as they appear in the various Eliot Tracts there is a consistent stress on the questions Indians ask, as the best indicators of their frame of mind, rather than their answers to the questions, but in general Eliot's idea of dialogue as an aid to proselytizing is a one-way street. The discourse was to be "by propounding certaine questions to see what they would say to them, that so we might skrue by variety of meanes something or other of God into them." On the whole, any sense of mutual adaptation is absent, and when we do get a sense of resistance from the Indians it is not dwelt on. In one instance, he targets the "Pawwaw" who is pointed out to him, asking him why he prays to "Chepian, the devil." Seeing that Eliot asks the questions with

> a sterne countenance and unaccustomed terrour, hee gave him no answer, but spake to other Indians that hee did never hurt any body by his *Pawwaw-ing*, and could not bee got by all the meanes and turnings of questions that might bee to give the least word of answer again.

In Mather's later, more programmatic account of this same scene, this silent resistance is interpreted as simple shame. "And the poor man was not able to stand or speak before him; but at last made promises of reformation."[25]

This sort of passive resistance may have been quite widespread, but we do have other, more intriguing and almost comic instances of a response Eliot chooses not to engage with directly. The serious tone of a meeting in which English visitors had been impressed by the Indians' "sober propounding of divers spirituall questions, their aptnessse to understand and beleeve what was replyed to them, [and] the readinesse of divers poore naked children to answer the chief questions in Catechism" is upset by "a malignant drunken" Indian (named elsewhere as George), who asks, "*Who made Sack? who made Sack?*" We are told that he "was soon snib'd by the other *Indians*, calling it a *Papoose* question," and that he was "seriously and gravely answered (not so much to his question as to his spirit) by Mr Eliot." It was perhaps easier for Eliot to finesse rather than answer this question, which he sees as impertinent. Actually, it is very pertinent, throwing into relief as it does the complexities of bringing civility to the Indians without many of its unwelcome accompaniments, such as alcohol. In another instance of resistance or skepticism, a young "desperado" being targeted by Eliot for drunkenness "brake out into a loud contemptuous expression; *So*, saith he; which we passed by without speaking again."[26] The tone of voice and the meaning of this one word are intriguing, seeming to throw Eliot's words back at him in a way he cannot handle and making it impossible for him to reinterpret, to impose his greater dialectical skills.

These impasses notwithstanding, Eliot clearly sees his task as an intellectual one and insists that "there is need of learning in Ministers who preach to Indians" more than there is in ministers who preach to an English congregation, "for these had sundry philosophicall questions, which some knowledge of the arts must help to give answer to." This goes along with a rational emphasis that also sees "no necessity of extraordinary gifts nor miraculous signes alway to convert the Heathens, who being manifest and professed unbeleevers may expect them as soon as any; (signes being given for them that beleeve not 1 Cor 14.22)."[27]

The control over the meaning and the way in which it manifests itself in an overwriting of the original Indian statement—the exercise of power reflected in rhetoric—is particularly clear in Mather's later accounts, such as *Magnalia Christi Americana*, where his overall providential framework leaves little room for even the pretense of real dialogue. In the pamphlet *Another Tongue*, referred to earlier, the overall intention is to present "A Glorious Christ Exhibited and Glorified," and while it does take the form of a sort of dialogue in the sense that it is initiated with a question, supposedly by the Iroquois, none of the questions sounds as if it comes from anywhere outside a Christian orthodoxy. They are simply feed lines for the answers, like the opening one "What are your thoughts?" or "where is the voice of God?" (answer: "lodged in the scriptures").[28]

Mather consistently contrasts the motives of New England missions with those of the Catholics, and his use and control of metaphor are worth particular attention. In a digression during his account of the Indian wars in *Magnalia Christi Americana*, he presents a supposed conversation between captured Indians and a Christian minister: "But now Bommaseen [the chief] is fallen into our hands let us have a little discourse with him." The main purpose here is to demonstrate to not only

Bommaseen and his people but also the reader the distortions of Christianity that have been taught by the Jesuits. Mather's minister, "considering, that the humour and manner of the *Indians* was to have their discourses managed with much of *similitude* in them; look'd about for some agreeable object, from whence he might with apt *resemblances* convey the ideas of truth into the minds of *Salvages*." He tells them, with appropriate "painting and pointing out the signs unto them," that Jesus has given religion like a good drink and the Bible is the cup. The Jesuits have put poison in the cup before giving it to the Indians, whereas the English, by translating the Bible into Indian languages, have "set the cup wide open" for them.[29] The poison represents the Catholic idea of confession to priests, but what is important for the present purposes is how the idea of the gift is turned round into the figure of the poisoned chalice. This is particularly effective, too, given the importance of the actual cup that would appear in Catholic communion, so that the figure becomes literal again.[30] Mather ascribes completely mercenary motives to the Jesuits and presents the Indians as astonished and grateful to find in the Puritan minister someone who could offer a way "to obtain the pardon of their sins and yet take no Bever-skins for it." Here again, then, is the conjunction of beaver and the gift of Christianity, and Mather insists that Catholic missionaries are "rarely employed but where *bever* and *silver* and vast *riches* are to be thereby gained."[31]

The trouble with figures of speech, though, is that they cannot always be controlled or used just by one side, as illustrated by the frequent misunderstandings over what is literal and what is not. The idea of a poisoned gift had occurred to the Indians, too, if only as an explanation of the diseases that accompanied encounters with whites.[32] Edward Winslow describes the accusation by Squanto (or Tisquantum as he calls him) that the English "had the plague buried in our storehouse; which, at our pleasure, we could send forth to what place or people we would, and destroy them therewith." When, in response to his accusations, the ground under the storehouse is dug up and barrels of gunpowder are found, Hobbamock, one of the other Indians, "asked him what it meant. To whom he readily answered, That was the place wherein the plague was buried." Winslow has just described Squanto's false accusations as "wicked," but what happens next reveals that the English are not above exploiting the suspicion for their own ends.

When asked by Hobbamock "if such a thing were, and whether we had command of it, one of the English answered, No; but the God of the English had it in store, and could send it at his pleasure to the destruction of his and our enemies." In this scene, the association of gunpowder (which could certainly be lethal) and plague and God moves between the literal and metaphoric, with Hobbamock trying to get a clear answer, and Squanto and the whites manipulating the connections. Interestingly, Mather's later account dismisses Squanto's charge as "a ridiculous rhodomontado," though he admits its usefulness in frightening the Indians. ("Thus was the tongue of a dog made useful to a feeble and sickly Lazarus.") But he immediately, with a sort of grim humor, underscores the association of the items in the cellar by adding, "Moreover, our English guns, especially the great ones, made a formidable report among these ignorant Indians," with the pun on "report" emphasizing the importance of backing up rumor and propaganda with real force.[33]

Shortly afterwards, Mather describes the ensuing plague of smallpox, which "getting in, I know not how, among them, swept them away with a most prodigious desolation." In spite of English assistance, "there was, it may be, not *one* in *ten* among them left alive; of those *few* that *lived* many also *fled* from the infection, leaving the country a meer *Golgotha* of unburied carcasses.[34] His insistence that the English used "all civility imaginable" and "fairly purchased" the land from the Indians rather than just taking it rings ironically to a modern ear, as Squanto's figure of destruction, Mather "knows not how," becomes literal.

Mather's strongly shaped account of earlier events shows this sort of linguistic control of Indians wherever they appear, and perhaps the clearest example of the play of figures of speech in Mather, and his concern to control them, comes in his description of King Philip. This "monster" has an angry altercation with Eliot, in which, "after the Indian mode of joining signs with words, he took a button upon the coat of the reverend man, adding That he cared for his gospel, just as much as he cared for the button." Such an act is bound to be punished, but Mather's description is striking in the way it brutally reduces Philip and in particular his ability to speak. "The world has heard what a terrible ruine soon came upon that monarch, and upon all his people. It was not long before the hand which now writes, upon a certain occasion took off the jaw from the exposed skull of that blasphemous leviathan."[35] The hand that writes silences the speaker—here it literally takes away the jaw of the blasphemer, and the brute reality of force suppresses the attempt to express opposition.

Roger Williams's position as skeptical outcast from the Puritan project combined with his substantial linguistic knowledge and experience of Indians gives his views of the work being done by Eliot and others special interest. In *The Bloody Tenant Yet More Bloody*, he delivers one of his keenest criticisms as part of a systematic polemic against John Cotton and, in particular, against the anomaly whereby dissenting Christians like Williams were excluded and persecuted, while Indians who were not even Christans were tolerated. Cotton's defense against this criticism had been that in fact the Indians were being Christianized. Williams's critique cuts to the heart of the whole missionary campaign, which needed to put a positive gloss on conversion activities and used Eliot as its prize exhibit. First, Williams flatly contradicts the claim that most Indians are moving toward Christianity and names four groups who "continue in their publike *Paganish Worship of Devils*." He further questions whether the sort of preaching and changing that is taking place is really very fundamental. While accepting with Cotton and Eliot that the conversion of nations (based on Rev. 15) "will not be great," he does not consider that any of the conversion activities are convincing. His reason is that even if the church's authority to send out apostles were accepted, none of the available preachers is linguistically capable "in any proprietie of their *speech* or *Language*," without which "no people in the World are long willing to heare of *difficult* and heavenly matters."[36]

Williams's authority for this is, first, that "The *Natives* themselves affirme, as I could instance in many particulars." His own personal experience testifies to the difficulties

> for any man to attaine a little *proprietie* of their *Language* in common things (so as to escape *Derision* amongst them) in many yeares, without abundance of *conversing* with them, in *Eating, traveling* and *lodging* with them,&c.which none of their *Ministers* (other affaires not permitting) could doe.

This echoes other heartfelt statements from Williams, claiming authority as someone who has ethnographically and linguistically paid his dues by living with the people themselves, and it is as a man keenly aware of the real difficulties of communication that he analyzes an incident described by Thomas Shepard, concerning Eliot. In the dialogue between Truth and Peace within which Williams's entire book takes place, Truth gives the instance in which

> Mr *Eliot* (the ablest amongst them in the *Indian Speech*) promising an old *Indian* a suit of Cloths the man (sayth the relation) not well understanding Mr *Eliots* speech, asked another *Indian* what Mr *Eliot* said. Peace replies Methinks, the *Native* not understanding such a *common* and *wellcome* promise of cloths upon *Gift*, would farre more hardly understand Mr. *Eliot's* preaching of the *garment of Righteousnesse Christ Jesus*, unto which Men mutually turne the deafe Eare &c.[37]

The purpose here seems less to belittle Eliot than to show the shaky nature of the whole enterprise. It also throws light on Gookin's description of the state of Christianization on Rhode Island, when he describes Williams as "skilful in the Indian tongue" but notes that

> God hath not honoured him, or any other in that colony that I can hear of, with being instrumental to convert any of those Indians; and yet there are very considerable numbers of Indians live nearby . . . I have observed that the Indians who live in these parts, generally are more indisposed to embrace religion, than any Indians in the country.

Gookin gives two reasons—"the averseness of the sachems" and the bad example of the English, "where civil government and religion run very low"—but one can ask whether Williams's realism about just what he was communicating may have made him see the possibilities of real conversion as a more distant prospect than did others in his situation. The footnote added by the editor in the Massachusetts Historical Society edition in 1792 confirms the Narragansett Indians' resistance: "Mr Williams made some laudable attempts to instruct them; but soon left off discouraged; conceiving that he could not with any propriety, preach christianity to them in their own language, without immediate inspiration."[38] The idea of propriety has already been used by Williams to describe linguistic competence, but here there seems to be the added idea of inspiration, pointing to the question, a fundamental one for Williams, of how thorough a conversion had to be.

In "Christenings Make Not Christians," Williams gives a variation on the "garment of righteousness" about which he was so ironic in his acount of Eliot's preaching. Williams notes that people may ask, why, given the opportunity, he did not make more conversions, why "hath there been such a price in my hand not improved?" In rejecting the idea of a merely superficial change, he images conversion in a set of dramatic contrasts of death and life. In a striking passage already discussed in chapter 4, he compares false or superficial conversion with dressing up a corpse. If appearances can be so deceptive, the whole idea of conversion at any level other than the most absolute is thrown into question, as in Eliot's image of the counterfeit "coyning" of Christians. This time, however, the criticism is aimed not at Catholics but at the Puritans themselves.[39]

In one of his few references to his own work at converting Indians, Williams emphasizes the gradual and difficult nature of the process. In the introduction to *A Key*, in a passage uncharacteristically positive about the prospects for conversion, he recounts his encounter with the dying Wequash, when he "closed with him concerning his Soule." Wequash recalls earlier conversations.

> Said he, *your words were never out of my heart to this present*; and said hee *me much pray to Jesus Christ . . . Me so big naughty heart, me heart all one stone! Savoury expressions* using to breath *from compunct and broken hearts*, and a sense of *inward hardnesse and unbrokennesse.*[40]

Here the sense of an inner core that has to be transformed (melted or broken down) is in contrast to the idea of changing an external garment or covering and reflects a continual questioning in missionary work and evangelizing in general about the nature of a true conversion. How much has to be changed, and how do we know for sure when it has? The stress on feeling in the preaching of the period of the Great Awakening gives a new twist to these questions, as is shown in the work of one specific preacher of this period, David Brainerd.

Though David Brainerd is relatively unknown today, he achieved widespread fame in the eighteenth and nineteenth centuries as a model of selfless dedication in a life devoted to missionary activity. John Wesley's recipe for reviving the work of God was "Let every preacher read carefully over *The Life of David Brainerd*," and popular accounts of Brainerd's life and work were widely available through Christian publishers well into the twentieth century.[41] Most of these recycled material from Jonathan Edwards's *The Life of David Brainerd*, which was based on Brainerd's diary, parts of which had already been published in 1746 in two books: *Mirabili Dei inter Indicos or The Rise and Progress of a Remarkable Work of Grace Amongst A Number of Indians in the Provinces of New Jersey and Pennsylvania, Justly Represented in A Journal, with General Remarks* and *Divine Grace Displayed.*[42]

In *The Life of David Brainerd*, Edwards uses almost exclusively those parts of the preacher's diary that deal with his anguished spiritual struggles, whereas the material in the other volumes, which are known, confusingly as the *Journal* concentrates more on his relation with his Indian congregations. While it is possible to see each text serving a polemical purpose (the journal was addressed to Brainerd's Scottish sponsors in the Society in Scotland for Propagating Christian Knowledge, whereas Edwards was presenting a case study of his own theological principles), the effect of Edwards's eminence has been to fix Brainerd as the saintly figure he presented him as and to ignore his dealings with his Indian congregations. Thus a picture has been propagated of heroic struggle against the elements, ill health, and heathen skepticism, with the Indians remaining anonymous. In fact, Brainerd's ministry was fairly brief and, if judged numerically in conversions, of limited success. After a brief spell with Mahican Indians near Stockbridge, he worked with the Delawares in Pennsylvania during 1744 and then, his only area of success, with Delawares at Crossweeksung in New Jersey. Constantly ill, he eventually succumbed to tuberculosis, dying at the home of Edwards, whose daughter nursed him until the end. His reputation is to a large degree the result of Edwards's desire to present him as a model of "true experimental religion."[43]

Brainerd's was a particularly tortured and gloomy life and ministry. Edwards acknowledged that Brainerd was "prone to melancholy and dejection of spirit" (91) and later views are likely to be closer to Patrick Frazier's assessment of him as "anxiety-ridden, melancholic manic-depressive, filled with guilt and self-loathing" or R. E. Day's description of him as "flagellant on horseback." Weddle argues that this persistent melancholy made Brainerd "at best an ambiguous example of Edwards' theology of religious experience," as melancholy could excite "enthusiastical vapours," which would be contrary to the picture he wants to present of Brainerd as steering between the Armenianism of good works and the excessive play of the "imagination."[44] If we look at Brainerd's own writings, though, we find, as well as this persistent melancholy and despair, some fascinating accounts of the dynamics of his relations with the Indians among whom he went to live.

Like other missionary enterprises, Brainerd's is couched in the language of a double benevolence. There is, first, the benevolence of the missionaries, who are bringing the good news, conferring a blessing and privilege, and, second and more fundamentally, the benevolence of God, who offers His unconditional love. The first of these was persistently questioned by Indians and skeptical whites alike, who challenged the idea of the unconditional gift, pointing to the hard economics of missions and schools whereby Indian land and labor were expropriated. Brainerd's self-sacrifice seems to have been personal and genuine, even if it was certainly played up for effect later. Throughout his writings we find the language of self-sacrifice. He longs to "spend and be spent for God" (415) and to "burn out in one continued flame for God" (402).

His mission was part of a larger undertaking, though, which the church represented as bringing the gift of God's benevolence to the Indians. This can be seen expressed in the sermon preached at Brainerd's ordination by Ebenezer Pemberton. The text is from Luke 14:23: "And the lord said unto the servant, Go out into the highways and hedges, and compel them to come in, that my house may be filled." This is an invitation that involves compulsion, and while Pemberton specifically rejects force, preferring what he calls "friendly violence," or "a lively representation of the power and grace of our Almighty Redeemer," he acknowledges the usefulness of invoking "the terrors of the Lord in array against the sinner." The invitation is to the "marriage supper" of Christ and ultimately a communion that will bind them, and it is to be reinforced by creating a psychological state of receptivity to their message. This is an offer they can't refuse.[45]

Brainerd's careful attention to the exact frame of mind of those being converted allows us a clear view of the importance of the idea of sovereignty, a giving that cannot be annulled by reciprocity. In his account of the conversions at Crossweeksung of an Indian woman and her husband we can see the issues spelled out. He refers to this particular woman on at least five occasions, though, characteristically, never gives her name or any details of her life. On her first appearance, she seems "in great distress for her soul. She was brought to such agony in seeking after Christ that the sweat ran off her face" (345). At the time he is preaching from Luke, the passage culminating in "ask and it shall be given you." At one level, this passage could easily be used to chime with Indian patterns of kinship and expectations of reciprocity ("If a son shall ask bread of any of you that is a father, will he give him a stone?"), but Brainerd uses it to make a rather different point. The man in the parable is given his three loaves not because he is a friend (which would be a tie of reciprocity) but because he asks. Because of his importunity, "he will rise, and give him as many as he needeth." In other words, the reason he receives has nothing to do with normal reciprocity, but is excessive and goes beyond the bounds of reason.

Six days later, Brainerd preaches from Matt. 19:16–22, where we find an account of the young man who has kept all the commandments and yet is told to sell all he has, give it to the poor, and follow Jesus. An indication of how closely Brainerd linked the Biblical texts to the specific occasion can be seen in his comments in his journal entry for that day on the presence of some newly arrived Indians, who had earlier lived among the Quakers and, like the young man in the Bible, had thought that living a "sober honest life" was "sufficient to salvation" (346). In contrast to this rational self-possession, the Indian woman appears "in a heavenly frame of mind." After trying to come to Jesus by her own efforts she had resigned herself to going to hell. Then, she tells him,

> "By by my heart be grad desperately." I asked her why her heart was glad. She replied, "Grad my heart Jesus Christ do what he please with me . . . Didn't me care where he put me, me lobe him for all." (347)

On a later occasion, when she gives further evidence of an "ecstacy of joy and desire," Brainerd in his journal entry measures her up against some revealing criteria. He accepts that we need to suspect great joys without "substantial evidence of their being well-grounded," but in this case he is convinced. "I scarce ever saw one appear more bowed and broken under convictions of sin and misery (or what is usually called a preparatory work) than this woman". He is satisfied that this does not come from any "sordid, selfish apprehension of her having any benefit whatsoever conferred on her" (370, 371).

Her husband has undergone a similar spiritual journey, described in revealing detail. Having heard Brainerd say that the aim was to be "emptied of a dependence on themselves and of all hope of saving themselves by their own doings," he had imagined this to be "an excellent frame of mind," (355) only to find that it was not a neutral state of waiting for God's grace, but a sense of self-loathing and unworthiness, accompanied by the belief that there was "nothing in such a sight to deserve God's love or pity" (356). Only when he has fully acknowledged his own lack of worth and power is he open to the intense vision of goodness that eventually comes to him. Even though Brainerd insists that he does not rely on "terror" in his sermons, there is still the crucial importance of instilling a sense of original sin and unworthiness. He remarks disappointedly, "They seem to have no consciousness of sin and guilt, unless they can charge themselves with some gross acts of sin."[46] Elsewhere he elaborates on this distinction, saying that they see sin only as a social wrong, "such as the light of nature condemns," whereas he wants to give them "a rational conviction that they are sinners by nature." Here the word "nature" does double duty, reflecting perhaps Brainerd's own difficulties in clarifying the distinction between evil in social and behavioral terms and in its metaphysical dimensions. The Indian man's sense of worthlessness creates both a need for something to reduce the sense of despair and the feeling that in a balanced or rational exchange he deserves nothing beyond just punishment. Elsewhere he describes the Indians "crying for mercy," and even, unusually, gives the phrases in the original language.[47]

One of Brainerd's most detailed accounts is of a man who had been a murderer, a powwow, (or conjurer), and a notorious drunkard but is reduced to a conviction of his own evil and undeservingness: "I had scarce ever seen any person more effectively brought off from a dependence upon his own contrivances for salvation, or more apparently to lie at the foot of *sovereign* [original emphasis] mercy," (392). Brainerd also mentions, though, that during the period of his preaching this man had murdered a young Indian, "which threw him into some sort of horror and desperation, so that he kept at a distance from me and refused to hear me preach" (391). The man also lost completely his "spirit of conjuration," such that "he don't now so much as know how he used to charm and conjure" (392). Where Brainerd sees purely the Word of God having its influence we may see a man in crisis for all sorts of other reasons connected with the breakdown of his culture. This might also be the place to point out that Brainerd's ministry is to a small remnant of a larger group who have already been moved and dispossessed. His lack of interest in their culture would make this irrelevant or a matter of some satisfaction for him, but it is, of course, crucial to note the difference in success between missionaries taking on intact cultures and those dealing with cultures already in crisis.

It is very noticeable just how often the Biblical text invoked is one which allows for the distinction to be made between rational expectations and good works, on the one hand and the unconditional gift, feeling, and grace on the other. The distinction is that between Martha and Mary and the "one thing needful," which I discussed earlier in relation to Eliot, and this idea pervades the thinking of Brainerd and his contemporaries. At the same time, it is important to Brainerd to steer a route between an excessive rationality, as in Armenianism, and the emotional excesses of the Moravians. This is illustrated clearly in how he deals with the central idea of the sovereignty of God. His hostility to the Indians who had been taught the doctrine of the sufficiency of good works was due to "their self-righteous disposition, their strong attachment to the covenant of works for salvation" (317). As he says dismissively, "They thought their state good and themselves happy" (318). The Covenant of good works is a sort of rational exchange and, taken far enough, requires no excess or sovereignty of God. Brainerd, though, wants to set up a different sort of rational balance. Once we accept that we are by nature and definition evil and undeserving, punishment from God is our rational expectation. At *that* point, God's irrational and excessive mercy comes in, so that what He gives is not a rational return for good works but an unconditional gift, as Brainerd's language insists: "the freeness and riches of his divine grace proposed without money and without price."[48] Thus he creates a need that cannot be satisfied, rationally but only by the sublime irrationality of grace and God's sovereignty. Brainerd has to confine all ideas of excess to God and the realm of the spirit, so that his sovereignty is about absolute power, but the Indians experience this initially as absolute personal powerlessness, only to be filled with God's sovereign power. As Georges Bataille says in a slightly different context, "The *evangelical* ethic is as it were, from beginning to end, an ethic of the sovereign moment."[49]

Brainerd's account of one of his larger and more successful meetings is remarkable for its detached understanding of the psychology of conversion. The excitement was such that "numbers could neither go nor stand," but what he particularly comments on is the relation of the individuals to the group

> Their concern was so great, each one for himself, that none seemed to take
> any notice of those about them, but each prayed as freely for themselves;
> and (I'm apt to think) were, to their own apprehension, as much retired as
> if they had been every one by themselves in the thickest desert . . . and so
> were every one praying apart, although all together. (308–9)

I think we can tentatively identify a certain sort of separate self here, created out of the fragmentation and decay of these Indians' traditional communal patterns, and connect this with what James Holstun identified in Eliot as the creation of a radical new subject, "the individual Praying Indian afflicted with a melancholic conscience and the right to make promises."[50]

The word "melancholic" here would be rejected as an ideal by Edwards and Brainerd, but it does point to a persistent phenomenon: the crying as well as the praying Indian. While this may have been more marked under the influence of the New Light preachers of the Great Awakening, Mather describes Eliot's initial successes in just these terms. "It broke his gracious heart within him to see, what floods of tears fell from the eyes of several amongst those degenerate salvages at the first addresses which he made unto them."[51] Brainerd also seems sometimes to judge the success of his preaching by the degree of "melting" in evidence. He even gives us an unwittingly revealing record of the ridicule it evokes from the Indian wits and skeptics, whom he describes as "asking my hearers how often they have cried, and whether they han't now cried enough to do the turn, etc." (323).

Like most other Christian missionaries, Brainerd displays little sense of the Indians as having anything at all to offer him, culturally or personally. He identifies few Indians by name, and even his interpreter, Moses Tatamy, on whom he greatly relied and who was himself baptized by Brainerd, gets little attention in his writings. In the sense it gives of isolation in an unsympathetic society, his account is reminiscent of early captivity narratives, which also demonstrate an ethnocentric mistrust of the alien culture, equating the non-Christian with the Satanic."[52] Some of Brainerd's descriptions of his reception by the Indians are unconsciously comic in their single-minded mistrust, such as when he arrives at a "sacred dance" and sits close to them, "with my

Bible in my hand, resolving if possible to spoil their sport and prevent them receiving any answers from the infernal world" (327), and when he describes being ignored, with crying children, unquelled by their mothers, by people "laughing and mocking at divine truths—Others playing with their dogs,—whittling sticks, and the like."[53] Overall, his aim was, like his predecessor Eliot's, to stamp Christianity upon the tabula rasa that he believed constituted Indian sensibility, and he differentiates the Indians only in terms of their receptivity or otherwise to his teachings. Unlike Eliot's emphasis on the need for education and civilization, though, in the time of the Great Awakening the stress on the role of the affections meant there was less concern for the sequential pattern of learning than for the sudden redemptive power of strong feelings.

Even so, there are places in Brainerd's writing where some sense of the existence, if not the validity, of Indian religion creeps in. In one of the most curious passages in his journal, he describes a meeting with an Indian who was "a devout and zealous reformer, or rather restorer, of what he supposed was the ancient religion of the Indians." Brainerd introduces him to us in a hyperbolic and dramatic way.

> But of all the sights I ever saw among them, or indeed anywhere else, none appeared so frightful or so near akin to what is usually imagined of infernal powers; none ever excited such images of terror in my mind as . . . (329)

He gives a detailed description of the man's clothing, mask, and rattle, but as the encounter goes on he records a surprising meeting of minds. Brainerd acknowledges that "he had a set of religious notions that he had looked into for himself, and not taken for granted upon bare tradition" and concludes, surprisingly, that "there was something in his temper and disposition that looked more like true religion than anything I ever observed amongst other heathens." One explanation for this openness may be the curiously similar roles of the two men. The Indian wants to revive a sense of religion among his increasingly degenerate people and has had to isolate himself from them in order to find his God. He even has thoughts "of leaving his friends and travelling abroad, in order to find some that would join him," just as Brainerd has done. With his rhetorical setting up of the horrific initial appearance, a stratagem that strikingly anticipates Ishmael's first response to Queequeg in *Moby Dick*, Brainerd seems to be both recognizing and denying the mirror image. Melville describes how, after the initial shock of the totally alien, Ishmael is brought through fellow-feeling and the obligations of human reciprocity ("What I require him to do for me, I should do for him") to bypass the absolute statement of sovereignty in the first commandment ("Thou shalt have no other Gods but me"). He is then able to embrace, along with Queequeg, a relativism that allows him to argue himself into worshipping with Queequeg his idol Yojo. There is nothing of this with Brainerd, of course, but there is the textual equivalent of a guilty start, as if he has gone too far, with the next paragraph after his sympathetic comments beginning with a reassertion of the party line: "But alas! how deplorable is the state of the Indians upon this river" (330).

In Brainerd's careful account of the vision of the converted conjurer, which I described earlier, there is a similar uneasy awareness of the ambiguous relation between pagan and Christian. In the vision, the man is admitted to the presence of a great man,

> clothed with the day, yea, with the brightest day he ever saw; a day of many years, yea of everlasting continuance! . . . Everything that was beautiful and lovely in the earth was upon him, and might be seen by looking on him. By the side of the great man stood his *shadow* or spirit; for he used the word *chichung*, the word they commonly make use of to express that of the man which survives the body, which word properly signifies a shadow.

This encounter took place before the conjurer's birth, and while on the earth he has been helped by this great man, who has sometimes appeared "in a special manner," as "all light, and not only all light himself but light all around him so that he could see through men." The language Brainerd uses here, so close to Biblical rhythms, and the unusually full account he gives suggest that he finds it difficult to know what to make of this experience. While he eventually dismisses it as a "mystery of iniquity," and declares that "these depths of Satan I leave to others to fathom," he is nevertheless uncomfortably aware that the powwow's spirit "seems to be a Satanical imitation of the spirit of prophecy that the church in early ages was favoured with."[54]

Like many other missionaries, Brainerd has a problem about the ambiguous gifts of civilization, ranging from alcohol to the Covenant of good works, but his final concern is with the Indians' spiritual life. Even his considerable efforts to safeguard their property are justified in terms of the threat debt poses to the development of a Christian community. He complains that they have lost their goods through trading for alcohol, "so they have not only lost their labour, but (which is infinitely worse) the impressions of divine things that were made upon their minds before."[55] Brainerd is in the paradoxical position of wanting to keep the Indian community intact in order to be able to change it, which places him in opposition to the market forces threatening them, in the form of land-hungry white neighbors. It is striking that in his account of how the money collected for the Indians was spent, four-fifths of it goes to paying off their debts to protect their land, and only one-fifth to paying a schoolmaster. His fear of their vulnerability through debt, added to the standard bourgeois attitudes of the time, means that although he preaches one sort of economic model of "the unsearchable riches of gospel grace" in religion,[56] in their daily life he advocates a cautious, possessive individualism as guaranteeing them economic independence. There is a contradiction, then, between the economic rationality of day-to-day trading and business and the economy of spiritual affairs. What Brainerd offers them on the spiritual side is neither balanced nor rational but excess, and the difficulties this gets him into can be seen in his account of the difficulties he encounters in explaining Christ's role in suffering and dying for others.

One difficulty, he says, is that the Indians have no legal sense of standing surety, or being responsible for paying each other's debts, something remarked on by others.[57] The way he chooses to explain Christ's ability to "pay off the debt of all"—in other words, to stand for us all—is through the analogy of gold's superior value to base metal, whereby "a small quantity of this will discharge a greater debt, than a vast quantity of the common copper pence."[58] This analogy reflects the slipperiness of the network of metaphors of debt, worth, and sovereignty with which he is working. The problem is that he tries to explain Christ in terms of equivalence via a common measure, whereas surely the point about Christ's sacrifice was that it expresses God's sovereignty, in overflowing beyond equivalence and measure, in excess. This is, in Bataille's terms, the accursed share and, according to the normal assumptions about primitive thought, is the last point that should need explaining to the Indians, especially in an economic metaphor, but we can see Brainerd's anxieties over presenting the Eucharist as too similar to a sacrifice. Looking back at his achievements as missionary and his administering of the Lord's Supper to those ready for it, Brainerd does deliberately seem to make the link. "From the time, when, as I am informed, some of them attending an *idolatrous feast and sacrifice* in honor to *devils*, to the time when they sat down at the Lord's table, I trust to the honor of God, was not more than a *full year*."[59]

Here he deliberately puts together the two ceremonies to demonstrate how the Christian one has replaced the other, and in doing so he also echoes the terms of Ebenezer Pemberton's ordination sermon for him described earlier, using the invitation to Christ's wedding feast. But it is crucial that the idea of the communion should be firmly controlled and not allowed to be seen as too similar to what Christians would believe primitive rites to be. Brainerd is at pains to explain to the Indians the Covenant of grace and the meaning of the sacrament as a seal or sign of that covenant, and he insists that

> They were likewise thoroughly sensible that 'twas no more than a seal or a sign, and not the real body and blood of Christ; that 'twas designed for the refreshment and edification of the soul, and not for the feasting of the body. (388)

However, the problems of first establishing a symbolic equivalence and then having to distinguish between Protestant and Roman Catholic versions of it through reliance on an interpreter might make us question his confidence, particularly since he elsewhere gives examples of some of the rather crude substitutes he has to use for concepts lacking in the Indians' languages.

By concentrating in detail on Brainerd's terms, I have been trying to show how he has to establish and explain his beliefs and how this involves him inevitably in a process of cultural translation. It is in metaphors of exchange and giving that we can see the complexities of missionary encounters—conversion, after all means translating, exchanging one state for another. In particular, we can see the complexity of Brainerd's position in relation to the idea of sovereignty. On the one hand, the autonomy of the self-possessed individual should relate nicely to the idea of a doctrine of good works. Jean Baudrillard sees the Church at this time as creating "a political economy of individual salvation,"[60] in which God, as trading partner, will respond rationally and appropriately and give us the equivalent of what we gave in life. On the other hand, this ignores the powerful stress on God's sovereignty, which takes him outside such a measure, or any measure, and on the importance of our own recognition of this excess and overflowing in our own spiritual life, through grace rather than good works. So we have the profound split between immeasurable grace and the secular world of calculation. It may well be that the Indians responded better to this combination than to the rational emphases of the earlier Puritans. Bataille argues that in separating out good works from grace, Calvinism enables capitalism to develop because it desacralizes the world and allows it as an autonomous realm outside the moral.[61] More important, perhaps, Calvinism combined with a stress on the fallen nature of humanity institutes a sort of scarcity economics of trust, what Lewis Hyde calls "a spiritual form of the scarcity economics that always accompanies private property."[62] In any case, what was actually happening as the message of the gospel, in whatever form, was sent on its way can only partially be estimated from missionary descriptions, especially given their resistance to the idea of any mixing or syncretism. Having looked at the message from the missionary perspective, it is now necessary to broaden the perspective with a look at some of the transformations of the ideas and the objects of Christianity as they enter a different system.

7

Conversion and Exchange

RELIGIOUS CONTACTS and exchanges never take place in isolation from the complex of other cultural, economic, and material interchanges, so that any attempt to control the meaning of cultural and religious exchanges inevitably runs into difficulties. The nature of the early missionaries' monotheistic message and their mission to convert means that we should not look to them for any interest in reciprocal exchange, or shared and mutually adaptive dialogue, but at the same time their very task of conversion involves a relation with the Indians different from that of diplomacy, trade, or military conquest. It could be argued that even when it was seen to be inadequate to the occasion, as in the exchanges between Captain John Smith and Powhatan, the European adventurers could operate within a template of diplomatic and political behavior—what Daniel Defert calls "the grid of universal diplomacy." This could cover feasts and various ceremonies of welcome and alliance, and did not actually require a shared mental agenda so much as a series of symbolic actions, the most infamous of which was perhaps the *Requerimiento.* Conversion, on the other hand, if it was to be anything more than perfunctory, required some interaction. As Defert puts it,

> To baptise, to inculcate a belief, initiate a life style and a hope for the future, to introduce a sexual code, to hear confessions, to keep guard over the orthodoxy of the faith—all these activities presuppose techniques and knowledge which did not derive from procedures proper to political domi-

nation, even when political and religious power were intermingled. Thus political power can inculcate its own language: religious power needs to penetrate the secrets of the native language.

Whereas for the diplomat a surface similarity or adaptation is enough, the missionary is involved in a more complex world of the devil's deception and mimicry, a treacherous play of similarity and difference.

> The observation of societies becomes a chapter in demonology. With what fascinated passion does the exhaustive extirpation of evil become the ethnography of a civilisation . . . The act of civil conquest generated homologies. Religious semiology, on the contrary, promulgated the strange Otherness of societies, the will to describe their difference.[1]

We may need to balance this view of the potential for a relativizing anthropology against an awareness of the impulse to control and authorize the message that was being given, as I show later, but it is also important to stress what was happening on the other side of the encounter.

During the seventeenth century, the native peoples of northeast America encountered a series of missionary enterprises that combined with varying degrees of contact with traders and settlers and the devastating effect of European diseases to create a profound challenge to their beliefs and social patterns. Without playing down the scale and destructiveness of the impact, recent research on these early contacts has tended to stress the remarkable strategies of adaptation and change on the part of the Indian communities, rather than just wholesale loss and destruction, and the missionary encounter and the idea of conversion need to be seen in this context. Conversion implies, at its simplest, changing something that is already present, and one of the recurrent questions is what exactly and how much is being changed.[2] Connected with this is the question of how far change might involve *ex*change, a two-way process, an altogether more problematic and threatening idea for Christian missionaries, given the exclusive and unilateral form of their Christian mission. The missionary enterprise entailed the dissemination of new ideas that were intended to replace or transform what was there before in a one-way transmission, but I shall show how, since the missionaries were involved in a complex network of exchanges— cultural, economic, and linguistic—what they entered into circulation, be it a word, an idea, or a religious object, took on a value given by its circulation within that particular material and discursive economy and could not be restricted or authorized only by its Christian origins.

In Indian societies of the Northeast, the missionaries were dealing with cultures that, for all their considerable diversity were alike in giving profound importance to redistribution, reciprocity, and circulation. There were well-established networks in which exchange was not merely a means to an end (material gain), but an end in itself, an enactment and reinforcement of a mutual relationship. By stressing the range of the cultural exchanges involved in the missionary encounter, I shall show some of the diversity of native responses, as well as the anxieties and crises of authority this diversity could create for the missionaries. In its most extreme form, this anxiety was a fear that the initial unilateral impulse behind conversion was falling foul of a reciprocity that might demand in return some converting or at least adaptation of the missionaries' own beliefs. Clearly, this could not even be contemplated—but what, after all, was the translating of Christian terms into native terms? How could one be sure which way the conversion was taking place at the linguistic level? And what about the adaptation and reuse of religious objects, such as rosary beads? In short, how was it possible to police and control the meaning of what was being introduced? Such questions involved the missionaries in a series of reciprocal and potentially relativizing and unsettling encounters, in which the terms of exchange needed to be controlled. In this chapter, I first outline some of the general terms.of these exchanges, with a brief comparative overview of Protestant and Catholic approaches. I then concentrate on some instances of the dissemination and dispersal of Christianity, but with a shift of emphasis to what may have actually been happening to the various material and intellectual ingredients as they found their way into the discursive economies of Indian life.

Apart from whatever adaptations and transformations were taking place as disparate elements of Christianity encountered another cultural reality, the missionaries were already involved in a set of interlocking and sometimes contradictory discourses from their own culture, as I show in chapter 6. Their situation made it impossible to keep the religious separate from the cultural and economic, particularly the linguistic and economic exchanges involved respectively in translation and trade. Not only was there a constant overlap of these areas in practice, but metaphors of value and exchange were inevitably fundamental to missionary discourse. In particular, the missionary enterprise inherited a complex language of benevolence, the bringing of an unconditional gift, represented in the absolute sacrifice of Christ, alongside the calculation and market mentality of trade and empire. The ideal may have been to give and not to count the cost, but the reality of the fur trade, Puritan land settlements, and financing of missionary activities from England and France actually involved a great deal of counting and accounting. The tendency has been to polarize Western and primitive cultures, stressing the excessive aspects of the latter and the rational and economic side of the former, but, as is implicit in my approach in chapter 6, to understand fully the missionary enterprise and its relation to Western expansion, we need to recognize the actual and rhetorical importance of unilateral giving and excess, the extravagant and exorbitant. This means that missionaries were in fact operating within two sorts of economy—possessive individualism and sacrifice and excess. Furthermore, we can find in European and Native American societies alike an important role for the idea of excess, for spending resources and energy rather than saving, and waste rather than use.

As should be clear by now, the idea of economy I am using refers to more than the circulation of money or goods. At a more general level, the two economies described above are not just trade and calculation versus the world of spiritual and self-surrender but also represent different discursive economies. In the one, things and words have fixed value and circulation can be controlled and regulated. In the other, the dissemination of meaning is endless and not guaranteed or controlled by any one fixed point of reference.[3] My argument is that missionaries moved uneasily between the two. They preached God's unconditional love and the need to give (a message of excess and sacrifice) at the same time they inculcated a value system based on self-possession (saving rather than spending). They were equally ambivalent about the communication of their message, in that they wanted to spread and disseminate (and the images are of abundance) but also to control and authorize. It is the movement of words, ideas, and objects within these various discursive economies that is the subject of this chapter.

In my examples from the Jesuit missionaries of New France and the Puritans of New England, both the similarities and the differences are important.[4] The Jesuits, unlike their predecessors the Recollets, believed that the best way to effect conversion was to keep the Indians in isolation from civilizing influences, which would corrupt rather than advance their understanding.[5] Christian doctrine and terms would be translated into native terms, and traditional Indian patterns of life and behavior would be changed only when necessary. While this policy created some friction with traders, who felt they were being excluded from contact and even accused the Jesuits of taking over the trade in furs, it coexisted with broader economic policy in that the success of the fur trade required Indians to remain relatively isolated and intact in their traditional patterns. In contrast, the Puritans of New England were settlers, living in proximity to Indians and in competition for their land. Largely committed to the idea of the depravity rather than nobility of the original Indians, Puritan divines insisted on civilization as a precondition of full conversion to Christianity. Crucial to John Eliot's enterprise were his pioneering work as translator of religious texts into Massachusett and the establishment of what came to be known as "Praying Towns," reflecting the Puritan belief that full conversion of Indians required both full understanding of the tenets of religious faith and a way of life likely to embody and encourage them. The self had to be reconstructed along Puritan lines, and this involved all aspects of life, including the secular. Though Eliot's early attempts to learn and use Indian languages were heavily publicized in fundraising efforts in London, the movement and the effort were increasingly expected to come from the Indian side.[6]

On the basis of this comparison, it is tempting to see the Jesuits as either more open to Indian ideas, less culturally aggressive and absolutist than the Puritans, or, put negatively, more superficial about the process of conversion, settling for the show rather than the substance. Certainly, the Puritans took the latter view in explaining the relative scarcity of the conversions they effected in comparison with the Catholics. For them, the Catholic use of religious paraphernalia chimed only too well with pagan superstition and magic as a threat to the purity of the Word. So unrelenting was the Puritan need for doctrinal correctness that it sometimes seems surprising that anyone met the criteria. Only later, under the influence of the Great Awakening, with its stress on emotion rather than intellect, do we find an easier access to grace.[7]

It is interesting, though, that the Indians themselves seem to have developed a highly charged style of preaching that anticipated the emotional intensities of the preachers of the Great Awakening. As Kathleen Bragdon says,

> native sermons were equally full of lamentations, self-condemnation, and pleas for pity. In this, as in their preference for monologues delivered with emotion and gesture, the native Christians of New England were early practitioners of a Christianity that became common among non-natives only during the Great Awakening.[8]

In spite of these differences, I shall bring out fundamental similarities between Protestant and Catholic by focusing on the missionaries' concern to control the message and meaning and the troubled response to unorthodox exchanges and conversions of significance beyond their control. Given the desire for the gift of Christianity to be unilateral—a benevolent imposition without the complications of negotiation, exchange, or dialogue—the ideal situation would be simply the introduction of new ideas into an empty space. This is altogether less messy than conversion of existing ideas and is as seductive as the myth of the virgin land that has operated for so long at the political level in North America. It appears as early as 1555 in Richard Eden's preface to the first English edition of Peter Martyr's *De Orbe Novo, The Decades of the New World of West India.* Eden sees the influence of civility as an inevitable effect of contact with Christians, just as "they that goo much in the soonne, are coloured therewith although they go not with such purpose." Unlike the Jews, who are already confirmed in a false set of beliefs,

> these simple gentiles lyvinge only after the lawe of nature, may well bee lykened to a smoothe and bare table unpainted, or a white paper unwritten, upon the which yow may at the fyrst painte or wryte what yow lyste, as yow can not uppon tables already paynted, unless you rase or blot owt the fyrste formes.[9]

This image is repeated in both Puritan and Jesuit thinking, where it is linked to the common ethnocentric characterization of the Indians in terms of what they lacked, whether writing, government, or religion. In New England, Eliot's ambition was to write and imprint no nother but Scripture principles in the *abrasa tabula s[c]raped board* of these naked people, that so they may be in all their principles a choice people unto the Lord.[10]

In New France, too, the Jesuits felt that the conversion of the Indians

would be all the easier, because—as upon a bare tablet, from which there was nothing to erase—we might without opposition impress on them the ideas of a true God.[11]

It is worth noting that the scraped board and the bare tablet represent different states, and Eliot's is in fact more accurate in its underlying implication that something has to be removed before the message can be applied. This relates back to the issue of nakedness examined in previous chapters, whereby the lack of Christian belief or European clothes represents not an alternative but an absence, in a binary system in which difference simply equals absence.

The realities of daily communication gave the lie to this idea of a complete absence of religion, though it is not uncommon to find confident statements of its absence followed immediately by quite detailed descriptions of what we would certainly recognize as religious practices. This is achieved by dismissing anything other than Christianity as less than religion, but even so there are some marked inconsistencies. Thomas Morton exhibits perhaps one of the clearest. He first insists that "these people are *sine fide, sine lege & sine rege*" (in opposition to William Wood's view, at which he takes a swipe in his rejection of a "wooden prospect"). Then in a later chapter he acknowledges that they are "not altogether without the knowledge of God" and describes their belief in "Kytan." What is in operation here is perhaps part of a larger stratagem of denial, whereby there is an initial premise of absolute privation, which then allows discussion of what is actually observably present, which is exactly the same pattern as the insistence on nakedness followed by descriptions of clothing, which we have already seen. Even when the existence of Indian religious beliefs and practices was acknowledged, there was a common assumption that the devil was being worshipped. Ironically, while this was clearly ethnocentric in extending inappropriate Christian categories, it did also allow Indian gods a real existence and efficacy, since Christians believed in the devil as a real being. This was denied by later skeptical or rationalist observers who, as a corollary to their more relativist and value-free position, could at best bracket the question of the validity of gods in general and deal with them entirely in terms of belief rather than reality. For Roger Williams, the real existence of satanic powers is so assumed that it prevents him from even observing native practices.

> For after once being in their Houses and beholding what their Worship was, I durst never bee an eye witnesse, Spectatour, or looker on, least I should have been partaker of Sathans Inventions.[12] (192)

A more nuanced approach was to see Indian religion as characterized by the same dualism of good and evil as Christianity. Edward Winslow's account of the Indians of New England, as encountered by the Pilgrims, shows the transition to this view. Though he originally wrote that the Indians lacked any religion, he tells us,

> therein I erred, though we could then gather no better; for as they conceive of many divine powers, so of one, whom they call *Kiehtan*, to be the principal and maker of all the rest, and to be made by none . . . This power they acknowledge to be good; and when they would obtain any great matter, meet together and cry unto him.

Having identified Kiehtan as a positive deity, Winslow seems to have to present the other major figure, Hobbamock, negatively: "this, as far as we can conceive, is the devil." This is in spite of the fact that he describes in some detail how Hobbamock is called on "to cure their wounds and diseases" and reports that those who communicate with him through visions and observances are clearly men of superior personal qualities ("of great courage and wisdom").[13] The problem for the modern reader is in finding where exactly this evil is supposed to reside that makes the distinction so absolute, but for Winslow the distinction between good and evil deities was a given.[14]

Though he was neither missionary nor divine, William Strachey gives an account of the Indians of Virginia that is revealing in this respect, not least for the sequence of ideas in the chapter on religion. None of the Indians, he tells us, have been discovered to be so "savadge and simple" as not to have a religion. To all things that are capable of being dangerous and beyond their control (this includes European guns and horses as well as thunder and fire), the Indians extend "their kind of divine worship." Their chief god, however, is

> no other, indeed, than the divell, whome they make presentments of, and shadow under the forme of an idoll, which they entitle Okeus, annd whome

they worship, as the Romans did their hurtfull god Vejovis, more for feare
of harme then for hope of any good.

But as the passage goes on, with a description of the control exerted
over the people by the priests in charge of the worship of Okeus, we
are given sight of another god,

> the great God (the priests tell them) who governes all the world, and makes
> the sun to shine, creating the moone and starrs his companyons . . . and by
> whose vertues and influences the under earth is tempered, and brings forth
> her fruicts according to her seasons, they calling Ahone; the good and pea-
> cable God requires no such dutyes, nor needes be sacrificed unto, for he
> intendeth all good unto them.

As Strachey develops the contrast, some of the characteristics of Okeus
begin to sound familiar. In contrast to the unconditional benevolence
of Ahone,

> the displeased Okeus, looking into all men's accions and examining the
> same according to the severe scale of justice, punisheth them with sick-
> nesses, beats them and strikes their ripe corne with blastings . . . Such is
> the misery and thraldome under which Sathan hath bound these wretched
> miscreants.[15]

On the one side is the overarching and unconditional gift, the benevolence of Ahone, and on the other is not sheer arbitrary evil but punishment, retribution based on harsh justice. This sounds more like two
aspects of Christianity, as exemplified by New and Old Testament
teaching, than devil worship, and Strachey's account can be read as revealing not so much a fuzziness about native belief as a difficulty in
aligning it with Christian terms. By beginning with the unwieldy and
unexamined idea of the devil and giving it precedence, Strachey renders
himself incapable of drawing the comparisons and conclusions that the
detailed descriptions in the rest of his chapter (which includes material
on burial practices and a translation of a creation story) would allow.

The same distinction between a benevolent god who does not need
to be appeased or worshipped and a malevolent one is found in Francis
Higginson's brief prospectus/report, *New England's Plantation*: "For
their Religion they doe worship two Gods, a good God, and an evill
God; the good God they call *Tantum* and their evill God whom they
fear will doe them hurt, they call *Squantum*." A further refinement is in
John Josselyn's 1675 account of New England:

They acknowledge a God who they call *Squantam*, but worship him they do not, because (they say) he will do them no harm. But *Abbamocho* or *Cheepie* many times smites them with incurable Diseases, scares them with his Apparitions and panick Terrours, by reason whereof they live in a wretched consternation, worshipping the Devil for fear.

The example that follows is an apparition of Cheepie gliding in the air, but, interestingly, he is described as "all wone *Englishman*, clothed with hat and coat, shoes and stockins, &c." William Simmons gives other instances where the conception or description of Cheepie/Hobbamock was affected by contact with Europeans or African-Americans.[16]

The most perceptive Puritan commentator on religion, as on so much else, is Williams, who, although in no doubt about the unilateral truth and necessity of Christian belief, nevertheless recognizes the plurality of gods in the Indian pantheon without needing to see a duality. As Neal Salisbury concisely puts it, Williams was able to see the Indians as "polytheists not crypto-monotheists." In a letter to John Winthrop, Williams comments,

> I find what I could never heare of before, that they have plenty of Gods or divine powers: the Sunn, Moone, Fire, Water, Snow Earth, the Beare etc are divine powers. I brought home lately from the Nahiggonsicks the names of 38 of their Gods all they could remember and had I not with feare and caution withdrew they would have fallen to worship O God (as they speake one day in 7).[17]

He shows a remarkable awareness of the way the Christian God was being assimilated as only one of many (one day in seven) and the problems this raised for its monotheistic claims. On this occasion as on others, Williams distances himself from their religion, but we also have here a sense of his real interest in what he has learned.

On the whole, though, the determination to ascribe evil to Indian religion meant a blinkered approach not only to its ideas but to its practitioners, and this was at the cost of a consistent blindness to the full role of what we would now recognize as shamans, who were partly equated with witches. There is a distinct lack of evidence, even at the level of hearsay, for shamans as practitioners of witchcraft in the sense of maleficium, or malign acts against others, whereas there is strong evidence, even from Puritans themselves, that these figures were healers in a long-standing and widespread shamanic tradition. The fact that these "Witches or Sorcerers" could "cure by help of the devill" did not make them any less of a threat to the Puritan enterprise.[18] As Alfred Cave puts it, "The shamans' crime in Puritan eyes was not that they did evil, but rather that they used their presumed alliance with the Devil to do good." Chretien Le Clercq, too, in his account of the Micmac is clear about his preconceptions:

> It is true that I have never been able to discover any pact, explicit or implicit, between the jugglers and the Devil; but I cannot persuade myself on that account that the devil is not predominant in their nonsense and their impostures.[19]

It is in the accounts of shamans and the determination to present them as malign that we see most clearly the limitations Christian ideology imposed, in that difference must be asserted even in the face of massive similarities. The contest for legitimacy between missionaries and shamans as upholders of traditional values is regularly presented in Christian accounts as evidence of the defeat of superstition, but it is worth looking more closely at some of the issues raised. Robert Conkling argues that the legitimation of Christian beliefs, as opposed merely to their imposition, was due to the priests' taking on the charismatic status of the shaman in contests with him,[20] but a closer look at the terms of these contests is necessary.

Accounts of the defeat of shamans involve a claim to two different sorts of superiority on the part of the whites. On the one hand, there is technology, for example, the impressive and unanswerable effect of a gun and the ability to predict an eclipse. On the other, there is the ability to produce or prevent rain or cure sickness by prayer. The confusion between these sorts of efficacy may have allowed Christianity to win out in these contests, and this overlapping area of magic, technology, and prayer raises some interesting questions about missionaries' belief and practice, given their insistence on distinguishing between Christian religion and pagan superstition. Stanley Tambiah has usefully summarized the distinctions to be drawn between Christianity, particularly the Protestant form, and what the missionaries saw as pagan practices. Whereas primitive religions saw the gods at work in nature and a part of it, capable of being induced to make things happen, the Judeo-Christian God was supposed to be sovereign and outside nature. While the role of miracles might need to be disputed, the rule was that God was not to be influenced directly, but that his will was sovereign and independent. A spell would claim to effect a change in nature; a prayer was more indirect. Tambiah also underscores the specifically Protestant associations of this and the connection with the more general desacralization of the world described by Max Weber.

> It was inevitable and logical given this formulation of God's sovereignty that Protestant theologians would hammer out the distinction between religious acts as primarily intercessionary in character, and magical acts as being coercive rituals ambitiously attempting to manipulate the divine . . . [For them] there was a fundamental distinction between prayer and spell, the former belonging to true religion, the latter to false religion.

Certainly for the Jesuits of New France, according to Bruce Trigger, their belief in God's intercessionary power was barely distinguishable from magic in Tambiah's description. They believed themselves to be

> serving a god who could intervene in human affairs at any moment . . . Moreover, while the Jesuits did not believe in magic in the strict sense of thinking that Roman Catholic rituals gave them the power to control nature automatically, they were convinced that their god would answer prayers for rain or good harvests, if this would convince the Indians of his glory and help to undermine the Indians' respect for their own shamans.

This is backed up by Conkling's description of the similarity of Jesuit and Indian attitudes. Whether seen negatively or positively, the elements of Christian ritual were believed to have an efficacy close to that of magic. As Conkling puts it, "The same Christian paraphernalia— baptismal water, crosses, images, rosaries—to which some Indians attributed evil power, others, like the missionaries themselves, attributed the power to cure."[21]

Whether in practice the Protestant position was so different is not clear, as Winslow's account of Squanto and the explanation of the plague in Chapter 6 indicate. Overall, though, the Catholics' greater use of ritual and ritual objects made them seem more like shamans than their Protestant counterparts, confirming the latter's suspicions about Catholic superstition. Protestant scrupulousness over ensuring that the real message is understood continued into later missionaries, as I have shown in David Brainerd's careful explanation of the covenant of grace and the sacrament as a seal or sign of that covenant. The Catholic missionaries encountering the Hurons and Iroquois were posed an additional problem by the central role of torture and the ritual eating of prisoners in these cultures. While they had to accept the presence of these practices (and even fell victim to them on some occasions, allowing them later to be presented as martyrs to the cause) the missionaries had an unexpected difficulty in preventing the Indians from equating the tortures of Hell as they described them with their own ritual tortures, which conferred respect and honor on those who withstood them bravely and therefore carried too many positive connotations for the Jesuits' liking.[22]

Baptism was the most important and visible religious activity that was likely to be considered shamanistic. For a long time, Indians assumed baptism to be a curing ceremony, at least partly because priests, although reluctant to baptize healthy Indians until they were sure they were genuinely converted, made a point of giving baptism to those they thought were on the point of death. As a result, large numbers of the baptized died, which may have done nothing for the priests' reputation as healers but did reinforce the idea that they had power of some description. Combined with the regular appearance of disease wherever missionaries had been, baptism seemed to the Indians to give strong evidence that they were witches. It is worth noting, though, that a fair number of those baptized and assumed to be dying did in fact recover, which might suggest that their ceremony worked regardless of their intentions, because of Indian belief in its efficacy. As Kenneth Morrison puts it, "thinking in terms of the vital symbols of traditional power, the Montagnais concluded that if baptism could kill, it might also cure."[23]

Although the Jesuits in particular gave a high priority to baptism,[24] they were also skeptical of how much was understood and were consequently reluctant to baptize prematurely, contrary to Protestant propaganda. Father Pierre Biard stresses the particular difficulty of dealing with nomadic and savage people. Even in South America, where "the people are not Savage but civilised; not wandering but stationary; not abandoned but under the watchful care of Pastors, namely in Peru and Mexico"—even there, premature baptisms led to

> a Synagogue of Samaritans rather than a Church of the faithful. For these who were too soon Baptised willingly came to Church but it was to mutter there their ancient idolatries. They observed the appointed saints' days but it was while carrying on their sacrifices, dances, and superstitions; they went to holy Communion, if it was desired, but without knowing either the *Creed* or *Confession*, and emerging from there, they went off to get Drunk and to sing to the Devil their usual sorceries.[25]

The first Indians Biard encountered had been inadequately catechized by his predecessor and had "accepted baptism solely as a sign of friendship"; they were unpleasantly surprised to discover that it entailed obligations like monogamy. Biard insisted that it needed to be seen like a contract, and his legal metaphor is revealing. Just as one cannot hold a person to an oath he or she does not understand, one cannot expect "a rational being of competent age to make a solemn profession of the law of God (which is done through Baptism)" when he has never been taught "the rules and duties of the profession." This is a long way from the emphasis later placed on the overwhelming power of grace and feeling by the preachers of the Great Awakening, but it also, as with the contemporary Puritan preachers, sits uneasily with a more general Christian insistence on the sovereignty of God and the unequivocal and absolute power of sacrifice, expressed in the gift of Christ. The rational contract may ultimately be a less useful way of conceiving of conversion than the idea, which Biard dismisses here, of a "sign of friendship" since within this can be invoked the full set of reciprocal obligations based on giving, exchange, and sacrifice.[26]

A broad idea common to Christian and Indian beliefs was the idea of an overall donor power, whose actions transcended any contractual sense of fairness or obligation, and as Morrison shows, there was enough resemblance between the Jesuits' concept of grace and the Montagnais idea of power for the conversion of ideas, if not souls, to take place. The fundamental Montagnais belief that "human beings and other-than-human persons were bound by webs of ritual exchange,"[27] combined with their fundamentally nondogmatic and flexible approach, enabled them to take over what seemed to work, but while the invocation of God's power may ultimately have stressed his benevolence, the short-term efficacy of the fear of his retributive power was not lost on the missionaries and seemed to be backed up by the devastating events being visited on the Indians. Morrison cites the example of a Montagnais, Nenaskoumat, who, having joined the French, loses most of his family through disease, which he also contracts. As the missionary Paul Le Jeune says, "It was enough to crush the spirit of a Giant, and to revive the ideas that many of the Savages had entertained, that to intend to become a Christian was to consent to depart from this world" (*JR* 14:137). Originally the congruence of ideas made it possible for the Montagnais to accept through baptism a Christian power that could be seen as a new manifestation of traditional categories, but such afflictions, combined with the Christian message of personal sin and guilt, had a cumulative impact. According to Morrison, "at the end of the 1630s the Montagnais had internalized the Jesuit theory of sin to such an extent that continuing crisis over which they had no control implied their overwhelming guilt."[28]

The refusal of Christian missionaries to recognize Indian religion as constituting a system of beliefs and practices comparable to their own was sustained by a working assumption that part of Indians' general deficiency was a lack of a spiritual dimension. As befitted their primitive state, they were chained to the material and animal levels. The response of one Indian when asked for his favorite prayer—"Give us today our food, give us something to eat. This is an excellent Prayer"—produces a resigned response from Jean de Brebeuf.

> I am not surprised at this Philosophy: Animalis homo, non percipit ea quae sunt Spiritus Dei. He who has never been at any school but that of the flesh, cannot speak the language of the Spirit. (*JR* 8:35)

As Michael Pomedi demonstrates, though, the Huron saw food and feasting as having strong and specific spiritual connections, and their translation of food terms makes this explicit, as he shows in the translation of precisely this passage from the Lord's Prayer.[29] Furthermore, de Brebeuf has just been describing the clear message given to the Indians of the material benefits to be gained from God, in helping them, for instance, with their hunt. This raises the questions of how to communicate the spiritual message and how far the translation and propagation of the Christian doctrine involved mixed messages about the material benefits. Missionaries found it necessary, after all, on top of the traditional exchanges of gifts, to give presents as inducement to attend to the gospel, and there was surely a clear awareness on the Indian side of the importance the French missionaries and traders attached to the purely economic advantages of the fur trade. There is no shortage in missionary accounts of Indian statements of blunt materialism, which perhaps irritated the missionaries as much for their accuracy in describing the Christians' underlying material agenda as for their intellectual naivety.

A fundamental issue was how the terms of Christianity were to be translated into Indian terms, and vice versa. This involved not just the Word but the belief system in which it operated. As long as the mission-

aries refused to recognize equivalent spiritual content in the Indian beliefs, they could not invoke any for comparison. Later in the same year
as the exchange described above there is a revealing account of the Jesuit response to the Indians' expressions of wonder at European me-
chanical products, particularly a chiming clock.

> But they have said all when they have said they are *ondaki*, that is *Demons;*
> And indeed we make profitable use of the word when we talk to them . . .
> "You think you are right when you see something extraordinary, in saying
> *ondaki*, to declare that those who make so many marvels must be Demons.
> And what is there so wonderful as the beauty of the Sky and the Sun?"
> (*JR* 8:109)

We might find a great deal of irony in this picture of a Jesuit reproving
the Indians for not seeing the spirit or "some beneficent *oki* and some
supereminent intelligence" in nature, given the prevailing modern view
that Christians exploited nature while Indians had a holistic and eco-
logically aware approach to it. We may need to adjust this picture,
therefore, by pointing out that Le Jeune is working his way to God,
rather than remaining at a celebration of nature, and he is able to develop his point only because he has already completely discounted the
validity of native beliefs. Rather than try to examine the full meanings
of the various Indian terms, missionaries usually made them fit the Pro-
crustean bed of their own religious terminology. Thus *demon* is used
(and in the original French), and *esprit* serves for soul and all similar
Indian concepts. On the other hand, when translating Christian ideas
into Indian languages the Jesuits were presented with real problems in
trying to avoid having the Christian concept swallowed up in a pre-
existent native category. Le Jeune's dismissive reference to 'ondaki'
does not mean that such terms can be entirely avoided when it comes
to translating the Christian message, as John Steckley has shown.[30]

The limitations of the way in which native terms are used and then
restricted by their translation into European cultural and linguistic
terms is well demonstrated in Williams's comments. In his description
of a concept similar to that described by Le Jeune, to be found among
the Indians of New England, he moves through a number of English
terms:

> There is a generall Custome amongst them, at the apprehension of any
> Excellency in Men, Women, Birds, Beasts, Fish &c. to cry out *Manittoo*,

that is, it is a God, as thus if they see one man excell others in Wisdome, Valour, strength, Activity &c. they cry out *Manittoo* A God: and therefore when they talk amongst themselves of the *English* ships, and great build- ings, of the plowing of their Fields, and especially of Bookes and Letters, they will end thus: *Manittowock* They are Gods: *Cummanittoo* you are a God &c. (191)

What the Indians are admiring (rather than worshipping) is the "Excel- lency" of technology and strangeness,[31] but Williams's translation of the term *Manittoo* as "God" means that he is able to make an immediate transition in order to transpose this term into general religious feeling and then Christianity.

A strong Conviction naturall in the soule of man, that God is; filling all things, and places, and that all Excellencies dwell in God, and proceed from him, and that they only are blessed who have that Jehovah their por- tion. (191)

Elsewhere Williams confirms the general use of the term—"*Manittooes*, that is, Gods, Spirits or Divine powers, as they say of every thing which they cannot comprehend" (175)—but once he has used a term from his own religion ("God"), he cannot allow such a term to float about. The sacred must be defined and located, and this reflects the general strat- egy of the chapter devoted to religion in *A Key*. In general, the Puritan suspicion and cultural isolationism meant that even toward the Praying Indians there was little sense of the possibility of a reciprocal relation.

WHAT WE have seen so far is that in spite of clear evidence of an Indian spirituality, the missionaries' preconceptions about the mate- rialist limitations of primitive mentality led them to dismiss it as a su- perstitious fetishism of objects conceived of as magical. If we take the idea of magic and fetishism in a cross-cultural situation a bit more seri- ously, however, and follow the leads of Marx and Michael Taussig dis- cussed in chapter 1, we can see that native categories of the magical or spiritual may embody a response to exchange rather than a retreat from it into something irrational and childlike. In fact, we can go further and suggest that some of the most influential anthropological formulations of how ideas of the magical or spiritual operate in primitive cultures turn out to involve just such exchanges, and it is worth looking briefly at Marcel Mauss's rather different account of *manitou* in his *General*

Theory of Magic. He quotes a Jesuit description of *manitou* as designating beings with souls and also

> all beings which still have no common name, which are not familiar. A woman who came across a salamander said she was afraid, thinking it to be a manitou. The people laughed at her, and told her the name of the animal. Trade beads are manitou's scales, and *cloth*—wonderful as it is—is said to be the skin of a manitou.[32]

Mauss's discussion also takes in other native terms from North America, such as *wakan* and *orenda*, as well as terms from elsewhere, particularly the Maori *hau* and *mana*, in an attempt to pin down the essence of the magical, but Claude Levi-Strauss's influential critique of Mauss focuses precisely on the point at which, instead of seeing the whole process of exchange as a system (i.e., structurally), Mauss concentrates on the discrete phenomena and, as Levi-Strauss puts it, "tries to reconstruct a whole out of parts; and as that is manifestly not possible, he has to add to the mixture an additional quantity which gives him the illusion of squaring his account." This is the idea of the spirit or magic, which can include the concepts of *mana, wakan, manitou,* and *orenda,* which are, in their respective cultures, "the conscious expression of a semantic function, whose role is to enable symbolic thinking to operate despite the contradictions inherent in it." Thus Levi-Strauss formulates his celebrated floating signifier, "a zero symbolic value, that is, a sign marking the necessity of a supplementary symbolic content over and above that which the signified already contains." This may seem a long way from Indian-European exchanges, but it is significant, I think, not only that many of the key terms in this influential debate come from North America, but that the specific examples Levi-Strauss gives involve trade goods. Mauss's original quotation includes more (nontrade) items and a wider general definition, but Levi-Strauss seems to isolate the trade items and, as if to underscore the point, adds examples from his own fieldwork of Indian reactions to imported red flannel and oxen. The point is that here we have something that does not fit into a closed system of representation and exchange, or discursive economy, and so has a special status both within and without the system.

> It has to be admitted that, like hau, mana is no more than the subjective reflection of the need to supply an unperceived totality. Exchange is not a

complex edifice built on the obligations of giving, receiving and returning, with the help of some emotional-mystical cement. It is a synthesis immediately given to, and given by, symbolic thought, which, in exchange as in any other form of communication, surmounts the contradiction inherent in it; that is the contradiction of perceiving things as elements of dialogue, in respect of self and others simultaneously.[33]

Levi-Strauss thus refuses the idea of an original lost unity or closed economy in arguing for the crucial necessity of the floating signifier. He anticipates Derrida's deconstruction of the idea of a restricted economy, but my point is that trade goods are very appropriate examples, in showing that all systems have a way of allowing for the new, and Levi-Strauss shows this to be not primitive but fundamental to symbolic thinking.

With Levi-Strauss's treatment of *manitou* in mind, we can see the Indian recognition of the English as possessing magical powers, not so much as deference to their power or technology as a reaffirmation of their own scheme of values, within which they were making sense of new alien phenomena.

Just as the floating signifier enables symbolic thought and allows the system to work, so ascribing *manitou* to something outside brings it in and allows the system to continue to function. As Salisbury puts it,

> Access to manitou was obtained above all through reciprocal exchanges with those who possessed it. In this way what [Roger] Williams called the "excellence" of manitou was distributed as widely as possible. To the Indians, material goods such as brass arrowheads, copper kettles, iron axes, glass beads and textiles were not only functionally or aesthetically valuable but actually transmitted some of the extraordinary power and brilliance behind their creation.[34]

This presents a picture of a complex Indian agenda, in which they Indians were not attracted just by the childish allure of trinkets or by utility, but were involved in fitting these objects into their own conceptual frameworks, one of which may have been that of foreignness itself, as a way of buttressing political power. As Nicholas Thomas argues, in a discussion of Polynesian first encounters, certain exchange may have "less to do with the particular features of the objects, than with the importation of a certain kind of foreignness that was seen as empowering rather than threatening."[35]

Although the missionaries may have conceived of their aim and activities as fundamentally spiritual, they did introduce a tangible set of ritual objects to which they seemed to ascribe magical properties, and it is interesting to see what happens to the material trappings of Christianity as well as its ideas and terminology, as they enter the discursive and spiritual economies of the Indian cultures. For Catholic and Protestant missionaries, the Bible would have been the most potent symbol not just of the technology of writing, like other books, but of the Word of God. The extent to which non-literate cultures conceived of writing as magic or powerful has been much debated,[36] and there are clear instances in North America of the association of the Bible with other dangerous powers, as in the report of the Huron dream, in which "they had seen black gowns in a dream . . . who were unfolding certain books, whence issued sparks of fire which spread everywhere, and no doubt caused the pestilential disease" (*JR* 20:31–33).

In addition to distributing Bibles and crosses, the Catholics used the rosary, incense, vestments, and images of all sorts, which had a close resemblance to the uses of religious and ceremonial objects in native religious practices, and we have a description of a sick man applying to his body "some Images, Rosaries and Crosses; for they make great account of these, using them against the molestations of the Demons" (*JR* 45:63).[37] Whether this is a "proper" use of Christian symbols is not clear, and the missionaries themselves are sometimes hesitant about ascribing power to objects. Biard's explanation for the cure of the son of the influential leader Membertou is cautious. Was it a miracle, as was suggested?

> For my part I scarcely know what to say; inasmuch as I do not care either to affirm or deny a thing of which I have no proof. This I do know, what we put upon the sufferer a bone taken from the precious relics of the glorified Saint Lawrence, archbishop of Dublin. (*JR* 2:19)

This sort of instance was sufficiently close to native practice to scandalize the Puritans, but the Catholic missionaries were also quite capable of being scandalized themselves by the uncontrolled and unauthorized uses to which Christian objects were put once they entered the circulation of cultural signs taking place among Indians as they responded to these new items. Le Clercq's account of the uses and misuses of elements of Christian ceremonial among the Micmac is revealing. As a result of seeing the respect accorded to missionaries, some of these barbarians have often been seen meddling with, and affecting to perform, the office and functions of missionary, even to hearing confession, like us, from their fellow-countrymen. So therefore, when persons of this kind wish to give authority to that which they say, and to set themselves up as patriarchs, they make our Gaspesians believe they have received some particular gift from heaven.

One man who claimed to have received "an image from heaven" had in fact "only a picture which had been given him when he was trading with our French." Significant here is the way in which the claim to have received a gift from supernatural donor powers chimes with the pre-established native religion rather than Christianity, but the fact that the picture is a trade object is also not without significance, as I elaborate later. A few pages later, Le Clercq gives another instance of what we might now call syncretism, in the case of a woman (he describes her as "a famous one," perhaps suggesting a pre-established shamanic status) who "had as the basis for all her ridiculous and superstitious devotions some beads of jet, which were the remains of an unthreaded rosary." She gives these to people, claiming that they are from heaven. Another woman has five mysterious rosary beads and wants Le Clercq to believe that they are "a present which Heaven had made to this pretended *religieuse*," but Le Clercq disabuses her of this idea by an act of conjuring. He palms one of them, making it disappear and reappear, thus demystifying the beads but also, ironically, playing the role of the "juggler" or shaman he is trying to replace.[38]

His approach to the woman is one of ridicule, and he tells us that as well as the beads she has "a King of Hearts, the foot of a glass, and a kind of medal" that she prostrates herself before "as before her divinities." She is from "the Crossbearer nation" and has decorated her cross with "beadwork, wampum, painting and porcupine quills." We have a glimpse here of a thoroughgoing syncretism that is recognized even by Le Clercq, despite the ironic use of the word "pleasing."

> The pleasing mixture thereof represented several and separate figures of everything which was in her devotions. She placed it [the cross] usually between her and the French, obliging them to make their prayers before her cross, whilst from her side she made her own prayers, according to her custom, before her King of Hearts and her other Divinities.[39]

Formerly the credulous object of ridicule, the woman is now revealed as a skilled intermediary, concretely embodying the ambivalent and Janus-faced aspects of spiritual power in a situation of crisis and change. Her cross that faces two ways, encrusted with different symbols of value, offers us a powerful image of cultural adaptation and connects her with the extensive recent debates over the role of Native American women as mediators and cultural brokers, as opposed to their cultural stereotyping as passive drudges.[40] For Le Clercq, though, such behavior reveals only "the error and the simplicity of this blind people, who have lived in the shades of Christianity without law, without faith, and without religion."[41]

Here again we find the litany of absences and the equation of anything less than pure Christianity with no religion at all. To live in "the shades of Christianity" is an interesting idea, though. At one level it might suggest the margins, where the light is not (yet) bright, a positive idea of transition, but here the idea of darkness seems to outweigh any gradualist optimism and points to another way of reading the phrase. We might want to argue that the darkness, the shade, is "of" Christianity also in that it is the creation of it, the projection of the Christian idea of evil and the devil onto a neutral ground, just as light creates shadow. What LeClercq saw as a misuse of Christian symbols we can more usefully see as their assimilation into a complex mixture of trade goods and objects traditionally valued for their exotic origins or associations.

It is not surprising that rosary beads are in this case being redistributed and recycled, given the well-established role of wampum and other beads in overlapping value systems, ranging from the monetary to the religious. The Jesuits gave glass beads as reward for Christian lessons learned because they knew the beads were valued, but the form of that value was multifaceted, as with wampum.

A good example of a mixing of functions is to be found in Father Pierre Millet's account of his attempts to get his Christian message across to his listeners by using familiar objects for demonstration. For one important meeting he sets up his materials carefully:

> In order to strike their imaginations by some kind of formal display, I hung up a fine large porcelain collar in the middle of the Cabin; placing on one side of it a map of the World, and on the other the image of Saint Louis, King of France. In another place, I put the portrait of the King and Monsieur the Dauphin. Beneath the porcelain collar I had put the Bible, on a desk covered with a handsome red cloth, below which was to be seen the

> Image of Our Lord,—who had at his feet all the symbols of the superstition
> and dissoluteness of these creatures, as if to indicate that he had overcome
> them. (*JR* 53:269)

What is intriguing is not only the mixture of native and Christian images of value (wampum and the king) but Millet's confidence that he
would be able to explain their relative meanings and values. It would be
interesting to know what "symbols of the superstition" he had gathered
together under the image of Christ, because it is easy to envisage a
scene in which, whatever construction he was putting on the various
objects, the Indian listeners would actually see a conjunction of recognizable religious objects being used by a priest in combination with his
own, so that he could be unwittingly acting out the same syncretism as
LeClercq's "religieuse."

Further evidence of Millet's approach can be found in an earlier
description of his teaching, where he lays out "various strings of porcelain beads to mark the number and variety of the things I taught them."
Sometimes he stretches out a cord and hangs from it

> a handsome porcelain collar, before my Chapel Altar to teach them that
> there was only one God; (2) a map of the whole world to show that he had
> made all things; (3) a little mirror, to signify that he knew all things; (4)
> some strings of glass beads to express the liberality with which he rewards
> all good actions; also some intruments of human Justice, to express to them
> that which God exercises in the flames of Hell. (*JR* 53:263)

Again, we have to wonder what his listeners would make of this, with
its strained analogies. Why would a mirror demonstrate omniscience,
for instance? It almost seems as if Millet is falling back on images of
the exotic with which to dazzle and impress the natives, and indeed his
objects do correspond with the early staples of trade used by Columbus
and Cartier: glass beads and mirrors.

In spite of the attempt to prescribe meaning and value, objects were
taken up into different systems. Silver medals and coins, for instance,
underwent fascinating transformations to express indigenous iconography and functions as well as various new forms altogether, as they became used in the fur trade. A surviving cross that has been engraved
with a picture of an Indian drinking from a bottle is a particularly eloquent indication of the adaptation of use and function of a religious

symbol, but one very different from LeClercq's "religieuse." Not only
does the object itself demonstrate a change of use, but it also actually
depicts the ambiguous nature of European gifts and innovations. Created apparently by a European trader for an Indian market, it raises
fascinating questions about the levels of ironic awareness of its meaning
by each side of the exchange. Was this a cynical joke by the European,
which was also shared, with an extra level of irony, by the Indian recipient?[42]

Such transformations of meaning and value not only show the inad-
equacy of trying to separate the economic and spiritual realms but also
throw into question that long-standing fundamental distinction between use value and exchange value that runs from Aristotle through
Marx. It is not just that the distinction does not hold as a way of distinguishing the different priorities between primitive and capitalist European economic systems. Once we expand the idea of use, as we need
to, to include the aesthetic and spiritual as well as the material and practical, it becomes clear that objects are often valued and used precisely
because they are exchanged across systems. Exchange is therefore not an
unfortunate foreign threat to the "proper" and domestic meanings and
values, and there is plenty of evidence to suggest that trade goods were
not just, or even primarily, used for their functional purposes to replace
existing technology. As Bruce White points out, the utility of a knife
was determined "by not only its sharpness but also the color of its
handle and the shape of its blade"; he sees every exchanged object having not just a single use but "a cultural trajectory, passing successively
and sometimes simultaneously through a variety of cultural contexts."[43]

We can see this clearly in Louis Hennepin's *A New Discovery of a
vast country in America, extending above Four Thousand Miles, between New
France and New Mexico*, in which he describes his chasuble being used
(against his will) as "an Ornament to cover the Bones of their Dead at
the celebrating [of] their most solemn rites" and then later being given
as a present to their allies. Elsewhere he comments, "If any Images were
given 'em, as a Crucifix, or a pair of Beads, they made use of 'em as
Jewels to adorn themselves with, esteeming them, as if they were so
many wrought Cups, or fine Porcelaine Vessels."[44] Where Hennepin
sees a change of use, though, others managed to see the wearing of
rosaries as an expression of piety.

so fondly do they preserve these that they wear them around their necks, even at preaching in New Holland, where the heretics have never been able to tear them away from even a single bead of their rosaries. (*JR* 57:95–97)

The importance of this transformation of the categories of sacred and secular as objects cross cultural systems is likely to be lost on someone like Hennepin, who is keen here to categorize the other culture as deficient or greedy. Elsewhere he describes a chief negotiating what seems to be a complex distribution of goods and gives instances of "What Tricks and Artifices were used by *Aquipaguetin* to cheat us handsomely of our goods." The chief makes the French, at periodic ceremonies,

> cover the Bones of their Deceas'd [which they have wrapped in a skin] with some of our *European* Merchandise, in order to dry up the Tears which he had shed for him . . . To appease the crafty, old Savage we strow'd on the Bones of the Deceas'd several pieces of *Marinico*—Tobacco, Hatchets, Knives, Beads and some bracelets of Black and White Porcelain . . . He gave us to understand, That what he had thus demanded of us was not for himself but the Dead, and to give the Warriours that he brought with him; and indeed he distributed amongst them whatever he took from us.[45]

A common aspect of the circulation of valuable trade objects was their physical dispersal, as they were literally broken up or cut into pieces. This may mean the change of use (metal or cloth being fashioned into different objects), but it can also suggest an aesthetic or spiritual property and even point to an aesthetics of the fragment that has been explored by Modernist artists and writers in this century. Indeed, it is perhaps only with the experience of the Modernist engagement with a fragmented and refashioned primitive as a realm of the aesthetic, as well as recent debates over the appropriation of religious and cultural objects in Western museums and galleries, that we are able to see what the missionaries could not: the full extent of the cultural as well as religious transformations that were taking place—in other words, just how much conversion was going on.[46]

I have tried to show here the ways in which what the missionaries introduced—whether words, ideas, or objects—immediately circulated within a set of economies, changing their nature in the process, or, like the Micmac woman's cross, facing both ways. Although part of the missionaries' rhetoric was that of dissemination, of spreading the Word and the seed, they were also concerned to authorize and define the proper interpretation of their cultural property. In this respect, though the Puritans criticized the Jesuits for syncretism and for being too close, in their use of ritual, to the superstitions of the Indians, the two denominations were as one in regarding any merging of Christian and pagan as absolutely unthinkable. The borders and boundaries needed to be policed, and while the message could be sent out, there could never be two-way traffic. The gift of God to the Indians was a one-way, not a reciprocal, process. Such isolationism of course went against Indian practice at all levels, and it is significant that, as Trigger has pointed out, much of the suspicion of Jesuits was at this level. "It is clear that almost all accusations of witchcraft resulted from violations of Huron norms concerning cooperation and reciprocity."[47] This was not just because of their need for privacy or their refusal to share what they had, but, at a fundamental level, their refusal to take. The Jesuits were aware of the need to be seen to be generous and were careful to provide presents to fit in with native customs. They were also convinced that they were giving the inestimable gift of God's Word, but they were incapable of understanding the need to take and to accord some respect for what the Indians believed. A particularly clear instance with which to conclude is their reaction to the ceremony known as the Feast of the Dead, one of the most important ceremonies among the Huron, which also spread to some Algonquian groups. Harold Hickerson's account of the Algonquian forms sees the rise and fall of the feast as reflecting a growing influx of goods and a communal response to this that stressed redistribution and exchange at a practical and a spiritual level.[48] Nicolas Denys, for instance, describes Indians throwing into the grave "bows arrows, snow-shoes, spears, robes of Moose, Otter, and Beaver," but also "when they were not yet disabused of their errors, I have seen them give to the dead man, guns, axes, iron arrow-heads, and kettles."[49]

European kettles were generally very popular, and Hennepin's explanation for their being put into the grave is that "they held all these to be much more convenient for their use than would have been their kettles of wood." Other sources, though, suggest a more complex valuation of the kettle, and even Hennepin mentions that the Indians he sees would not touch the kettle "without covering their hands first in something of castor-skin" or accept it as a gift because it had a spirit within it. Laurier Turgeon, demonstrating how the European-made kettle became invested with a complex of values that went well beyond its utility, shows that though the kettle did fit in with pre-existing belief systems (such as the color-symbolism explored by George Hamell), it also actively gained power by its provenance as coming from outside. Turgeon argues that the kettles seemed to be reserved for ceremonial and ritual use, as in feasts, including cannibal activities, and were associated with group cohesion and identity. Of particular interest is the kettles' relation to the Feast of the Dead, the central activities of which are described in metaphors of cooking and the kettle. Kettles were systematically destroyed or, rather, made nonfunctional in terms of their original purpose, so that they could function in a different way. As Turgeon puts it, "The copper kettle served as a catalyst for identity formation *because* it was an appropriated object. The act of appropriation, more than the object itself, produced the creative tension involved in identity formation."[50]

In the Feast of the Dead, those who had died since the last ceremony were disinterred and their bones all buried together in one place, representing and reinforcing the unity and friendship of their descendants, who marked this with feasts and the exchange of gifts.[51] As well as the many items buried with the dead, which as elsewhere included a notable number of trade goods and other items of value like wampum,[52] the ceremony had a crucial role in the redistribution of goods, to which the mingling of bones was a symbolic corollary. As Trigger argues, the fact that after the increase in their trade and material wealth the Huron chose to elaborate the Feast of the Dead, "a ritual that depended so heavily on redistribution and making offerings to the dead," is evidence of the ways in which they were incorporating new items and new wealth into the traditional patterns. The Jesuits opposed the sheer waste of burying goods with the dead, as well as the continual redistribution, as dissipating the prosperity of those they wished to wean away from tribal values, and as Indian hegemony waned the influence of the French was used to restrict what they saw as waste and excess. In another way, of course, as Hugh Amory points out, grave goods are almost the quintessence of private property, removed forever from circulation, and it is interesting to see the account of the Jesuit Bigot recording his success in combatting this and forcing them to recirculate goods: "I make them give in public the articles Left by the Savages when they die" (*JR* 62:39). Of course, this acts to prevent the other circulation, the other economy they enter, as secular, trade, and traditional objects are min-

gled in the grave, and in fact the Jesuits explicitly drew the line when it
came to mixing the bones of Christians with pagans in reburials. Even
in death, it seems, the Christian must not be assimilated into those processes of inclusion and circulation so fundamental to the Indians and
so threatening to the purity of the Christian gospel.

Among the many European goods found in Indian graves, a particularly interesting item was found in a Mashantucket Pequot grave: a tiny
medicine bundle preserved by its chemical reaction with the metal
spoon with which it was buried was found to contain a piece of wool
cloth and a page from an English-language Bible. As Amory argues,
this is a good example of one of Nicholas Thomas's "entangled objects"
in the way that it has changed its status, but he also points out the similarities with the ways in which small Bibles were used by Europeans as
talismanic objects. "On some level, it matters little whether we describe
small-format Bibles as European medicine bundles, or this medicine-
bundle as an Indian Bible."[53]

THE GIFT of religion, then, cannot be separated from other exchanges, and neither can the message be authorized and kept from
changing. In a much later text, we find an account that, in its self-
conscious framing of a particular episode, as well as its echoing of earlier themes, serves as a conclusion to this section. The incident is recorded in Stephen H. Long's account of an expedition to the source of
St. Peter's River in 1833, and the terms of his description are themselves worth dwelling on. Long begins with a description of the scene
at Fort Geary, overlooking the confluence of the Assiniboin and Red
Rivers. As a set-piece scene, it is carefully structured to stress the peaceful mixing and coexisting of European and Indian. There are domestic
cows, a European import, but also a young buffalo bull, with groups of
Indian lodges and Indian tents. Long and his companions watch from
their vantage point the Indian boys in canoes as well as the Canadian
carters passing, urging their horses on in French. Together with the
children "of every possible shade of colour between the red and the
white" this all offers "food for pleasant contemplation." Then, though,
we are introduced to "an object which once observed rivetted our attention." It is "the sight of a crazed woman standing alone in a canoe."
She has "a soft expression of melancholy beauty, such as is often seen
in the women of mixed European and Indian blood," and her eyes have

"a wild and particularly interesting expression," which seems to correspond to her song, "a melancholy air, that struck our ear melodiously and sweetly as we heard it from a distance." Long questions whether "it was but the effect of an association of ideas, which led a melancholy interest to her voice," but in fact discovers that she was

> a half-breed whose insanity was suppose to have sprung from a religious melancholy. Being one of those whom the missionaries had converted, she had become very pious, but her intellect was too frail for the doctrines which had been taught to her; in endeavouring to become familiar with them, she had been gradually affected with a malady, which at that time seemed incurable.[54]

One of the stock occasions for pathos, the solitary Indian maiden representing a dying race—an idea already used by Long in recounting stories associated with places on his travels—is here combined with the idea of religious melancholy.[55] We have a European import that did not blend, a graft that did not "take," in contrast to the scene of harmonious mixing we have just been given. The wind then takes the woman out of reach, but the next day she reappears and

> with much modesty presented to us a small parcel of papers neatly folded up and secured by a thread; she desired that it might be give to her mother in Montreal. There was no superscription. We opened it, it contained but a printed sheet of a religious tract. Having performed her errand, she made a slight inclination and passed away.[56]

Long at this point moves briskly on, but let's dwell for a moment on this scene, in which, in an ironic and pathetic reversal, the gift of Christianity is returned without a proper destination or address, to become one of those dead letters that Herman Melville describes at the end of "Bartleby the Scrivener": "On errands of life, these letters speed to death." The seed, to take up a metaphor used by missionaries and by Melville, too, in his story, is scattered but unpropagated. Here, in contrast to the other elements in Long's description of the scene, we have a hybridity that is sterile, a seed that has withered, a message that has not been disseminated. This haunting episode is of course a late and an isolated one, and Long's account perhaps illustrates as much as the legacy of missionary failure the later colonists' readiness to turn any case of Indian pathos or failure into an occasion for the exercise of the poetic and picturesque. By the nineteenth century, an aesthetic response is likely to move into the place where earlier a religious or moralistic reaction would have been. In the manner of the vanishing American, having done her errand, the woman "passed away," but we are not told what happened to the returned Christian tract.

Having invoked Melville's dead letters, I want to close with an episode that at first glance seems distant from Indian-missionary contact. In Melville's *Billy Budd, Sailor* the young Billy, about to be unjustly or sacrificially hanged, is counseled by the chaplain. Billy, "the young barbarian," seems not to absorb the chaplain's message about the need for him to die and about "the thought of salvation and a Savior." He has the common sailor's general skepticism, an attitude Melville describes as

> not wholly unlike the way in which the primer of Christianity, full of transcendent miracles, was received long ago by any superior *savage*, so called . . . Out of natural courtesy he received, but did not appropriate. It was like a gift placed in the palm of an outreached hand upon which the fingers do not close.[57]

Here we have in one haunting image the theme of this chapter—a gift, variously received but not appropriated—or received and returned—or received and transformed. Melville's image also reminds us of the situation of power in which this gift is offered. Unlike other early exchanges involving barter, negotiation, and dialogue, this gift is imposed. It is a free gift but one that the Indians are not free to refuse, and if we pursue the analogy with Billy further we find his fate—to be sacrificed in the name of a larger good, namely, an order and authority into which he was conscripted without his agreement—chiming well with the fate of the Christian Indians. Furthermore, not only is he sacrificed to sustain military order, but the political and military brutality that murders him is inextricably entangled by Melville with the language of Christian sacrifice and submission. This produces some of Melville's most complex and disturbing ironies, in a text that, as the culmination of a lifelong concern with the meaning of the primitive and a questioning of the values of his own society and of Christianity, offers an unexpected but devastating insight to the psychic economies of Christianity and power I have been exploring here.

Notes

Introduction

1. Neil Whitehead, "The Historical Anthropology of Text," 62. There are already fine readings of specific moments of initial encounter, in particular from Eric Cheyfitz, Stephen Greenblatt, and Michael Taussig, who also develop analyses of the rhetoric and ideology underlying the accounts and to whom I return later in the book. James Axtell's many works offer a wide-ranging account of early encounters. For early trade encounters specifically, see his *After Columbus: Essays in the Ethnohistory of Colonial North America*, 144–81.

2. Christopher Columbus, *The Diario of Christopher Columbus's First Voyage to America, 1492–3*, 65–69.

3. Fernando Colon, *The Life of the Admiral Christopher Columbus by his son Ferdinand*, 60.

4. Antonio Gómez-Moriana, "Narration and Argumentation in the Chronicles of the New World," 109–10.

5. Peter Martyr, *De Orbe Novo, The Eight Decades of Peter Martyr D'Anghira*, 1:61.

6. Gómez-Moriana, "Narration and Argumentation," 111, 112.

7. Gerald Sider, "When Parrots Learn to Talk, and Why They Can't," 5.

8. Stephen Greenblatt, *Marvelous Possessions*, 70.

9. See Patricia Seed, *Ceremonies of Possession*, and "Taking Possession and Reading Texts." For an older but detailed account, see Arthur S. Keller, Oliver J. Lissitzyn, and Frederick J. Mann, *Creation of Rights of Sovereignty*. See also Beatriz Bodmer, *The Armature of Conquest*, 125–6, and L. C. Green and Olive P. Dickason, *The Law of Nations and the New World*.

10. H. P. Biggar, ed., *The Voyages of Jacques Cartier*, 64.

11. Eric Cheyfitz, *Poetics of Imperialism*, 205.

12. Greenblatt, *Marvelous Possessions*, 6.

13. Steven Connor, *Theory and Cultural Value*, 57.

14. Cheyfitz, *Poetics of Imperialism*, 35, 36.

15. "Metaphor, therefore, is determined by philosophy as a provisional loss of meaning, an economy of the proper without irreparable damage, a certainly inevitable detour, but also a history with its sights set on, and within the horizon of, the circular reappropriation of literal, proper meaning." Jacques Derrida, "White Mythology," 270.

16. My overall approach in this book is to try to integrate such theoretical debates over economy and representation into my account without trying to engage with the debates in any detail, given their complexity. For a detailed and influential critique of the traditional view of metaphor, see Derrida, "White Mythology." For important essays on which I have relied in trying to develop a view of economy appropriate to my subject matter, see Jacques Derrida, "From Restricted to General Economy" and "Economimesis." See also Jean-Francois Lyotard, *Libidinal Economy*, and Jean Baudrillard, *Symbolic Exchange and Death*. For an ambitious attempt to create a unified theory, see Jean-Joseph Goux, *Symbolic Economies*. I refer to many of these works in more detail elsewhere in the book, but even when they are not explicitly cited, my approach reflects an attempt to integrate some of their insights.

17. Francis Jennings, *The Invasion of America*. For a discussion of the contentious nature of such terms, see Ariana Hernández-Reguant, "The Columbus Quincentenary and the Politics of the 'Encounter.'" The danger, as she points out, was that "the word *encounter* hid the negative consequences of the enterprise and seemed to suggest the peaceful and egalitarian fusion of two groups and cultures" (23). A good example of the ways in which the whole process can be made to sound entirely polite and consensual is U.S. President Harry S. Truman's breathtaking characterization in 1946 of the appropriation and theft over several centuries of vast areas of Indian land as "the largest real estate transaction in history" (quoted in Harvey D. Rosenthal, "Indian Claims and the American Conscience," (45)).

18. Richard White, *The Middle Ground*, x, ix.

19. Roger Williams, *A Key into the Language of America*, 83.

Chapter 1

1. Alexander Young, *Chronicles of the Pilgrim Fathers*, 134.

2. William Bradford, *Of Plymouth Plantation*, 66.

3. Thomas Morton, *New English Canaan*, 106.

4. See Francis Jennings, *The Invasion of America*, 135–45, for an account of Puritan uses and misuses of this doctrine.

5. Cotton Mather, *Magnalia Christi Americana*, 1:72.

6. Jack Weatherford, *Indian Givers*; see also his *Native Roots*.

7. Thomas Hutchinson, *The History of the Colony of Massachusets-Bay*, 468–90.

8. Stephen Greenblatt, *Marvelous Possessions*, 110.

9. The anthropological literature on the gift is huge, but the debates have tended to focus on societies where the idea of the gift most differs from that in

Western society. Thus the favored areas, in the wake of Bronislav Malinowski and Marcel Mauss, have been Polynesia and the Pacific Northwest of America. While I draw on these debates here, I should make clear at the beginning that I have deliberately avoided making connections with what might seem the obvious area for discussions of exchange and giving, namely, the potlatch of the Northwest. This is partly because my focus is on the points of interchange and exchange in a different geographical area and in a period much earlier than the documented potlatch period, but also because I want to avoid carrying over a ready-made idea of exchange that would too crudely distinguish these Indian societies from the European. Taking a different tack, Christopher Bracken's work in *The Potlatch Papers* distinguishes itself from most historical and ethnographic studies of potlatch by concentrating on the Canadian representation of it, and his concern for textual production and general theoretical orientation bring his work close to my own concerns at many points.

10. Marshall Sahlins, *Stone Age Economics*, 85.

11. See Hayden White, "The Fetish of the Primitive."

12. See James Carrier, "Gifts, Commodities, and Social Relations" and, more fully, his *Gifts and Commodities*.

13. For a penetrating account of the development of economic thinking that, although not dealing with the influence of the New World, uses many of the same theorists as my own account toward a different end, see Judith Still, *Feminine Economies*.

14. Interestingly, it is in the discussion of the most scandalously bestial and uncivilized aspect of the New World, cannibalism, where we also find the idea of a self-sustaining economy contrasted with Europe. Rather than an asocial feeding frenzy, cannibalism in its earliest representations contains within itself an image of a balanced and reciprocal society, sustaining and feeding upon itself, which can throw into relief other more parasitic forms of social organization in Europe. Jean de Lery makes the comparison with the operation of credit in Europe: "In the first place, if you consider in all candor what our big usurers do, sucking blood and marrow, and eating everyone alive—you will say that they are even more cruel than the savages I speak of" (*History of a Voyage to the Land of Brazil*, 132). Montaigne, drawing on de Lery as well as André Thevet, may be echoing this in his remark, "I think there is more barbarity in eating a live than a dead man." *Essays of Montaigne*, 1:209. Certainly, his description of the reciprocal relations between eater and eaten among the cannibals, with the prime motive being revenge (a reciprocal relation) rather than expansionism or greed for more land or property, continues de Lery's theme of cannibalism as social ritual rather than the ultimate threat to social order. For Montaigne, as David Quint puts it, "Their cannibalism and the warfare that literally feeds it are superfluous products of a culture that, however simplified, possesses its own logic." David Quint, "A Reconsideration of Montaigne's *Des Cannibales*," 174. It is this complex role of excess and sacrifice (what Georges Bataille calls the "accursed share") operating alongside and within Western thinking about economy that makes the encounter with the New World and its representation so complicated.

15. Morton, *New English Canaan*, 57, 58.

16. Robert Beverley, *The History and Present State of Virginia*, 225, 233.

17. In the original French, "qu'ilz s'en retournèrent touz nulz, sans alcune chose avoir sur eulx". H. P. Biggar ed., *The Voyages of Jacques Cartier*, 53.

18. Gordon Sayre, *Les Sauvages Americains*, 152.

19. Edward Winslow, *Good News from New England*, in Young, ed., *Chronicles of the Pilgrim Fathers*, 228.

20. Paul J. Lindholdt, ed., *John Josselyn, Colonial Traveller*, 99.

21. Reuben G. Thwaites, *The Jesuit Relations and Allied Documents*, 46:103. Subsequent references to this collection are incorporated into the text using the abbreviation *JR* and the page number.

22. Indians themselves were also painfully aware of this parasitic relation, in which by creating a need, the giver becomes the eventual taker, as is reflected in a later report by James Logan, a Pennsylvania official, in 1736:

> When sober . . . they justly complain'd that they were reduced by it to the extreamest poverty, and that it "Sucked away all their blood flesh and spirits['] (this was their language) and that they were now left but Skin and bone, and could subsist no longer. (Quoted in Daniel Richter, *Ordeal of the Longhouse*, 266)

23. Maria Campbell, *Halfbreed*, 137.

24. Baron Lahontan, *New Voyages to North America*, 1:258.

25. Richard White, *The Middle Ground*, 480.

26. John Long, *Voyages and Travels of an Indian Interpreter and Trader*, 85–86.

27. Daniel Gookin, *Historical Collections of the Indians of New England*, 1:188.

28. In his passionate denunciation of the evils of alcohol, Chretien Le Clercq sees it undermining the idea of the rational basis of trade. The trade is "fraudulent, and liable to restitution in proportion to what the thing is worth, according to the customs of trade, these barbarians not having in their drunkenness the liberty nor the judgement which is necessary for concluding a deed of sale or purchase, which requires a free and mutual consent from both parties." *New Relations of Gaspesia*, 255.

We can see a similar position being worked out by John Eliot, who, perhaps because he realizes the impossibility of keeping alcohol out of reach, develops the idea of the free rational consumer, using but not being used. He refers to "that adventitious sin which we have brought unto them, Drunkenness, which was never known to them before they knew us *English*." But he sees his duty as to teach them the wisdom "to be able to bridle their own appetites, when they have means and opportunity of high-spirited enticements. The Wisdom and power of Grace is not so much in the beggarly want of these thengs, as in the bridling of our selves in the use of them. It is true Dominion, to be able to use them, and not to abuse ourselves by them." He is presenting rational choice as better than the protection from making that choice at all, which would be a degrading condition of "beggarly want." *A Brief Narrative of the Progress of the Gospel*, 28.

29. Richard White, *The Roots of Dependency*, 82, 58.

30. John Lawson, *A New Voyage to Carolina*, 240, 244, 246.

31. Sir William Johnson quoted in Wilbur R. Jacobs, *Wilderness Politics and Indian Gifts*, 28.

32. White, *The Middle Ground*, 129.

33. Mary Black-Rogers, "Starving and Survival in the Subarctic Fur Trade."

34. Black-Rogers, "Starving and Survival," 641.

35. Further evidence of this use of pity and the demonstration of abject dependence as a cultural performance is to be found in accounts of Dakota Indians weeping and presenting themselves as helpless children cited by Bruce M. White, "Encounters with Spirits," 385.

36. Michael Taussig, *Mimesis and Alterity*, 90, 95.

37. While Beverley's oppositions were in general currency through the eighteenth century, it was only with Lewis Henry Morgan that the idea of a society organized in terms of kinship as opposed to individuals and classes began to be possible. Morgan's work, based partly on the Iroquois, and the fieldwork of Ely Parker was then extensively used by Marx and Engels in developing a critique of capitalism by contrasting a society of acquisitive individuals with a communal society, where family and kin are deciding factors. By the twentieth century, the growing emphasis in sociology and anthropology on the power of society itself as opposed to the individual and the influence of the work of Malinowski and others working with societies that placed great value on gift exchange meant the elevation of ideas of reciprocity and exchange. This was at not only the empirical but the methodological level, as demonstrated in functionalist and later structuralist approaches. The key figure here is Marcel Mauss, but the significance of his work continues to be disputed. The most detailed debates over gift exchange have inevitably been based on evidence from societies where the gift has been most consistently recognized as a key element of social organization. The specifics of such a specialist debate would take me well beyond my needs or competence, but the way Mauss has been used in wider debates requires us at least to see what is at stake here.

38. Carrier, "Gifts, Commodities, and Social Relations," 120.

39. Sahlins, *Stone Age Economics*, xii.

40. For a useful discussion of some of Sahlins's ideas, see Nurit Bird-David, "Beyond 'The Original Affluent Society.'"

41. Sahlins, *Stone Age Economics*, 95, 133, 140, 134.

42. Ibid., 170. Taussig has a wonderfully elliptical description of a postcapitalist utopia, along the lines of Sahlins, as "weak chiefs, sharing" (*Mimesis and Alterity*, 99).

43. Jacques Derrida, "From Restricted to General Economy." The best brief account Bataille gives of his position is the essay "The Notion of Expenditure" in his *Visions of Excess;* for a fuller account, see his *The Accursed Share*.

44. Julian Pefanis, *Heterology and the Postmodern*, 22.

45. Jacques Derrida, *Given Time: 1: Counterfeit Money*, 24.

46. Pierre Bourdieu, *Outline of a Theory of Practice*, 171, 177–8.

47. We find a similar use of it in 1727 by Father Du Poisson, who warns, "We know from experience that the more one gives to the Indian, the less probability there is of his being contented, and that gratitude is a virtue of which he has not the least idea." Quoted in Cornelius J. Jaenen, "The Role of Presents in French-Indian Trade," 235.

48. See also Kenneth M. Morrison, "Montaganais Missionization in Early New France," 6–10, for a discussion of the role of the idea of the gift in Montagnais religion.

49. Jonathan Parry, "*The Gift*, the Indian Gift and the 'Indian Gift.'"

50. C. A. Gregory, *Gifts and Commodities*, 8.

51. Gregory, *Gifts and Commodities*, 12, 19.

52. Marilyn Strathern, *The Gender of the Gift*, 143.

53. Sahlins, *Stone Age Economics*, 83.

54. Jean Baudrillard, *For a Critique of the Political Economy of the Sign*, 130, 137. I am following Baudrillard's sweeping critique here for the leverage it gives me on some key terms, rather than as a definitive critique on Marx. A different view of the importance of use value can be found, for instance, in Gayatri Spivak, who argues for the continuing importance of the idea. See "Scattered Speculations on the Question of Value" in her *In Other Words: Essays in Cultural Politics*.

55. Nicholas Thomas, *Entangled Objects*, 11.

56. Quoted in Gregory, *Gifts and Commodities*, 12.

57. Arjun Appadurai, *The Social Life of Things*, 11, 13.

58. Bruce M. White, 'Encounters with Spirits," 395. See also Igor Kopytoff, "The Cultural Biography of Things," and Calvin Martin, "The Four Lives of a Micmac Copper Pot."

59. Karl Marx, *Karl Marx: A Reader*, 64–65.

60. Quoted in Maurice Godelier, *Perspectives in Marxist Anthropology*, 160.

61. Marx, *Karl Marx: A Reader*, 68.

62. William Pietz, "The Problem of the Fetish," 9:6–7. Pietz's detailed, authoritative, and fascinating exploration of the history and contemporary significance of the idea of the fetish is spread across several articles. See Bibliography. See also for a wider range Emily Apter and William Pietz, *Fetishism as Cultural Discourse*. For an account of early encounters that uses Pietz, see Wyatt MacGaffey, "Dialogues of the Deaf."

63. For discussions of this passage, see Arthur Ray and Donald Freeman, *Give Us Good Measure*, and Calvin Martin, *Keepers of the Game*. A phrase from the original French version is used for the title of a collection of essays on the fur trade: Bruce Trigger, Toby Morantz, and Louise Dechene, *Le Castor Fait Tout*.

The literature on the fur trade in general and even on the issue of how to conceptualize the economic behavior of each side is immense. I do not pretend to deal with it except in selective instances, but it will be evident that my treatment of economic and noneconomic exchanges parallels many of the fur trade debates. For a brief summary and discussion of the formalist/substantivist debates, see Bruce G. Trigger, *Natives and Newcomers*, esp. 183–94. (For a fascinating account of the ways in which the beaver's social organization and productivity were represented by Europeans in ways parallel to those used by Indians, and the ideological implications of this, see Sayre, *Les Sauvages Americains*, chap. 5.)

64. Ronald L. Trosper, "That Other Discipline," 205.

65. Karl Marx, *Karl Marx: Selected Writings*, 180.

66. Marx quoted in William Pietz, "Fetishism and Materialism," 134.

67. In the Florentine Codex, for instance, we find a native description of the Spanish lust for gold, which makes the same point.

> And when they have given them these [precious objects], they appeared to smile; they were greatly contented, gladdened. As if they were monkeys they seized upon the gold. It was as if there their hearts were satisfied, brightened, calmed. For in truth they thirsted mightily for gold; they stuffed themselves with it; they starved for it; they lusted for it like pigs. (Quoted in Jose Rabasa, *Inventing America*, 111)

68. Michael Taussig, *The Devil and Commodity Fetishism in South America*, 127–8, 11, 4–5, 21.

Chapter 2

1. Jean-Pierre Sanchez, "Myths and Legends in the Old World," 1:221.

2. Peter Martyr quoted in Stelio Crio, "Classical Antiquity, America," 404.

3. Peter Martyr *De Orbe Novo*, 1:413. We find the same concern in Montaigne, in his essay on the sumptuary laws of his time, which were designed to limit conspicuous consumption by controlling the wearing of expensive clothing and materials. He dismisses the laws as only making more desirable what they are attempting to control. "The right method would be to create in humanity a contempt for gold and silk, as vain and useless things" (*Essays of Montaigne*, 1:263).

4. Martyr, *De Orbe Novo*, 2:113, 355.

5. Montaigne, *Essays of Montaigne*, 2:363.

6. Ibid., 377.

7. Pierre Clastres, *Archeology of Violence*, 116. Clastres' earlier and more considered work, *Society Against the State*, has been used widely to keep open the possibility of thinking about society in nonstate terms.

8. Michael Taussig, *The Magic of the State*, 124, 127.

9. Georges Bataille, *The Accursed Share*, 3:198.

10. Francis Jennings quoted in Cornelius J. Jaenen, "French Sovereignty and Native Nationhood," 22–23. For a fuller account of this, see Olive P. Dickason, "Concepts of Sovereignty." Sakej Youngblood Henderson, in an account of treaty making as understood from the native point of view, notes that Europeans' idea of sovereignty does not necessarily translate easily: "Few, if any, of the First Nations have a tradition of theological absolutism or hierocratic traditions. Indeed, the typical interpretation of sovereignty in the Cree language is 'pretending to be God' (*mandohkasowin*)" ("Empowering Treaty Federalism," 246).

11. Sir Walter Raleigh quoted in Louis Montrose, "The Work of Gender in

the Discourse of Discovery," 9. Surprisingly, Montrose does not make the connection with the Latin phrases. See also Roy Strong, *Gloriana.*

12. Richard Hakluyt, *The Principal Navigations,* 10:447.

13. Sir Walter Raleigh, *The Discoverie,* 196.

14. I draw extensively on Mary Fuller's account of Raleigh's text, as found in *Voyages in Print.*

15. Raleigh, *The Discoverie,* 165. Gesa Mackenthun points out intriguingly that a recently discovered manuscript containing material subsequently censored gives clear evidence of the purchase of Indian wives, which certainly undermines Raleigh's claims (*Metaphors of Dispossession,* 179).

16. Fuller, *Voyages in Print,* 28.

17. See Barbour's introduction in *The Jamestown Voyages,* 2:321–6. Given the problematic nature of Smith's accounts of his dealings with Powhatan, we cannot rely on his versions of Powhatan's statements as an accurate record of what the chief said or thought. I mainly use the accounts as paradigmatic of the relations of power and of European thinking, but, like other commentators, I respond to the temptation to speculate. For a thorough overall account, see Frederick W. Gleach, *Powhatan's World and Colonial Virginia.*

18. Barbour, *The Jamestown Voyages,* 2:393–4, 438–9.

19. Ibid., 2:411, 413.

20. John Barth's comic account of the Pocahontas story in *The Sotweed Factor* similarly presents it in terms of a man's inability to satisfy. A more searching account of the changing representations of gift-giving and the power relations involved is to be found in Bernadette Bucher's analysis of a De Bry illustration in which a native woman brings a basket of fruit to the Spanish conquerors. Bucher traces the changes made to the woman's appearance in successive versions as part of a series of transformations of episodes of gift-giving—including that of the fruit offered by Satan in the Garden of Eden—that reflect the contradictions in the imperial role. In the Biblical scene, the monstrous tempter offers a gift that brings the Fall, but here the monstrous one is the taker, not the giver. "A native figure, an autochthone, brings in all good faith, in a gesture of welcome, some of the fruits of her land to the foreigners. In return, she will be expropriated, tortured and reduced to slavery" (*Icon and Conquest,* 69). Bucher sees these contradictions as accounting for the transformation of the woman into a monstrous old hag, but beyond this she connects the failure of reciprocity here, via Edmund Leach's reading of Genesis in conjunction with Oedipus, with incest taboos and eventually cannibalism.

21. Barbour, *The Jamestown Voyages,* 2:414.

22. The Virginia assembly quoted in L. C. Green and Olive Dickason, *The Law of Nations,* 232–3.

23. Eric Cheyfitz, *Poetics of Imperialism,* 81. Myra Jehlen uses the coronation scene, together with early accounts of cannibalism, to engage in a debate with Peter Hulme over the dangers of too easily assuming the power of the discursive realm and our inability to go beyond it. She stresses the role of ruptures and incoherencies in the text, as representing the failure of language to exert absolute control, but also as a challenge to our contemporary rereadings, to find ways of allowing

for the possibility of agency rather than settling for the analysis of a self-sealing discourse of empire. See Myra Jehlen, "History Before the Fact," 687, 689. and Hulme's response, "Making No Bones," 179–86. See also Mackenthun, *Metaphors of Dispossession*, 199–207.

24. Nicholas Canny quoted in Jeffrey Knapp, *An Empire Nowhere*, 2.

25. Barbour, *The Jamestown Voyages*, 1:153. For other examples, see Karen O. Kupperman, "Presentment of Civility."

26. Helen C. Rountree, *Pocahontas's People*, 11.

27. Cheyfitz, *Poetics of Imperialism*, 217–8.

28. Richard White, *The Middle Ground*, 37–40.

29. Barbour, *The Jamestown Voyages*, 2:414.

30. William Strachey, "A True Reportory."

31. Barbour, *The Jamestown Voyages*, 2:411, 413, 392.

32. As Arthur Ray and Donald Freeman show, even in direct dealings with Europeans the element of gift exchange was still significant for Indian traders, and fur trading institutions adapted accordingly. Before and after the strict trading, there was a substantial exchange of gifts, which the Indians associated with prestige and the white traders saw as maintaining customer loyalty. While the whites gave items they knew would be regarded as status objects by the Indian trading captains, as well as luxuries and utility items, the Indians gave furs, and although initially they were presumably meant in the full spirit of gift, Ray and Freeman note that the quality of these furs decreased, suggesting that "the Indians also consciously began to use the traditional forms of the gift-exchange as a means to their own economic gain." They conclude that "the spirit behind the gift-exchange waned as the trade developed" (*Give Us Good Measure*, 241–2).

33. Martin H. Quitt, "Trade and Acculturation at Jamestown," 247. Quitt gives a usefully detailed account of what he sees as a shift in exchanges between colonists and the Powhatan people from what he calls unbalanced gift-giving, where the two sides were not aware of a common agenda or criterion of exchange value, to a more balanced barter, as their leader Powhatan learns and adapts to the trade patterns of the English.

34. Barbour, *The Jamestown Voyages*, 2:424, 428. Describing the alliance created between Europeans and Algonquians a little later, Richard White points out that "because it was largely Algonquian in form and spirit, [it] demanded a father who mediated more often than he commanded, who forgave more than he punished, and who gave more than he received" (*The Middle Ground*, 143). The striking similarity between these supposedly Algonquian values and the description of Elizabeth on her portrait should warn us against assuming clear-cut differences between cultures and leadership styles. For a detailed discussion of the importance of kinship terms and reciprocity (and the misunderstandings of them), see Peter Hulme, *Colonial Encounters*, 147–56.

35. William Strachey, *The Historie of Travaile*, 51–53.

36. For the reverse phenomenon, see William M. Hamlin, who notes the frequency of the incidence of natives attributing divinity to Europeans and relates this to romance tropes. Hamlin points out that "the early voyagers and colonists were, in a sense, *inhabiting* Renaissance romance; their accounts and their ethnographic

endeavours employ rhetorical conventions familiar to us from the Spanish chivalric romances" ("Attributions of Divinity in Renaissance Ethnography," 429–30).

The famous meeting between Cortes and Moctezuma as described in Cortes's second letter provides a fascinating parallel in that Cortes is intent on establishing Moctezuma as a subject of Charles, even while insisting that he is not interfering with Moctezuma's status in his own kingdom. The negotiations with Moctezuma are carried out with chivalric and aristocratic manners, and the uneasy move between coercion (when he is put in chains for a time) and deference to nobility is similar to that in Captain John Smith. The lavish gifts given to Cortes in advance of the meeting can be seen as both tributes demonstrating subservience and marks of sovereignty and nobility, and it is not until the meeting that the agendas become clearer. In Cortes's account, Moctezuma is immediately prepared to recognize Charles's authority within native terms, as the long-promised Quetzalcoatl, but also to demystify his own authority as divine ruler. He is at pains to deny the stories Cortes will have been told of his fabulous wealth and his divinity.

> I also know that they have told you the walls of my houses are made of gold, and that the floor mats in my rooms and other things in my household are likewise of gold, and that I was, and claimed to be, a god; and many other things besides. The houses as you see are of stone and lime and clay. Then he raised his clothes and showed me his body, saying, as he grasped his arms and his trunk with his hands, "See that I am of flesh and blood like you and all other men, and I am mortal and substantial." (Hernan Cortes, *Letters from Mexico*, 86).

It is intriguing to see this exposure of the body as a subjection to colonial surveillance and very different from the gift of garments from Powhatan. See also Jose Rabasa, who views the encounter in terms of Hegel's master-slave relation, with its emphasis on recognition (*Inventing America*, 109). Rabasa also uses the Florentine Codex to suggest ways in which a native account of the dialogue can be tentatively reconstructed.

37. Strachey, *The Historie of Travaile*, 81. This passage is quoted by Stephen Potter, who argues that the Algonquian weroances consciously sought to incorporate the trade with Europeans into the existing system of tribute, thus controlling the flow of European goods ("Early English Effects on Virginia Algonquin Exchange," 153).

38. See David B. Quinn, *The Roanoke Voyages*, 1:100.

39. Strachey, *The Historie of Travaile*, 103–4.

40. Henry Spelman, *Relation of Virginia*, 17.

Chapter 3

1. Philip Barbour, *The Jamestown Voyages*, 2:414.

2. See Christian Feest's entry on Powhatan's mantle in Arthur McGregor, *Tradescant's Rarities*.

3. Steven Mullaney, "Strange Things, Gross Terms, Curious Customs"; James Clifford, *The Predicament of Culture*, 117–51.

4. See Thomas Keenan, "The Point is to (Ex)Change It," 161, for a discussion of this point. Keenan brings out the meaning of *ungeheuer* as 'monstrous' as well as 'immense'.

5. George R. Hamell, "The Iroquois and the World's Rim," 454.

6. Denise Albanese, *New Science, New World*, 44; Susan Stewart, quoted in ibid., 46.

7. Margaret Hodgen, *Early Anthropology*, 165.

8. Michel de Certeau, "Writing vs Time," 40, 41, 43, 50. For a useful discussion of the idea of the new scriptural economy and a careful critique of de Certeau, see Jose Rabasa, *Inventing America*, especially chap. 2.

9. Richard Hakluyt quoted in Mary Fuller, *Voyages in Print*, 151, 152.

10. Stephen Greenblatt, *Marvelous Possessions*, 12.

11. Sir Walter Raleigh, *The Discoverie*.

12. This narrative trope was not confined to belated English adventurers, but was already a part of the Spanish textualization of the New World. Beatriz Pastor Bodmer describes the mixture of mythic and fabulous elements with details of actual discovery that constitutes a "narrative discourse of failure" in *The Armature of Conquest*, chap. 3.

13. James Rosier, *A True Relation of the Most Prosperous Voyage*, n.p.

14. Mary C. Fuller, "Raleigh's Fugitive Gold," 46–47. In a parallel discussion, Jeffrey Knapp develops the idea that as isolationist and distinctly lacking in the colonial successes of its rivals, England uses a self-justifying but uneasy rhetoric that to validate a nonexpansionist, supposedly nonmaterialist approach plays with the idea of trifles, expressed characteristically in the idea of tobacco and of profits and wealth going up in smoke, as opposed to the real wealth of gold (*An Empire Nowhere*, esp. chap. 5). See also Neil L. Whitehead, who offers a useful warning against assuming that Raleigh's text is entirely rhetorical rather than referential. Whitehead points out the ways in which the text may indeed be reflecting native beliefs and practices, even at those points where Raleigh has been accused of imposing his own agenda, such as his accounts of Amazons and the presence of gold. In the extensive introduction to his edition of *The Discoverie* and in "The Historical Anthropology of Text," Whitehead makes the case for the ethnographic significance of Raleigh's text, which has been played down in the concentration on his European preconceptions.

15. The indebtedness is demonstrated on both sides. Laurence Keymis, in his introductory Latin poem to Raleigh's text, dedicates his account "Ad Thomam Hariotum Matheosis & universae Philosophiae peritissimum." Keymis reworks the theme of the endless productivity of the sun, (echoing my discussion of Queen Elizabeth's portrait in chapter 1) but allies it to the land of Guiana:

> This land has gold, and gems the color of grass.
> It is always spring there: there the prodigal earth yearly
> Teems, it puts down the sun in fertility.

Muriel Rukeyser's translation, in her *The Traces of Thomas Hariot*, 141.

16. Raleigh, *The Discoverie*, 113.

17. Thomas Harriot, *A Briefe and True Report*, 6. The most detailed commen-

tary on text and pictures is to be found in David Beers Quinn, *The Roanoke Voyages*, vol. 1.

18. Quinn, *The Roanoke Voyages*, 1:315.

19. Harriot, *A Briefe and True Report*, 31.

20. Raleigh, *The Discoverie*, 176.

21. David Beers Quinn, *Set Fair For Roanoke*, 199; Rukeyser, *The Traces of Thomas Hariot*, 106.

22. Harriot, *A Briefe and True Report*, 56.

23. On the question of Harriot's possible atheism, see Quinn *The Roanoke Voyages*, 1:376, and Jean Jaquot, "Thomas Harriot's Reputation for Impiety," 164–87. It is intriguing, too, that Harriot is explicitly named in the notorious charges laid against Christopher Marlowe, who is claimed to have affirmed that "Moyses was but a Jugler, & that one Heriots being Sir W Raleighs' man can do more than he." He also suggested that if Christ wanted the sacrament to be held in greater reverence, "it would haue bin much better being administered in a Tobacco pipe" (quoted in Rukeyser, *The Traces of Thomas Hariot*, 127–8). This could be seen as a startling anticipation of the syncretism developed by Indian tribes, and the equation of peyote and the host in peyotism. Stephen Greenblatt pursues the possible subversions in Harriot's text, with his alleged slur on Moses in mind, by focusing on his account of the Indians' response to the Europeans' superior technology and their willingness to ascribe divinity to it and its providers. Rather than accepting this only as the usual complacent assumption of Indian naivety, Greenblatt sees it in the context of Harriot's reputation as atheist and juggler, as raising a more subversive idea: "the very core of the Machiavellian anthropology that posited the origin of religion in an imposition of socially coercive docrines by an educated and sophisticated lawgiver on a simple people" (*Shakespearian Negotiations*, 27).

24. Mary B. Campbell, "The Illustrated Travel Book," 186–9.

25. Fuller, *Voyages in Print*, 49.

26. Rukeyser, *The Traces of Thomas Hariot*, 105.

27. Oviedo quoted in Kathleen A. Myers, "The Representation of New World Phenomena," 189–90.

28. Greenblatt, *Marvelous Possessions*, 104, 182.

29. These full grammatical studies and dictionaries are beyond the scope of this chapter. For useful accounts of the Jesuit endeavours in North America, see Victor Egon Hanzeli, *Missionary Linguistics in New France*, and Rudiger Schreier, 'Take Your Pen and Write. Learning Huron." For a recent comprehensive overview, see Ives Goddard, "The Description of the Native Languages."

30. Fuller, *Voyages in Print*, 50.

31. I am greatly indebted to Daniel J. Slive of the John Carter Brown Library for allowing me to use his unpublished catalogue of an exhibition, *Amerindian Languages in the Colonial World*, held at the library in 1997. The catalogue presents a valuable list of early texts containing or devoted to Indian languages.

32. Peter Martyr, *De Orbe Novo Decades* (Alcala de Henares, 1516). A facsimile of the 1530 edition is available (Rome, 1983).

33. Eric Cheyfitz, *Poetics of Imperialism*, 42–43. See also Peter Hulme, *Colonial Encounters*, esp. 69–70.

34. See Maria de las Nievas Olmedillas de Pereiras, *Pedro Martir de Angleria*, who gives details of Martyr's exoticisms and their influence, including a "vocabulario exotico," though she does not discuss the "Vocabula Barbara."

35. Since Antonio Nebrija, the creator of Latin grammars, was involved, the linguistic material may well have had some connection with him rather than Martyr. See also Felix G. Olmedo, *Nebrija: Debelador de la Barbarie*, 57.

36. Richard Eden, *The Decades of the New World*. This is reprinted in Edward Arber, *The First Three English Books on America*. The original edition gives the word lists a complete page at the beginning of the book, whereas they are squeezed down at the end of the list of contents in Arber's reprint.

37. Greenblatt, *Marvelous Possessions*, 91.

38. Sebastian Munster, *A treatise of the Newe India*.

39. Alonso de Ercilla y Zuniga, *La Araucana*, n. p. following 468.

40. William Wood, *New England's Prospect*, 117. For some reason, in the 1639 edition this reads "if they can get no proof" rather than "no profit," though this is not noted by Vaughan.

41. Greenblatt, *Marvelous Possessions*, 103.

42. I use here the original English edition, Jacques Cartier, *A Shorte and Briefe Narration*, but the standard text with notes of variants and with English translation straight from the French is H. P. Biggar's *The Voyages of Jacques Cartier*. Biggar gives a longer list of words, with the variants between editions.

43. For a comparison of the two available lists and a linguistic analysis, see the Appendix to the Hakluyt Society's edition of the Princeton text, *The Historie of Travell into Virginia Britain*, 174–214.

44. E. Arber and A. G. Bradley, *Travels and Works of Captain John Smith*, 45. For a detailed analysis of these words, with comparisons with other sources, and showing the degree of likely borrowing from Harriot and Strachey, see Philip L. Barbour, "The Earliest Reconnaisance of the Chesapeake Bay Area." Karen Robertson sees the list of words as "remarkably prescient in its anticipation of the consequences of the proces of contact" and distinguishes eight rough groupings "around substantives for humans, shelter, clothing and resources" ("Pocahontas at the Masque," 562). Jeffrey Knapp, *An Empire Nowhere*, 211.

45. Gabriel Sagard, *The Long Journey*, 17.

46. Perspective can be seen as a way of ordering or laying out the natural resources of the country, so that it almost becomes synonymous with *prospect* in the sense of site for exploration, or *prospectus*. Thomas Morton heads one chapter "A Perspective to view the Country by," and it consists simply of a list of the virtues of the country's soil, air, weather, and natural abundance, so that like Harriot's and Williams's, Morton's text is "discovering," opening up for our controlled and appraising centralized view an otherwise inchoate mass. In a prefatory poem from a certain S. W. to William Wood, praising his work, the poet underscores this role for Wood:

> And thine experience thus a Mount dost make,
> From whence we may *New England's Prospect* take.
>
> (Wood, *New England's Prospect*, 21)

His experience gives him and us a vantage point from which we take in the prospect and gain a perspective. Interestingly, de Lery is one of the few to acknowledge explicitly the difficulty of gaining or keeping a perspective when confronted with strangeness, when he complains that "by reason of their diverse gestures and behaviour, utterly different from ours, it is a very difficult matter to express their true proportion, either in writing or in painting" (de Lery quoted in Paul Hulton's introduction to Harriot, *A Briefe and True Report*, xiii).

47. Charles de Rochefort, *Histoire Naturelle e Morale*, 527. The lack of Christian terminology and of Christian concepts themselves is often linked to the idea of Indians as incapable of abstract thought per se. Biard talks of the difficulties in trying to preach the gospel without any of the necessary terms:

> Besides, as these Savages have no formulated Religion, government, towns nor trades, so the words and proper phrases for all these are lacking: Holy, Blessed, Angel, Grace, Mystery, Sacrament, Temptation, Faith, Law, Prudence, Subjection, Authority, etc when will you get all these things you lack? Or how will you do without them? (Reuben G. Thwaites, *The Jesuit Relations*, 3:195–7).

48. Jean de Lery, *History of a Voyage;* Michel de Certeau, *Writing and History*, 223. The crucial role of the noble savage, both in and out of dialogues with Europeans, in the work of Montaigne and Diderot has been extensively documented, but not so often in relation to America and French travelers there. For a useful and wide-ranging attempt to fill this gap, see Gordon M. Sayre, *Les Sauvages Americains*. One of the most interesting instances of this is Baron Lahontan's *New Voyages to North America* of 1735, where we find a brief list of Huron and Algonkian words organized alphabetically, with some grammatical information, and then a dialogue, which, rather than growing directly out of the linguistic interchange, is separate and programmatic. The articulate and rationalist Indian, Adario makes all the usual noble savage criticisms of money, private property, and the principle of interest and is given the last word, when he voices the hope that "one Day you may give the name of *Savage* to all the *French*, who will be wise enough to follow exactly the true rules of Justice and Reason" (*New Voyages to North America*, 2:184). Lahontan manages a witty combination of ideas of nakedness and clothing, or propriety and property, when Adario, answering the criticism that nakedness is improper, says,

> I allow that in a Nation where the distinctions of property are acknowledg'd, you are very much in the right of it, to cover not only such parts as ought not to be named, but even all the parts of the Body. What use would the *French* make of their Gold and their Silver, if they did not imploy it in providing themselves with fine Cloaths? (2:104)

It is worth contrasting this with another eighteenth-century dialogue in which a quite different universal human behavior is demonstrated. James Isham offers us a few pages of what he claims is typical trading conversation, and there we have a vivid sense of a common and narrow agenda of hearty and hard bargaining for furs. See E. E. Rich, *James Isham's Observations and Notes*, 49–54.

49. de Lery, *History of a Voyage*, 189.

50. Louis Hennepin, *A New Discovery of a vast country*, 2:79, 81. (On a more flippant level, William Wood slips into his brief word list a word for which he gives only a Latin translation. Only in the 1639 edition do we find it given in blunt English as 'kiss my arsehole'.); Alexander Whitaker, *Good News from Virginia*, 27.

51. Quoted in Peter Hulme and Neil L. Whitehead, *Wild Majesty*, 61. Perhaps the most bizarre instance of the enumeration of parts of the body is to be found in the brief list of words at the end of the first voyage of Martin Frobisher, from "the language of the people of *Meta Incognita*," which consists of words translated as 'hand', 'nose', 'eye', 'tooth', 'head', 'ear', 'leg', 'foot', 'a pair of breeches', 'coat', 'knife', 'ship', and then separate words for 'thumb', 'the foremost finger', 'the middle finger', 'the fourth finger', and 'the little finger' (Richard Hakluyt, *The Principal Navigations*, 622).

52. de Lery, *History of A Voyage*, xxiii, xxxvi, 62.

53. Ibid., 66, xxv, 68.

54. de Certeau, *Writing and History*, 226–8, 233. De Certeau is of course working within the terms developed by Levi-Strauss (who also uses de Lery) and critiqued by Derrida, and while his use of these oppositions is penetrating, it is not clear how far he subscribes to them and would therefore be susceptible to Derrida's deconstructive criticisms of Levi-Strauss. See also Rabasa, *Inventing America*, and Hulme, *Colonial Encounters*, for two of many discussions of the representations of America as female, focusing on Jan van der Straet's picture *America*.

Chapter 4

1. The fullest scholarly edition is Roger Williams, *A Key into the Language of America, or An Help to the Language of the Natives in that part of America called New England* (1643), ed. John J. Teunissen and Evelyn J. Hinz. References are to this edition unless otherwise indicated, and page numbers are given in the text. The most detailed linguistic commentary is provided in the edition edited by J. Hammond Trumbull as *Publications of the Narragansett Club*, no. 6 (1874), reprinted in Williams, *The Complete Writings*.

2. Cotton Mather, *Magnalia Christi Americana*, 2:499.

3. See Johannes Fabian, *Time and the Other*, and James Clifford and George Marcus, *Writing Culture*.

4. See David Beers Quinn, *Set Fair For Roanoke*, xxii.

5. Peter Albinus, *A Treatise on Foreign Languages*, 61.

6. Cf. the quotations from Matt. 13, with which one of the Eliot Tracts begins, "The Kingdom of Heaven is like to a graine of mustard seed" and "The Kingdom of Heaven is like unto Leven" (Thomas Shepard, *The Day-breaking, if not the Sun-Rising*).

7. Teunissen and Hinz want the book to be seen as "careful, deliberate and aesthetically oriented" (30), but their own reading of the text as having an overall pattern that moves not only in a sequence from birth to death but thematically from primitive to civilized in a "structure which could be called elegiac" and a

theme that they compare with the Fall (36) is arguable. The Williams they present, who "with all his heart admires the natural Indian" but whose theology tells him otherwise and whose book ends apocalyptically ("The American Garden—has *become* the American Wilderness; the dream has become the nightmare. This is the boxed key that has been revealed"), I find not much more convincing than Ola Winslow's description of Williams as a writer without a "shadow of ambitious authorship, of literary scholarship" (*Master Roger Williams*, 162).

8. Gordon Brotherston, "A Controversial Guide to The Language of America," 86.

9. Ives Goddard, "The Description of the Native Languages," 19. See also William Simmons, "Narragansett."

10. John Canup, *Out of the Wilderness*, 143.

11. Ibid., 144.

12. This mix of repetition and randomness may sound to a modern reader like Gertrude Stein or a modern performance poem. The poet Rosmarie Waldrop (*A Key into the Language of America*) uses some of the words in the Williams original, both Indian and English, to make a new book, with the same chapter headings and the same combination of commentary, word list, and poem in each chapter. She "tries to get at the clash of Indian and European cultures by a violent collage of phrases from Williams with elements from anywhere in my Western heritage" (xxii). The result is a complex and difficult book that is perhaps ultimately less interested in Williams (and consequently less interesting about him) than in developing a new poem expressing her own particular "immigrant's take" on America.

13. Eric Wertheimer, "'To Spell Out Each Other,'" 2.

14. For another example, see the way Williams moves to, or at least strategically uses, an Indian point of view in a letter he wrote in 1669 to John Whipple, in which he complains of the greed of some of his countrymen in overturning land agreements.

> What God can that be, Say the Indians, that is followed by such Extortioners, Cheatours and Lyers, as his Servants and Worshippers? For my Selfe it is a terrible matter in mine eyes, that (beside the many cries of the English) the cry of these Barbarians *Commootin Commootin* [stealing] should knock at Heaven gate agnst us. (Williams, *The Correspondence*, 598)

15. Brotherston notes that when his charter was granted, special mention was made of his "printed Indian labours" ("Controversial Guide," 85).

16. Reprinted in Williams, *The Complete Writings*, 7:31–41.

17. Williams, *The Correspondence*, 452.

18. See Keith W. Staveley, "Roger Williams and the Enclosed Gardens of New England," for a useful discussion of this idea in Williams. While Staveley shows that theological and land disputes have an overlapping rhetoric in Williams, because of his own marginal position between the garden and the wilderness, he does not develop the implications of Williams's linking this idea with the idea of a key and unlocking the "language of America." In the Song of Solomon we find the parallel images of "a spring shut up, a fountain sealed."

19. Perry Miller's (*Roger Williams: His Contribution*) stress on the importance of Williams's typological approach in giving him intellectual as well as spiritual leverage against the church authorities has been influential, but his assumption that Williams was unusual in using typology has been extensively challenged. See, for instance, Thomas M. Davis, "The Traditions of Puritan Typology"; Ursula Brumm, *American Thought and Religious Typology;* Sacvan Bercovitch, "Typology in Puritan New England"; and Jesper Rosenmeier, "The Teacher and the Witness." Although there was certainly a Protestant reaction against allegorical reading and its elaboration into fourfold readings in favor of more literal readings of the Bible, this literalism never excluded typology in its fundamental form of finding in the Old Testament "types" that prefigured or foreshadowed New Testament events or figures, who would become their "antitype." This way of reading required two literal or historically based items to be matched up, demonstrating God's purpose and design across time and ensuring the reliability of the reading, unlike the merely fanciful elaborations of allegory.

20. John Cotton quoted in Miller, *Roger Williams: His Contribution*, 185–6.

21. This is the basis, argues Miller, of Williams's celebrated defense of religious liberty. For more detail, see Richard Reinitz, "The Separatist Background of Roger Williams' Argument." In his reply to John Cotton, "Mr Cotton's Letter Lately Printed, Examined and Answered," Williams pursues his critique of the New England church and his defense of separatism. The church can justify its break with Rome, itself an act of separatism, through Biblical instances, but it is not prepared to see Williams's break as justifiable by the same logic, and Williams's argument with Cotton specifically engages the question of how to interpret his actions through type and antitype.

> Mr Cotton having made a locall departure from Old England in Europe to New England in America, can he satisfie his owne soule, or the soules of other men, that he obeyed that voice *come out of Babel my people, partake not of her sins,&.* Doth he count the very Land of England literally Babel and so consequently Egypt and Sodome, Revel.11.8 and the land of new England Judea, Canaan? (*The Complete Writings*, 1:76)

22. Williams, *The Complete Writings*, 7:32–3, 36. Williams is using the words *ethnicke* and *heathen* interchangeably here, and they indeed have an intriguingly close etymology. Until the mid-nineteenth-century *ethnic(ke)* was indeed used exclusively to mean "heathen."

23. Later, in fact, he suggests that the Indians are descendants of Jews. The question of their origins had some significance in terms of their convertibility to Christianity, as is clear from the differences between Cotton and Eliot. According to Puritan millenarian thinking, the Jews, as God's original chosen people, would be forgiven by Him en masse at the end of history, and only after their Jews' conversion would any significant numbers of Gentiles be converted. Until then, there would be "a seal set upon the hearts" of Gentiles. It was important, then, for missionaries to see Indians as Jews, if there was to be much prospect of conversion. See Richard W. Cogley, "John Eliot and the Origins of the American Indians," and

James Holstun, "John Eliot's Empirical Millenarianism," who sees the experiment of the Praying Towns as part of a larger effort of utopian enclosure in New England. The first text Eliot preached upon to the Indians, according to Thomas Thorowgood, was Ezek. 37:9–10 on the dry bones, which Thorowgood describes as foretelling the conversion of Israel. In his letter to Thorowgood, Eliot talks of the scattered Ten Tribes, the dry and scattered bones, being reunited. "He that can gather together the scattered dust of the dead bodies of men, and raise them up at the resurrection, he also can find the lost Israel" (Thorowgood, *Jewes in America*; Eliot's sermon is printed in the Appendix to Edward Winslow, *The Glorious Progress*).

24. Staveley, "Roger Williams and the Enclosed Gardens," 270.

25. An indication of the use of the word *nakedness* can be found in an interesting textual change to James Rosier's 1605 account. He describes Indian women as reluctant to come forward to meet the English visitors, "whether it were in regard of their own natural modestie, being covered only as the men with the foresaid beavers skins, or by the commanding jealousy of their husbands" (*A True Relation of the Most Prosperous Voyage*, n.p.). In Samuel Purchas's account, this line becomes "whether it were in regard to their own natural modesty being naked" (*Hakluytus Posthumus, or Purchas his Pilgrimes*, 18:343). This change is noted by Karen O. Kupperman, "Presentment of Civility," who offers a good discussion of this issue.

26. Brotherston has linked this with his larger argument that the presence of Indian writing has been systematically overlooked or misrepresented in white accounts ("Controversial Guide," 93–94). For a useful survey, see Peter Wogan, "Perceptions of European Literacy." See also Gordon Sayre, *Les Sauvages Americains*, chap. 4, for a discussion that links writing, clothing, and wampum.

27. Williams, *The Complete Writings*, 7:37.

28. See Olive P. Dickason, *The Myth of the Savage*, and Alan Hunt, *Governance of the Consuming Passions*. Hunt points out that the impulses behind such laws became increasingly influenced by protectionist rather than hierarchical considerations and were in any case undermined by the increased emphasis on consumption. Nonetheless, the emphasis on clothing as a marker of social position in the period cannot be ignored. See also the comments on the stylized clothing of the Pictish figures included in Thomas Harriot as perhaps "the epidermal version of displaced Elizabethan sumptuary laws—a displaced aristocratic body whose very extravagance of decoration confirms the racial superiority of the early British" (Denise Albanese, *New Science, New World*, 195).

29. See Daniel K. Richter, *The Ordeal of the Longhouse*, 76.

30. Nathaniel Hawthorne, *Tales and Sketches*, 360.

31. Thomas Morton, *New English Canaan*, 135.

32. Here we could be said to have fetishism in its sexual and Freudian sense, but the fact that it is explicitly linked to its sumptuary status, too, is significant. Leopold von Sacher-Masoch's *Venus in Furs* offers some interesting reflections on the significance of fur. In the novel, the recurring fetishistic image of a woman naked except for furs is expressed in a painting composed as a counterpart to Titian's *Venus with a Mirror*, and Severin points out the "symbolic meaning which fur

has acquired as the attribute of power and beauty," which caused its use by nobility for display as well as by painters such as Titian. His explanation for this contains some rather surprising nineteenth-century science (fur creates an electricity that is connected to heat and to sexual excitement). This explains, he says, the influence of cats upon impressionable people but also great men of intellect. To which Wanda replies, with an irony that seems not to deflect him, "A woman wearing furs, then, is nothing else than a large cat, an augmented electric battery?" Leopold von Sacher-Masoch, *Venus in Furs*) (New York, 1965), 45.

33. Francis X. Moloney, *The Fur Trade*, 23–25. In Morton's *New English Canaan*, there is a sharp vignette of a minister described as an assiduous trader in beaver. On Sunday he warns off others from trading with an Indian who appears with "a gode Beaver coate," only to take him aside himself "where, (with the helpe of his Wampampeack, hee had in his pocket for that purpose in a readinesse,) hee made a shifte to get that beaver coate, which all their mouthes watered at; and so deceaved them all" (155).

34. See Howard Miller Chapin, *The Trading Post*; Charlotte Taylor, "A Frontier Entrepot"; William A. Turnbaugh, "Roger Williams: A Key," 139–41.

35. Williams does record borrowings of two English words for 'money' and 'paying'. "The *Indians* are ignorant of *Europes* Coyne; yet they have given a name to ours, and call it *Moneash* from the *English* Money," and "*Cuppaimish* I will pay you, which is a word newly made from the *English* word pay" (152, 161). This raises interesting questions about whether economic conceptions were being borrowed along with the words, given that the only other borrowed words Williams notes seem to be for new items such as European animals. This is particularly significant in relation to the status of the native wampum, the subject of Chapter 5, and whether, as Williams assumes, it operates in exactly the same way as English money, given its other functions. Similarly, the appearance here of a verb for 'pay' raises questions about the idea of a return that is not reciprocal and the depth of penetration of European ideas. According to Louise Burkhart, in her study of religious influences, "the process of linguistic acculturation is such that nouns are borrowed more easily than verbs . . . Thus while the things of religion could come to have foreign names the acts of religion did not" (*The Slippery Earth*). This might lead us to see the verb form here as particularly significant.

Another intriguing instance of the possible impact of borrowing words and their relation to economic ideas is found in the annotations in an Eliot Bible. The annotations are written in Massachusett and translated as 'I,I Nanahdinnoo, own this forever. Because I bought it with my money and not with assookuhkatchagmoon' (Ives Goddard and Kathleen J. Bragdon, *Native Writings in Massachusett*, 397). The emphasis on personal property, demonstrated by writing, and the fact that it is in the Bible is an almost too perfect demonstration of the values of civility Eliot propounded to the Christian Indians (see chapter 6), but what is left unanswered here is the exact nature of the opposition between different sorts of buying, and money, and the extent to which this shows the influence of English economic practices.

36. Even here, though, he follows it up with a characteristic plea for reassur-

ance to be given by John Winthrop to Miantunnomu, in whom he sees "some sparks of true Friendship," in order to guarantee the help of his troops (Williams, *The Correspondence*, 101).

37. Roger Williams, *The Bloody Tenent*, 217.

38. Keith W. F. Staveley, "Roger Williams: Bible Politics," 77. Benjamin Nelson, *The Idea of Usury*, xxiii, xxv. According to E. A. J. Johnson, although aspects of early American economics have "a definite medieval flavour," in retaining guiding moral principles such as the just price, on the subject of interest and usury there was no sign of any greater reluctance to accept it than there was in Europe (*American Economic Thought in the Seventeenth Century*). See also Bernard Bailyn, *The New England Merchants*.

39. Alexander Young, *Chronicles of the Pilgrim Fathers*, 240–1.

40. Ibid., 242.

41. Williams, *The Complete Writings* 6:407; idem., *The Correspondence*, 165, 485.

42. John Garrett, *Roger Williams: Witness*, 40; Williams, *The Correspondence*, 752.

43. This included a keen awareness of the exploitative uses of alcohol by white traders. Williams's own trading practice excluded what he referred to in a later letter as "that bloudie Liquour trade," but in a defense against charges that he himself had acquired land from Indian sachems too drunk to know better, he reveals a comprehensive cynicism about white dealings with Indians. Even while insisting on the sobriety of his own partners in the deal, he challenges the relevance of the accusation, with an attack on the prevailing standards of Indian-white commerce:

> And if the Natives had Liquours and were distempered before or after, what is that to the invalidating or aspersing of a Business? If so, what Contracts, what Purchases among Merchants or others in this Countrey, or any Countrey shall stand and be Effectuall? (Correspondence, 489)

One significant absence in Williams's *A Key* is, in fact, any mention of alcohol, which he is here admitting to be ubiquitous and fundamental to trade. This may be partly explained by his wish to present a fairly positive view of America to England, but it also perhaps reflects the more general desire to see alcohol as an unfortunate extra rather than a prerequisite, as I discuss in chapter 1.

Chapter 5

1. John Eliot, "Some Unpublished Correspondence," 454–5.

2. William Kellaway, *The New England Company*, 157. The reasons given by Cotton Mather for moving to English reflect the concern to "Anglicise" the Indians, but we could follow the logic of John Eliot's own argument and say that English had already become the key language because of its distribution through the trade networks.

3. October 8, 1652, Guildhall MS 7938 (this is a copy of the Bodleian manuscript).

4. Lynn Ceci, "Wampum as a Peripheral Resource," 51; Roger Williams, *A Key into the Language of America* (page numbers are given in the text). The literature

on wampum is extensive, though often narrow in focus. The older standard accounts include Frank G. Speck, "The Functions of Wampum"; William A. Beauchamp, "Wampum and Shell Articles," and William B. Weeden, *Indian Money*. Recent general studies are George S. Snyderman, "The Functions of Wampum," and Don Taxay, *Money of the American Indians*. Jerry Martien's *Shell Game* is an idiosyncratic account of a poet's obsession with wampum and his view of modern capitalist America. By turns indulgent and perceptive, a lament for a gift economy overwhelmed by capitalism, the book's central message is that "They began with a gift and turned it into money. This is how the New World was 'conquered'—not with a bang, but one crooked deal at a time" (54). Ceci's work, beginning with her doctoral dissertation thesis in 1977, "The Effects of European Contact and Trade," marked a new direction, and her recent work building on this is cited in this chapter as my argument develops.

5. Immanuel Wallerstein, *The Modern World System*, vol. 2. See also Eric R. Wolf, *Europe*, esp. chaps. 3 and 6. For an important application of this approach, see Denys Delage, who refers to the Dutch awareness of "the pre-Columbian wampum trail, which ran from Long Island (the principal producer of wampum) to the Richelieu via the Hudson, then up the Saint Lawrence to the entire Canadian shield inhabited by the Algonkian peoples." (*Bitter Feast*, 104). Criticism of the world-system approach has focused on, among other things, its lack of attention to diversity and ethnohistory in its concern for a trajectory that links all peoples, but for my purposes here this sense of interlinkedness is important. For a discussion of the problems and advantages of such an approach, see Thomas D. Hall, "Native Americans and Incorporation."

As part of his theme of Indian giving, Jack Weatherford, also using a world-system approach, offers the useful reminder that the influx of gold and silver to Europe allowed the conditions for the full development of a market economy, so that, ironically, the effect of contact was not just to bring Indians into a market economy but to create the market economy itself in its fullest form. The Indians, then, "gave" the West the market economy by creating greater liquidity and circulation of wealth, thereby moving the emphasis from land as property and also creating the dynamic by which Europe reached out to the rest of the world for goods. (Jack Weatherford, *Indian Giving*, 10–20).

6. William Wood, *New England's Prospect*. 81.

7. William A. Turnbaugh, "Roger Williams: A Key," 137.

8. Isaak de Rasiere quoted in Kevin A. McBride, "The Source and Mother of the Fur Trade," 40.

9. Ceci, "Wampum as a Peripheral Resource," 61; idem., "The Effects of European Contact," 262–4.

10. Weeden, *Indian Money*, 15; Thomas Morton, *New English Canaan*, 41; William Bradford, *Of Plymouth Plantation*, 203.

11. Ceci, "Wampum as a Peripheral Resource," 59.

12. Daniel K. Richter, *The Ordeal of the Longhouse*, 85. Given the importance of wampum to the Iroquois, it is not surprising that they have a number of myths and traditions describing its origin within their culture. Arthur Parker's "Constitu-

tion of the Five Nations" recounts how Hayonwhatha finds the shells at the bottom of a lake, strings them, and establishes them as a means of consolation, to be used in the Condolence ceremonies (William Fenton, *Parker on the Iroquois*, 116–7). In *Money of the American Indians*, Taxay gives a brief general survey of these accounts (110–8). For the scientific version of origins, see Lynn Ceci, "Tracing Wampum's Origins."

13. For instance, E. A. J. Johnson in *American Economic Thought* manages to ignore the role of Indians and wampum almost entirely.

14. *Records of the Virginia Company, of London*, vol. 3, August 12, 1621, (U.S. Government Printing Office, 1933). I am indebted to Rebecca Bach for pointing out this passage to me.

15. J. Franklin Jameson, *Narratives of New Netherlands*, 86, and quoted in George R. Price, "Wampumpeag"; Harmen Meyndertsz van den Bogart, "A Journey into Mohawk and Oneida Country," 3, 9.

16. Richard LeBaron Bowen, *Rhode Island Colonial Money*, 2, 4.

17. Morton, *New English Canaan*, 41.

18. John Josselyn, *John Josselyn, Colonial Traveller*, 142–3.

19. Thomas Shepard, *The Day-breaking*, 19.

20. Kathleen Bragdon, *Native People of Southern New England*, 97; Daniel Gookin, *Historical Collections*, 152.

21. Patricia E. Rubertone, "Archaeology, Colonialism," 40, 41, 42.

22. Paul A. Robinson, Marc A. Kelley, and Patricia E. Rubertone, "Preliminary Biocultural Interpretations," 123. See also William A. Turnbaugh, "Community, Commodities," who argues that the Narragansett leaders successfully adapted community-oriented transactions in order to assert more personal control over the flow of wampum and other valuable goods in the new situation created by the European presence.

23. Deborah B. Gewertz and Frederick K. Errington, "Duelling Currencies," 163. On a world scale, the role of shell money in the form of cowrie shells is an interesting parallel to wampum, and there seem to have been moments in which the two independent currencies met. James W. Bradley points to the Dutch joint involvement in slaves and furs, for instance, in *The Evolution of the Onondaga Iroquois*, 179–80.

24. Richter, *The Ordeal of the Longhouse*, 28–29. See also Shepard Krech III, "The Early Fur Trade." Though dealing with a different area and the nineteenth century, Krech is similarly concerned with the ways in which trade beads play into pre-existent patterns of value and distribution, in this case, the familiarity with dentalia shells. This allows him to question the assumption that a demand for European goods necessarily entails dependency (as opposed to mutual dependence) and a loss of cultural autonomy.

25. Teunissen and Hinz point out that Williams's mention of breeches is a reference to the Geneva Bible's use of "breeches" (rather than the King James version's "apron") to describe the garment made by Adam and Eve from fig leaves after the Fall (Williams, *A Key*). They suggest that the reference emphasizes "the Adamic

condition of the Indian," but surely the implication is also that the Indian, like the European, is postlapsarian. This image is made more complex when we consider the associations of wampum with wealth and power in all their manifestations.

26. See Speck, "The Functions of Wampum," 63.

27. Quoted in W. H. Holmes, "Art in Shell of the Ancient Americans," 234.

28. Mary Rowlandson, *A Narrative of the Captivity, Sufferings and Removes of Mrs Mary Rowlandson*, reprinted in Alden T. Vaughan and Edward W. Clark, *Puritans Among the Indians*, 66.

29. Mitchell R. Breitwieser, *American Puritanism*, 158. Acknowledging the more comprehensive view of exchange that might be generated out of Marcel Mauss's tradition, Breitwieser makes the interesting suggestion that Rowlandson's extreme physical and psychological condition meant that she narrowed her view of Indian behavior to what was necessary for her to survive. She was "studying the captors, seeking at least pattern where reason is wanting," in "a kind of urgent assiduousness," and the many Indians who over the years have suffered individually and collectively the cultural and sometimes physical equivalent of her fate at white hands should be seen as similarly dislocated from their cultural patterns.

30. John Lawson, *A New Voyage to Carolina*, 203, 194.

31. Ibid., 225.

32. Snyderman, "The Functions of Wampum," 489.

33. Robert Beverley, *History and Present State of Virginia*, 233, 225, 227.

34. Father Joseph Lafitau, *Customs of the American Indians*, 310. A similar ambiguity over something that appears to have both public symbolic and currency value seems to be present in the reference to the Delaware chief who "would have Resigned his Crown before now, but as he had the keeping of the public treasure (that is to say, the Counsell Bagg) Consisting of Belts of Wampum, for which he buys Liquor" (quoted by Timothy J. Smith, "Wampum as Primitive Valuables," 244). See also Gabriel Sagard's description of the Indians as laying in "a kind of stock of wampum necklaces, glass beads, axes, knives, and in general all that they gain and obtain for the community," which he refers to as a "treasury" (*The Long Journey*, 266).

35. Baron Lahontan, *New Voyages to North-America*, 1:36. In the original French edition, the wording makes clear that "business" in its widest sense was meant: "On ne sauroit faire aucune affaire, ni entrer en negotiation avec les Sauvages" (*Nouveaux Voyages*, 1:48).

36. Richard White, *The Middle Ground*, 21–2.

37. Reuben G. Thwaites, *The Jesuit Relations and Allied Documents*, 41:165. Subsequent references to this collection are incorporated into the text, using the abbreviation *JR* and the page number.

38. For a detailed account of this occasion, with extensive discussion, see Francis Jennings, M. A. Drake, and D. R. Miller, *The History and Culture of Iroquois Diplomacy*.

39. Fenton, *Parker on the Iroquois*, 20.

40. Speck, "The Functions of Wampum," 60; Louis Hennepin, *A New Discovery of a Vast Country*, 1:56, 2:137; Cornelius Jaenen, "The Role of Presents," 237.

41. Lafitau, *Customs of the American Indians*, 311.

42. Richter, The Ordeal of the Longhouse, 47; George Snyderman, "Functions of Wampum," 493.

43. Holmes, "Art in Shell of the Ancient Americas," 235; Weeden, *Indian Money*, 33, 20.

44. Ibid., 6, 15.

45. Ibid., 10; Bragdon, 112; Natalie Zemon Davis, *Women on the Margins*. Rowlandson also mentions that it was the woman's task to make "girdles of wampum" (Vaughan and Clark, *Puritans Among the Indians*, 61). Writing in 1924, Edwin Stanley Welles describes the making of wampum as needing "patience nurtured in drudgery" as well as deftness and skill, so that "it may not be presumptuous to conjecture that much of the work in making it, was performed by the toiling Indian women." He also cites evidence that it was made by white women in New Jersey as late as the 1840s, to sell to the Indian traders for use in the West (*Some Notes on Wampum*, 10, 24).

46. Weeden, *Indian Money*, 13.

47. Ibid., 40.

48. Welles, *Some Notes on Wampum*, 26.

49. See Ian Hodder, "Toward a Contextual Approach to Prehistoric Exchange," 199–211, for a brief outline of the positions and their implications for precontact exchange.

50. Snyderman, "Functions of Wampum," 470.

51. Bradley, *The Evolution of the Onondaga Iroquois*, 222–3, 107, 180.

52. Michael K. Foster, "Another Look at the Function of Wampum," 110; Sir William Johnson quoted in N. Jaye Fredrickson, *The Covenant Chain*, 15.

53. Francis Jennings, "The Constitutional Evolution," 94, 96.

Chapter 6

1. The seal of the Governor and Company of Massachusetts Bay shows an Indian, with the English words "Come over and help us" coming out of his mouth. This early example of the ventriloquism that was to become a crucial part of the ideological justification for settlement and missionary activity adapts a statement referring in context specifically to religious need, to make the Indian more comprehensively needy and desirous of the English presence.

2. Hakluyt, *The Original Writings and Correspondence*, 216.

3. Ibid., 332.

4. Robert Johnson, *Nova Britannia: Offering Most Excellent Fruites by Planting in Virginia*, 1:13, 12 (this is the pagination of the document only, as the volume is not paginated).

5. Alexander Whitaker, *Good Newes From Virginia*, D2, 9, 11, 21, 24.

6. Ibid., 32.

7. John Eliot quoted in Edward Winslow, *Glorious Progress of the Gospel*, Appendix, 27.

8. Herbert's concern may have been more a rhetorical critique of spiritual pov-

erty in England and the threats from France ("When Sein shall swallow Tiber, and the Thames/By letting in them both pollutes her streams") than any real sense of Indian benefit, but this did not stop Daniel Gookin from quoting this passage in *Historical Collections of the Indians*, 1:160.

9. Cotton Mather, *Another Tongue brought in*, 3. The pamphlet is often catalogued under "anonymous," and according to Ives Goddard, "probably derives from materials prepared by Bernardus Freeman" ("The Description of the Native Languages," 23–4).

10. See also Thomas Shepard, who, in his prefatory epistle to the "Christian Reader," encourages English sponsors and merchants to "take *incouragement* from hence to *scatter* the beames of light, to *spread* and propagate the *Gospel* into those dark *corners* of the earth; whither you *traffick* you take *much* from them, if you can *carry* this to them, you will make them an *abundant* recompence" (*The Clear Sunshine of the Gospel*, C).

11. Samuel de Champlain, *Works*, 6:137.

12. Reuben G. Thwaites, *The Jesuit Relations and Allied Documents*, 23:113–5 (subsequent references to this collection are incorporated into the text using the abbreviation *JR* and the page number). See James P. Ronda, "The European Indian," 388.

13. Francis Jennings provides the most skeptical reading of Puritan activities and in particular the disparities between the Puritans' rhetoric of righteousness and benevolence and their self-interested policies and actions. He disputes, for instance, Eliot's early missionary claims, pointing out that Eliot tries to take credit for Mayhew's successes at Martha's Vineyard. See *The Invasion of America*, esp. 22–253.

14. Cotton Mather, *Magnalia Christi Americana*, 1:506. Mather's comments on Eliot come mostly in the form of an extended commentary on a letter from his father, Increase Mather, to Holland on the subject of Eliot's ministry, reflecting his view of Eliot's central importance in the ideological justification of Puritan policies. See Constance Post, "Old World Order in the New."

15. Thomas Shepard, *The Day-breaking*, 19, 35.

16. John Eliot, *The Indian Grammar Begun*, title page; Mather, *Magnalia Christi Americana*, 1:511.

17. Henry Whitfield, *The Light appearing*, 23.

18. In contrast, see Paul de Man, writing about Walter Benjamin's essay on translation: "The translation is the fragment of a fragment, is breaking the fragment—so the vessel keeps breaking, constantly—and never reconstitutes it; there was no vessel in the first place" (de Man, *The Resistance to Theory*, 91).

19. Hakluyt, *The Original Writings and Correspondence*, 215.

20. Vicente L. Rafael, *Contracting Colonialism*, 34, 38, 21.

21. John Eliot, *The Logick Primer*, 21.

22. There seems to be a symbolic importance to the creation of the Massachusett Bible, which is brought out incidentally in Daniel Gookin's letter to Prince Charles, where he combines the printing of the Bible and the establishment of an Indian college at Cambridge, "a house of brick" and "a structure strong and

substantial," respectively, suggesting the role of the Bible as institutional foundation. According to Gookin's account, the cost of printing the Bible was six times
the cost of the next largest item, which was keeping two boys at college for a year,
on the list of accounts sent to the Commissioners in London (*Historical Collections
of the Indians*, 176, 218).

23. William Simmons, *Spirit of the New England Tribes*, 42. In a rather later
instance, Joseph Fish, the missionary to the Narragansetts, recounts the vision of
the Narragansett Indian Tobe Cowyass, who

> said he had, Sometime ago, been home, (meaning, to Heaven). Had Seen
> the Great God and that he was a great Gentleman. Had seen Jesus Christ.
> A handsome Man. Seen also a Multitude of Folks in Heaven, Resembling
> Butterflies of Many Colours, etc. Strange, Gross Horrible Ideas and no-
> tions of the heavenly World! I corrected them as far As I then Could. (W.
> Simmons, and C. L. Simmons, *Old Light On Separate Ways*, 93)

24. Whitfield, *The Light appearing*, 36.

25. Shepard, *The Day-breaking*, 3, 26; Mather, *Magnalia Christi Americana*,
1:511.

26. Shepard, *The Clear Sunshine of the Gospel*, 20, 11.

27. Shepard, *The Day-breaking*, 21.

28. Mather, *Another Tongue*, 5–6.

29. Idem, *Magnalia Christi Americana*, 2:546.

30. In the 1760s, John Heckewelder collected a story from Delawares and
Mahicans that combines the topos of the initial encounter with the Dutch with the
suspicion of a poisoned cup—which turns out to contain alcohol. See Colin G.
Calloway, *The World Turned Upside Down*, 35–38.

31. Mather, *Magnalia Christi Americana*, 2:523.

32. See also *JR* 3:105–9, where Indian suspicions are mentioned, only to be
denied. Stephen Greenblatt discusses this pattern of misunderstandings and mis-
representations in relation to Thomas Harriot's report that the Indians suspected
that disease was being transmitted by "invisible bullets" (*Shakespearian Negotiations*, 21–65).

33. Edward Winslow in Alexander Young, *Chronicles of the Pilgrim Fathers*, 292;
Mather, *Magnalia Christi Americana*, 2:53, 72. See Thomas Morton, *New English
Canaan*, 104–5, for a slightly different version. Eric Cheyfitz, reporting the intim-
idating show of power in the English use of guns in another encounter, takes up
the same metaphor, describing it as an "English oration, in which the gun is a
prime piece of eloquence, pronounced to persuade the Indians and the English
themselves, no doubt, of English power. In this context, the momentary force of
Captain John Smith is as much a matter of oratorical, or dramaturgical skills, as it
is of military strategy" (*Poetics of Imperialism*, 65).

34. Mather, *Magnalia Christi Americana*, 1:72.

35. Ibid., 1:514. For an account that places this incident in the wider context
of the campaign for literacy and conversion, see Jill Lepore, "Dead Men Tell No
Tales."

36. Roger Williams, *The Bloody Tenent Yet More Bloody*, 218.

37. Ibid., 219, 220. The incident is described by Shepard, who does make a great deal of the old man's gratitude, expressed in his remark, "God, I see is mercifull," and in his ability to "see not only God in his Cloths, but mercy also in a promise of a cast off worne sute of Cloths" (*The Clear Sunshine of the Gospel*, 18).

38. Gookin, *Historical Collections of the Indians*, 210.

39. Roger Williams, *The Complete Writings*, 7:37.

40. Roger Williams, *A Key into the Language of America*, 88.

41. John Wesley quoted in Joseph A. Conforti, *Jonathan Edwards*, 69.

42. These, in one volume, were usually referred to confusingly as "Brainerd's Journal." Edwards omitted some of the diary material that had already appeared, so the two volumes are largely complementary. Later editors sometimes combine both sets of material but then edit out material fairly cavalierly, so that there is no one complete and reliable version of Brainerd's own writings. Norman Pettit's edition of Edwards's *Life of David Brainerd* gives a useful summary of the textual history, as well as new material on Edwards's revisions of Brainerd, but his emphasis is inevitably on Brainerd as a model of Edwards's ideas rather than on Brainerd's own experiences as missionary. Future references to *The Life* are to this volume, and page numbers are incorporated into the text. References to the journal are to the version included in Jonathan Edwards, *The Life of the Rev. David Brainard, Missionary to the Indians* (London 1818) as *The Rise and Progress of a Remarkable Work of Grace*. If material appears in both *The Life* and the journal, references are given for *The Life*, as the more generally accessible text.

43. Brainerd, *Rise and Progress*, 299. For the limitations of Edwards's own missionary experience, see P. Frazier, *The Mohicans of Stockbridge*, 90–94. He never learned an Indian language and reportedly spent thirteen hours a day in his study. His son, Jonathan Edwards Jr., growing up among Indians, spoke Mohegan well and wrote one of the most interesting early accounts of the language.

44. Dwight, *Memoirs*, v; Frazier, *The Mohicans of Stockbridge*, 58; R. E. Day, *Flagellant on Horseback*; D. L. Weddle, "The Melancholy Saint."

45. Ebenezer Pemberton in Brainerd, *Rise and Progress*, 478, 479.

46. Ibid., 398.

47. Ibid., 453, 335.

48. Ibid., 417.

49. Georges Bataille, *The Accursed Share*, 2/3:438.

50. James Holstun, "John Eliot's Empirical Millenarianism," 137. A parallel interpretation of the Catholic confessional, using Foucault, is to be found in Rafael, who sees a need for the narrative of sin,

> without which there can be no possibility of asserting and reasserting the economy of divine mercy . . . Confession was crucial because it produced a divided subject who was then made to internalize the Law's language. The penitent became "the speaking subject who is also the subject of the sentence." (*Contracting Colonialism*, 103)

51. Mather, *Magnalia Christi Americana*, 1:510.

52. Richard Pointer, in one of the few accounts of Brainerd to go beyond his relation to Edwards, argues for a greater influence of his Indian encounters on Brainerd than I do here, including the role of Moses Tatamy. "'Poor Indians' and the 'Poor in Spirit,'" 418ff.

53. Brainerd, *Rise and Progress*, 457.

54. Ibid., 446, 447.

55. Ibid., 460.

56. Ibid., 362.

57. See, for instance, J. P. Reid, *A Better Kind of Hatchet*, 46, for examples of the attempt to ensure that an Indian's relatives agreed and accepted a transaction, because the debt would be binding on them, too.

58. Brainerd, *Rise and Progress*, 456.

59. Ibid., 425.

60. Jean Baudrillard, *Symbolic Exchange and Death*, 145.

61. Bataille, *The Accursed Share*, 1:122–3.

62. Lewis Hyde, *The Gift*, 127.

Chapter 7

1. Daniel Defert, "The Collection of the World," 15.

2. The process was often described as "reducing" the Indians to Christianity, which has some misleading modern connotations but meant in English 'turning towards'. It also, of course, echoes the Spanish policy of *reduccion* in Paraguay and elsewhere. Vicente Rafael glosses the Spanish *reducir* as "to reduce a thing to its former state, to convert, to contract, to divide into small parts, to contain, to comprehend, to bring back into obedience ... Bodies were to be 'reduced' to centralized localities subject to the letter of the law, just as Tagalog was to be 'reduced' to the grammatical terms of Latin" (*Contracting Colonialism*, 90).

3. My approach here follows the distinctions Jacques Derrida made in his influential discussion of Georges Bataille, "From Restricted to General Economy."

4. For a useful survey of missionary activity, see Henry Warner Bowden, *American Indians and Christian Missions*. For a useful reminder of the limitations of Anglophone scholarship on the Jesuits, see Luca Codignola, "The Battle is Over," and for Protestant activity in the Northeast, see R. Pierce Beaver, "Protestant Chuches and the Indians."

5. For Jesuit policy, see George R. Healy, "The French Jesuits and the Idea of the Noble Savage." For a summary of Recollet policy, see Bruce G. Trigger, *The Children of Aataentsic*, 376–81. The North American ventures were influenced by accounts of successes in Paraguay. For a summary in English of recent approaches to Latin American missions, see Erick Langer and Robert H. Jackson, *The New Latin American Mission History*, esp. 1–45.

6. See Kenneth Morrison, "'That Art of Coyning Christians.'"

7. See A. Heimert and P. Miller, *The Great Awakening*.

8. Kathleen Bragdon, "Gender as a Social Category," 585.

9. Richard Eden, *The Decades of the New World*, 57.

10. John Eliot, "The Learned Conjectures," 27.

11. Le Jeune quoted in James P. Ronda, "The European Indian," 388.

12. Thomas Morton, *New English Canaan*, 27, 49; Roger Williams, *A Key into the Language of America*, (references are to this edition unless otherwise indicated, and page numbers are given in text.)

13. Edward Winslow, in Alexander Young, *Chronicles of the Pilgrim Fathers*, 356, 359. The same opposition may be found in many early accounts. See Edward Johnson, *Wonderworking Providence;* William Strachey, *The Historie of Travaile*, 82–83; and John Josselyn, *John Josselyn, Colonial Traveller*, 95.

14. Cf. Kathleen Bragdon: "The partial similarities between Native beliefs in Cautantouwit and Abbomocho and the Christian belief in God and the Devil were only that; the opposition of good and evil expressed in the Christian concept had no exact equivalent in the beliefs of the Ninnimissinuock. Cautantouwit's distant benignity was less significant than the more local and powerful, if more ambivalent forces of good and evil embodied in Abbomocho" (*Native People of Southern New England*, 190). On this point, and for a good general account of the different presuppositions, see Charles L. Cohen, "Conversion Among Puritans and Amerindians," 239. Louise M. Burkhart also argues that the tendency to think in moral absolutes, especially of good and evil, meant that missionaries had to falsely align native categories. "Indigenous forms of thought could be right or wrong, good or bad, but they could not be simply different" (*The Slippery Earth*, 27).

15. Strachey, *Historie of Travaile*, 82, 83.

16. Francis Higginson, *New England's Plantation* C4; Josselyn, *John Josselyn*, 95; William Simmons, *Spirit of the New England Tribes*, 118.

17. Neal Salisbury, *Manitou and Providence*, 136; Roger Williams, *The Correspondence*, 146.

18. Thomas Shepard quoted in Alfred A. Cave, "Indian Shamans and English Witches," 251.

19. Cave, "Indian Shamans and English Witches," 252. The Puritan mindset seems also to have blinded them to the true status of two of their most important intermediaries, who were clearly shamans and whose names seemed to indicate this, one of them even being called Hobomok. See Frank Shuffleton, "Indian Devils and Pilgrim Fathers." Chretien Le Clercq, *New Relations of Gaspesia*, 216.

20. Robert Conkling, "Legitimacy and Conversion in Social Change"; see also Kenneth M. Morrison, "Towards A History of Intimate Encounters."

21. Stanley J. Tambiah, *Magic, Science, Religion*, 17; Trigger, *The Children of Aataentsic*, 503; Conkling, "Legitimacy and Conversion in Social Change," 13.

22. John Steckley, "The Warrior and the Lineage."

23. Kenneth Morrison, "Baptism and Alliance," 420.

24. Trigger, *The Children of Aataentsic*, 503.

25. Reuben G. Thwaites, *The Jesuit Relations and Allied Documents*, 3:145. Subsequent references to this collection are incorporated into the text using the abbreviation JR and the page number.

26. Cf. Vicente L. Rafael's punning title, *Contracting Colonialism*. He sees the Tagalogs restricting the influx of Christian ideas by a process of (mis)translation

and by converting the particular Christian ideas of gift and reciprocity into their own. "The Tagalog's interest in contracting Christianity and colonialism stemmed from their fear of being overcome by *hiya*, that is, of being barraged by gifts and signs that they might not be able to read and would be unable to control" (127). Contracting, then, is like the missionaries' reduction, a process of control and conversion. There is also, though, the idea of contracting an illness, virus, or parasite, which does not play by the rules, or the contract, and cannot be controlled. Serge Gruzinski, in a fascinating and detailed account of the interaction of native and Catholic religions in Mexico, quotes an early reference to the use of idols as "the barter of passions" (*The Conquest of Mexico*, 168).

27. Morrison, "Baptism and Alliance," 418.

28. Ibid., 432.

29. Michael M. Pomedi, *Ethnophilosophical and Ethnolinguistic Perspectives*, 52–53.

30. See John Steckley, "Brebeuf's Presentation of Catholicism," for a detailed examination of the ways Brebeuf used or avoided the forms of the verb *aki*. For a useful more general account, see Peter A. Dorsey, "Going to School with Savages."

31. Cf. Thomas Harriot, who lists the many technological wonders that were "so straunge unto them that, and so farre exceeded their capacities to comprehend the reason and meanes how they should be made and done, that they thought they were rather the works of gods then of men, or at the leastwise that they had bin given and taught us of the gods" (*A Briefe and True Report*, 27).

32. Marcel Mauss, *A General Theory of Magic*, 114–5.

33. Claude Levi-Strauss, *Introduction to the Works of Marcel Mauss*, 47, 63, 64, 58.

34. Neal Salisbury, "Religious Encounters in a Colonial Context," 502. Here and in later chapters I also draw on Salisbury's larger earlier study, *Manitou and Providence*. See Constance Crosby, "From Myth to History," 183–209, for a discussion of the meaning of *manitou* or *manit*.

35. Nicholas Thomas, "The Cultural Dynamics of Peripheral Exchange," 27. For a fuller discussion of these issues in a Polynesian context, see his *Entangled Objects*.

36. See Peter Wogan, "Perceptions of European Literacy," 407–27, for a useful and skeptical survey of this theme.

37. See Conkling, "Legitimacy and Conversion in Social Change," 13, for further instances, and Margaret J. Leahey, "Iconic Discourse: Aspects of French/Native Language Encounter," which discusses the circulation of visual images as part of "the Jesuit arsenal of wonderworks" (3), including magnets, clocks, pictures, books, and emblems.

38. Le Clercq, *New Relations of Gaspesia*, 229, 231.

39. Ibid., 232–3. Le Clercq devotes a chapter of his book (143–58) to a description and discussion of the origins of the widespread use of the cross among this particular group. He sees it as explicitly pre-Christian but auguring, like a rainbow, God's ultimate design for the Indians. How far this would now be explained by assuming earlier Christian influences and syncretistic responses to them is beyond my scope here, but it certainly means that in this particular instance Le Clercq and, presumably, the woman he is describing see the cross as more, and other than, a Christian symbol.

40. Natalie Zemon Davis argues in her account of Marie de L'Incarnation that women described by Marie, who continued to bury grave goods of beaver and wampum, "sustained and required a religious sensibility much more hybrid than she knew or allowed" (*Women on the Margins*, 127). Marie would have shared with them an acceptance of the importance of women speaking on sacred things, argues Davis, who suggests that there was a role for women as soothsayers and seers, as opposed to the political and public rhetoric of the men's world of oratory. She also points out that women strung the wampum belts that accompanied male diplomacy and rhetoric.

41. Le Clercq, *New Relations of Gaspesia*, 233.

42. Reproduced in N. Jaye Fredrickson, *The Covenant Chain*, 33.

43. Bruce M. White, "Encounters with Spirits," 395. See also the highly influential series of articles by George R. Hamell on pre-existing categories of the sacred and valuable, particularly Christopher L. Miller and George R. Hamell, "A New Perspective on Indian-White Contact" and George R. Hamell, "Trading in Metaphors" and "The Iroquois and the World's Rim."

44. Louis Hennepin, *A New Discovery*, 210, 124.

45. Ibid., 198.

46. See James Clifford, "On Ethnographic Surrealism," in his *The Predicament of Culture*, and A. David Napier, *Foreign Bodies*.

47. Trigger, *Children of Aataentsic*, 67. Salisbury points out that traders were not harmed at all ("Religious Encounters," 504).

48. Harold Hickerson, "The Feast of the Dead."

49. Nicolas Denys, *The Description and Natural History*, 439.

50. Hennepin, *A New Discovery*, 213; Laurier Turgeon, "The Tale of the Kettle," 21, my emphasis. See also Calvin Martin, "The Four Lives of a Micmac Copper Pot."

51. Elisabeth Tooker, *An Ethnography of the Huron Indians*, 139. See also *JR* 39:29–33.

52. In a useful overview of scholars' interpretations of the increased use of trade goods in burials, and the complex mix of resistance and adaptation of economic and aesthetic values, Bragdon also raises the possibility of "sacrifices" of wealth to promote renewal. She notes that "the distribution of the cemeteries is closely associated with the centers of wampum manufacture and trade, arguing for a link between chiefly lineages and the control of wealth" (*Native People of Southern New England*, 242). The problems involved in interpreting grave goods as necessarily the ideological representation of existing social relations is concisely discussed in the context of southern New England by Elise M. Brenner, "Sociopolitical Implications of Mortuary Ritual Remains," 147–81.

53. Hugh Amory, "The Trout and the Milk: An Ethnobibliographical Talk," 63. My thanks to Norman Fiering for pointing out this reference. See also an intriguing reference to a "curiosity" from the Pottawatomie tribe that had been exhibited, consisting of "four small rolls or strips of parchment, closely packed in the small compartments of a little box, or locket, of about an inch cubical content. On these parchments are written in a style of assured elegance, and far more beautiful

than print, portions of the Pentateuch, to be worn as frontlets, and intended as stimulants of the memory and moral sense" (Electa F. Jones, *Stockbridge, Past and Present*, 270–1). This had been kept out of Europeans' sight in a medicine bag and was claimed to date back many centuries. I am indebted to Hilary Wyss for pointing out this reference and generously sharing with me her research on Christian Indians.

54. Stephen H. Long, *Narrative of an Expedition*, 74.

55. The issue of gender in relation to religious conversion is one I have not attended to at all here. For a useful survey of recent debates and studies, see Pauline Turner Strong, "Feminist Theory and the 'Invasion of the Heart.'"

56. Long, *Narrative of an Expedition*, 75.

57. Herman Melville, *Billy Budd, Sailor*, 121. I am indebted to Colin Harrison for drawing my attention to the implications of this passage and sharing many perceptive insights into the dynamics of gift-giving and exchange arising out of his work on Melville.

Bibliography

Albanese, Denise. *New Science, New World.* Durham, N. C., 1996.

Albinus, Peter. *A Treatise on Foreign Languages and Unknown Islands.* Translated by Edmund Goldsmid. Edinburgh, 1884.

Allen, David G., and Robert A. White. *The Work of Dissimilitude: Essays from the Sixth Citadel Conference on Medieval and Renaissance Literature.* Newark, N.J., 1992.

Amory, Hugh. "The Trout and the Milk: An Ethnobibliographical Talk." *Harvard Library Bulletin* 7, no. 1 (1996): 50–65.

Appadurai, Arjun, ed. *The Social Life of Things: Commodities in Cultural Perspective.* Cambridge, 1986.

Apter, Emily, and William Pietz, eds. *Fetishism as Cultural Discourse.* Ithaca, N.Y., 1993.

Arber, Edward, ed. *The First Three English Books on America.* Birmingham, 1885.

Arber, E., and A. G. Bradley, eds. *Travels and Works of Captain John Smith.* Edinburgh, 1910.

Axtell, James. *The European and the Indian: Essays in the Ethnohistory of Colonial North America.* New York, 1981.

———. *The Invasion Within: The Contest of Cultures in Colonial North America.* New York, 1985.

———. *After Columbus: Essays in the Ethnohistory of Colonial North America.* New York, 1988.

Bailey, A. G. *The Conflict of European and Eastern Algonquian Cultures, 1504–1700.* Toronto, 1969.

Bailyn, Bernard. *The New England Merchants in the Seventeenth Century.* Cambridge, Mass., 1955.

Barbour, Philip L., ed. *The Jamestown Voyages under the First Charter, 1606–1609.* 2 vols. Cambridge, 1969.

———. "The Earliest Reconnaisance of the Chesapeake Bay Area: Captain John

Smith's Map and Indian Vocabulary (Part 2)." *Virginia Magazine of History and Biography* 80 (1972): 21–51.

Bataille, Georges. *Visions of Excess: Selected Writings, 1927–1939.* Translated by A. Stoekl. Minneapolis, Minn., 1985.

———. *The Accursed Share.* 3 vols. Translated by R. Hurley. New York, 1991 and 1993.

Baudrillard, Jean. *Symbolic Exchange and Death.* Translated by Iain H. Grant. London, 1993.

———. *For a Critique of the Political Economy of the Sign.* Translated by Charles Levin. St Louis, Mo., 1981.

Beauchamp, William M. "Wampum and Shell Articles Used By New York Indians." *Bulletin of the New York State Museum* 8 (1901): 321–477.

Beaver, R. Pierce. "Protestant Churches and the Indians." In *History of Indian-White Relations.* Edited by Wilcomb Washburn, Vol. 4 of *Handbook of North American Indians*, edited by William C. Sturtevant. Washington, D.C., 1988.

Bercovitch, Sacvan. "Typology in Puritan New England: The Williams-Cotton Controversy Reassessed." *American Quarterly* 19 (1967): 167–91.

———, ed. *Typology and Early American Literature.* Amherst, Mass., 1972.

Beverley, Robert. *The History and Present State of Virginia.* Edited by Louis B. Wright. 1705. Chapel Hill, N. C. 1947.

Biggar, H. P., ed. *The Voyages of Jacques Cartier.* Ottawa, Ontario, 1924.

Bird-David, Nurit. "Beyond 'The Original Affluent Society': A Culturalist Reformulation." *Current Anthropology* 33, no. 1 (1992): 25–47.

Black-Rogers, Mary. "Starving and Survival in the Subarctic Fur Trade: A Case for Contextual Semantics." In *Le Castor Fait Tout: Selected Papers of the Fifth North American Fur Trade Conference, 1985.* Edited by Bruce Trigger, Toby Morantz, and Louise Dechene. St. Louis, Mo., 1987.

Bodmer, Beatriz Pastor. *The Armature of Conquest: Spanish Accounts of the Discovery of America, 1492–1589.* Stanford, Calif., 1992.

Bourdieu, Pierre. *Outline of a Theory of Practice.* Cambridge, 1977.

Bowden, Henry Warner. *American Indians and Christian Missions: Studies in Cultural Conflict.* Chicago, 1981.

Bowen, Richard LeBaron. *Rhode Island Colonial Money and Its Counterfeiting.* Concord, N. H., 1942.

Bracken, Christopher. *The Potlatch Papers: A Colonial Case History.* Chicago, 1997.

Bradford, William. *Of Plymouth Plantation.* Edited by Samuel Eliot Morison. New York, 1952.

Bradley, James W. *The Evolution of the Onondaga Iroquois: Accommodating Change, 1500–1655.* Syracuse, N.Y., 1987.

Bragdon, Kathleen. *The Native People of Southern New England: 1500–1650.* Norman, Okla., 1996.

———. "Gender as a Social Category in Native Southern New England." *Ethnohistory* 43, no. 4 (1996): 573–92.

Brainerd, David. *The Rise and Progress of a Remarkable Work of Grace.* London, 1818.

Breitwieser, Mitchell R. *American Puritanism and the Defense of Mourning: Religion, Grief and Ethnology.* Madison, Wisc., 1990.

Brenner, Elise M. "Sociopolitical Implications of Mortuary Ritual Remains in 17th-century Native Southern New England." In *The Recovery of Meaning: Historical Archaeology in the Eastern United States.* Edited by Mark P. Leone and Parker B. Potter. Washington, D.C., 1988.

Brotherston, Gordon. "A Controversial Guide to The Language of America." In *1642: Literature and Power in the Seventeenth Century.* Edited by F. Barker et. al. Proceedings of the Essex Conference on the Sociology of Literature Colchester, Essex, 1981.

Brumm, Ursula. *American Thought and Religious Typology.* New Brunswick, N.J., 1970.

Bucher, Bernadette. *Icon and Conquest: A Structural Analysis of the Illustrations of De Bry's Great Voyages.* Chicago, 1981.

Burkhart, Louise M. *The Slippery Earth: Nahua-Christian Moral Dialogue in Sixteenth-Century Mexico.* Tucson, Ariz., 1989.

Calloway, Colin, ed. *New Directions in American Indian History.* Norman, Okla., 1988.

———. *The World Turned Upside Down: Indian Voices from Early America.* Boston, 1994.

Campbell, Maria. *Halfbreed.* Toronto, 1973.

Campbell, Mary B. "The Illustrated Travel Book and the Birth of Ethnography: Part 1 of De Bry's *America.*" In *The Work of Dissimilitude: Essays from the Sixth Citadel Conference on Medieval and Renaissance Literature.* Edited by David G. Allen and Robert A. White. Newark, N.J., 1992.

Canup, John. *Out of the Wilderness: The Emergence of an American Identity in Colonial New England.* Middletown, Conn., 1990.

Carrier, James. "Gifts, Commodities, and Social Relations: A Maussian View of Exchange." *Sociological Forum* 6, no. 1 (1991): 119–36.

———. "The Cultural Dynamics of Peripheral Exchange." In *Barter, Exchange and Value: An Anthropological Approach.* Edited by C. Humphrey and S. Hugh-Jones. Cambridge, 1992.

———. *Gifts and Commodities: Exchange and Western Capitalism since 1700.* London, 1994.

Cartier, Jacques. *A Shorte and Briefe Narration of the Two Navigations and Discoveries to the Northwest parts called Newe France,* London, 1580.

Cave, Alfred A. "Richard Hakluyt's Savages: The Influence of 16th-Century Travel Narratives on English Indian Policy in North America." *International Social Science Review* 60, no. 1 (1985): 3–24.

———. "Indian Shamans and English Witches in Seventeenth Century New England." *Essex Institute Historical Collections* 128 (1992): 239–54.

Ceci, Lynn. "The Effects of European Contact and Trade on the Settlement Patterns of Indians in Coastal New York, 1524–1664." Ph.D. diss., City University of New York, 1977.

———. "Tracing Wampum's Origins: Shell Bead Evidence from Archeological Sites in Western and Coastal New York." In *Proceedings of the 1986 Shell Bead Conference: Selected Papers.* Edited by Charles F. Hayes. Rochester Museum and Science Center, Research Records no. 20. Rochester, N.Y., 1989.

———. "Wampum as a Peripheral Resource." In *The Pequots in Southern New England.* Edited by L. Hauptman and J. D. Wherry. Norman, Okla., 1990.

Chapin, Howard Miller. *The Trading Post of Roger Williams, with Those of John Wilcox and Richard Smith.* Providence, R. I., 1933.

Cheyfitz, Eric. *The Poetics of Imperialism: Translation and Colonization from The Tempest to Tarzan.* Expanded edition. New York, 1997.

Clastres, Pierre. *Society Against the State: Essays in Political Anthropology.* New York, 1987.

———. *Archeology of Violence.* New York, 1994.

Clifford, James. *The Predicament of Culture: The Poetics and Politics of Ethnography.* Berkeley, Calif., 1988.

Clifford, James, and George Marcus, eds. *Writing Culture.* Berkeley, Calif., 1986.

Codignola, Luca. "The Battle Is Over: Campeau's *Monumenta* vs. Thwaite's *Jesuit Relations,* 1602–1650." *European Review of Native American Studies* 10, no. 2 (1996): 3–10.

Cogley, Richard W. "John Eliot and the Origins of the American Indians." *Early American Literature* 21, no. 3 (1986–7): 210–25.

Cohen, Charles L. "Conversion among Puritans and Amerindians: A Theological and Cultural Perspective." In *Puritanism: Transatlantic Perspectives on a Seventeenth-Century Anglo-American Faith.* Edited by Francis J Bremer. Boston, 1993.

Colon, Fernando. *The Life of the Admiral Christopher Columbus by his son Ferdinand.* Translated by Benjamin Keen. New Brunswick, N.J., 1992.

Columbus, Christopher. *The Diario of Christopher Columbus's First Voyage to America, 1492–3.* Translated by Oliver Dunn and James E. Kelley Jr. Norman, Okla., 1989.

Conforti, Joseph A. *Jonathan Edwards, Religious Tradition and American Culture.* Chapel Hill, N. C., 1995.

Conkling, Robert. "Legitimacy and Conversion in Social Change: The Case of French Missionaries and the Northeastern Algonkian." *Ethnohistory* 21, no. 1 (1974): 1–24.

Connor, Steven. *Theory and Cultural Value.* Oxford, 1992.

Cortes, Hernan. *Letters from Mexico.* London, 1972.

Crio, Stelio. "Classical Antiquity, America, and the Myth of the Noble Savage." In *The Classical Tradition and the Americas.* Edited by Wolfgang Haase and Meyer Reinhold. Vol. 1. New York, 1994.

Crosby, Constance. "From Myth to History, or Why King Philip's Ghost Walks Abroad." In *The Recovery of Meaning: Historical Archeology in the Eastern United States.* Edited by Mark P. Leone and Parker B. Potter. Washington, D.C., 1988.

Davis, Natalie Zemon. *Women on the Margins: Three Seventeenth-Century Lives.* Cambridge, Mass., 1995.

Davis, Thomas M. "The Traditions of Puritan Typology." In *Typology and Early American Literature.* Edited by Sacvan Bercovitch. Amherst, Mass, 1972.

Day, R. E. *Flagellant on Horseback: The Life Story of David Brainerd.* Philadelphia, 1950.

de Certeau, Michel. "Writing vs. Time: History and Anthropology in the Works of Lafitau." *Yale French Studies* 59 (1980): 37–64.

de Champlain, Samuel. *Works*. Edited by H. P. Biggar. Toronto, 1936.

Defert, Daniel. "The Collection of the World: Accounts of Voyages from the Sixteenth to the Eighteenth Centuries." *Dialectical Anthropology* 7, no. 1 (1982): 11–20.

Delage, Denys. *Bitter Feast: Amerindians and Europeans in Northeastern North America, 1600–64*. Translated by J. Brierley. Vancouver, British Columbia, 1993.

de Lery, Jean. *History of a Voyage to the Land of Brazil, Otherwise Called America*. Translated by Janet Whatley. 1578. Reprint, Berkeley, 1990.

de Man, Paul. *The Resistance to Theory*. Minneapolis, 1986.

Dennis, M. *Cultivating a Landscape of Peace: Iroquois-European Encounters in Seventeenth-Century America*. Ithaca, N.Y., 1993.

Denys, Nicolas. *The Description and Natural History of the Coasts of North America*. Edited by William F. Ganong. Toronto, 1908.

Derrida, Jacques. "From Restricted to General Economy; A Hegelianism without Reserve." In *Writing and Difference*. Translated by Alan Bass. Chicago, 1978.

———. "Economimesis." Translated by R. Klein. *Diacritics* 11, (1981): 3–25.

———. "White Mythology: Metaphor in the Text of Philosophy." In *Margins of Philosophy*. Translated by Alan Bass. New York, 1982.

———. "Plato's Pharmacy." In *Dissemination*. Translated by B. Johnson. Chicago, 1991.

———. *Given Time: 1: Counterfeit Money*. Translated by Peggy Kamuf. Chicago, 1992.

Dickason, Olive P. *The Myth of the Savage and the Beginnings of French Colonialism*. Edmonton, Alberta, 1984.

———. "Concepts of Sovereignty at the Time of First Contacts." In *The Law of Nations and the New World*. Edited by L. C. Green and Olive P. Dickason. Edmonton, Alberta, 1989.

Dorsey, Peter A. "Going to School with Savages: Authorship and Authority among the Jesuits of New France." *William and Mary Quarterly* 55, no. 3 (1998): 399–420.

Duran, Bonnie. "Indigenous Versus Colonial Discourse: Alcohol and American Indian Identity." In *Dressing in Feathers: The Construction of the Indian in American Popular Culture*. Edited by S. Elizabeth Bird. Boulder, Colo., 1996.

Dwight, Sereno E. *Memoirs of the Rev. David Brainerd, Missionary to the Indians*. New Haven, Conn., 1822.

Eden, Richard. *The Decades of the New World of West India*. 1555. Reprinted in *The First Three English Books on America*. Edited by Edward Arber. Birmingham, 1885.

Edwards, Jonathan. *The Life of David Brainard*. Vol. 7 of *Works of Jonathan Edwards*. Edited by Norman Pettit. New Haven, Conn., 1985.

Eliot, John. "The Learned Conjectures of Reverend Mr. John Eliot touching the Americans, of new and notable consideration, written to Mr. Thorowgood." In *Jewes in America*. Edited by Thomas Thorowgood. London, 1660.

———. *The Indian Grammar Begun: or An Essay to Bring the Indian Language into RULES, For the Help of Such as Desire to Learn the Same, for the Furtherance of the Gospel among them*. London, 1666.

———. *A Brief Narrative of the Progress of the Gospel among the Indians of New England in the year 1670.* Boston, 1868.

———. *The Logick Primer.* Cambridge, Mass., 1672.

Ercilla de Zúñiga, Alonso de. *La Araucana.* Madrid, 1590.

Etienne, M., and Leacock, E., eds. *Women and Colonization.* New York, 1980.

Fabian, Johannes. *Time and the Other: How Anthropology Makes Its Other.* New York, 1983.

Feest, Christan F. "Powhatan's Mantle." In *Tradescant's Rarities. Essays on the Foundation of the Ashmolean Museum, 1683, with a Catalogue of the Surviving Early Exhibition.* Edited by Arthur McGregor. Oxford, 1983.

———. "The Collecting of American Indian Artifacts in Europe, 1493–1750." In *America in European Consciousness, 1493–1750.* Edited by K. O. Kupperman. Chapel Hill, N. C., 1995.

Fenton, William, ed. *Parker on the Iroquois.* Syracuse, N.Y., 1968.

Fitzhugh, William M., ed. *Cultures in Contact: The Impact of European Contacts on Native American Cultural Institutions A. D. 1000–1800.* Washington, D.C., 1985.

Foster, Michael K. "Another Look at the Function of Wampum in Iroquois-White Councils." In *The History and Culture of Iroquois Diplomacy.* Edited by F. Jennings, M. A. Drake, and D. R. Miller. Syracuse, N.Y., 1983.

Frazier, P. *The Mohicans of Stockbridge.* Lincoln, Neb., 1992.

Fredrickson, N. Jaye. *The Covenant Chain: Indian Ceremonial Trade Silver.* Ottawa, Ontario, 1980.

Fuller, Mary C. "Raleigh's Fugitive Gold: Reference and Deferral in *The Discoverie of Guiana.*" *Representations* 33 (1991): 42–64.

———. *Voyages in Print: English Travel to America, 1576–1624.* Cambridge, 1995.

Garrett, John. *Roger Williams: Witness Beyond Christendom, 1603–1683.* London, 1970.

Gewertz, Deborah B., and Frederick K. Errington. "Duelling Currencies in East New Britain." In *Occidentalism: Images of the West.* Edited by James G. Carrier. Oxford, 1995.

Gleach, Frederick W. *Powhatan's World and Colonial Virginia: A Conflict of Cultures.* Lincoln, Neb., 1997.

Goddard, Ives. "The Description of the Native Languages of North America before Boas." In *Language.* Edited by Ives Goddard. Vol. 17 of *Handbook of North American Indians,* edited by William C. Sturtevant. Washington, D.C., 1996.

Goddard, Ives, and Kathleen J. Bragdon. *Native Writings in Massachusett.* Philadelphia, 1988.

Godelier, Maurice. *Perspectives in Marxist Anthropology.* Cambridge, 1977.

Gomez-Moriana, Antonio. "Narration and Argumentation in the Chronicles of the New World." In *1492–1992: Re/Discovering Colonial Writing.* Edited by R. Jara and N. Spadaccini. Minneapolis, Minn., 1989.

Gookin, Daniel. *Historical Collections of the Indians of New England.* Vol. 1 of *Collections of the Massachusetts Historical Society.* 1792. Reprint, Boston, 1806.

Goux, Jean-Joseph. *Symbolic Economies: After Marx and Freud.* Translated by Jennifer Curtiss Gage. Ithaca, N.Y., 1990.

Gregory, C. *Gifts and Commodities*. London, 1982.

Green, L. C., and Olive P. Dickason. *The Law of Nations and the New World*. Edmonton, Alberta, 1989.

Greenblatt, Stephen. *Shakespearian Negotiations: The Circulation of Social Energy in Renaissance England*. Oxford, 1988.

———, ed. *Representing the English Renaissance*. Berkeley, Calif., 1988.

———. *Marvelous Possessions: A Wonder of the New World*. Oxford, 1991.

Gruzinski, Serge. *The Conquest of Mexico: The Incorporation of Indian Societies into the Western World*. Cambridge, 1993.

Haase, Wolfgang, and Reinhold Meyer, eds. *The Classical Tradition and the Americas*. Vol. 1. New York, 1994.

Hakluyt, Richard. *The Principall Navigations Voiages Traffiques & Discoveries of the English Nation*. 12 vols. 1598–1600. Reprint, Glasgow, 1904.

———. *The Original Writings and Correspondence of the Two Richard Hakluyts*. London, 1935.

Hall, Thomas D. "Native American and Incorporation: Patterns and Problems." *American Indian Culture and Research Journal* 11, no. 2 (1987): 1–30.

Hamell, George R. "Strawberries, Floating Islands, and Rabbit Captains: Mythical Realities and European Contact in the Northeast during the Sixteenth and Seventeenth Centuries." *Journal of Canadian Studies* 21 (1986–7): 72–94.

———. "Trading in Metaphors: Another Perspective Upon Indian-European Contact in Northeastern North America." In *Proceedings of the 1982 Glass Trade Bead Conference*. Edited by Charles F. Hayes. Rochester Museum and Science Center, Research Records no. 16. Rochester, N.Y., 1983.

———. "The Iroquois and the World's Rim: Speculations on Color, Culture and Contact." *American Indian Quarterly* 15 (fall 1992): 451–69.

Hamlin, William M. "Attributions of Divinity in Renaissance Ethnography and Romance: Or Making Religion of Wonder." *Journal of Medieval and Renaissance Studies* 24, no. 3 (1994): 415–47.

Hanzeli, Victor Egon. *Missionary Linguistics in New France: A Study of Seventeenth and Eighteenth Century Descriptions of American Indian Languages*. The Hague, 1969.

Harriot, Thomas. *A Briefe and True Report of the New Found Land of Virginia*. 1588. Facsimile edition, New York, 1972.

Hauptman, Laurence, and James D. Wherry. *The Pequots in Southern New England: The Fall and Rise of an American Indian Nation*. Norman, Okla., 1990.

Hawthorne, Nathaniel. *Tales and Sketches*, New York, 1982.

Healy, George R. "The French Jesuits and the Idea of the Noble Savage." *William and Mary Quarterly* 15 (1958): 143–67.

Heimert, A., and P. Miller, eds. *The Great Awakening*. Indianapolis, Ind., 1967.

Henderson, James (Sakej) Youngblood. "Empowering Treaty Federalism." *Saskatchewan Law Review* 58 (1994): 241–329.

Hennepin, Louis. *A New Discovery of a vast country in America, extending above Four Thousand Miles, between New France and New Mexico*. 2 vols. London, 1698.

Hernandez-Reguant, Ariana. "The Columbus Quincentenary and the Politics of the 'Encounter'." *American Indian Culture and Research Journal* 17, 1 (1993): 17–35.

Hickerson, Harold. "The Feast of the Dead among the Seventeenth Century Algonkians of the Upper Great Lakes." *American Anthropologist* 62 (1960): 81–107.

Higginson, Francis. *New England's Plantation, or a Short and True Description of the Commodities and Discommodities of that Countrey.* London, 1630.

Hodder, Ian. "Toward a Contextual Approach to Prehistoric Exchange." In *Contexts for Prehistoric Exchange.* Edited by Jonathon E. Ericson and Timothy K. Earle. New York, 1982.

Hodgen, Margaret. *Early Anthropology in the Sixteenth and Seventeenth Centuries.* Philadelphia, 1964.

Holmes, W. H. "Art in Shell of the Ancient Americans." In *Second Annual Report of the Bureau of American Ethnology.* Washington, D.C., 1883.

Holstun, James. "John Eliot's Empirical Millenarianism." *Representations* 4 (fall 1983): 128–53.

Hulme, Peter. *Colonial Encounters: Europe and the Native Caribbean, 1492–1797.* New York, 1986.

———. "Making No Bones: A Response to Myra Jehlen." *Critical Inquiry* 20 (1993): 179–86.

Hulme, Peter, and Neil L. Whitehead, eds. *Wild Majesty: Encounters with the Caribs From Columbus to the Present Day: An Anthology.* Oxford, 1992.

Humphrey, Caroline, and Stephen Hugh-Jones, eds. *Barter, Exchange and Value: An Anthropological Approach.* Cambridge, 1992.

Hunt, Alan. *Governance of the Consuming Passions: A History of Sumptuary Laws.* New York, 1996.

Hutchinson, Thomas. *The History of the Colony of Massachusetts-Bay.* Boston, 1764.

Hyde, Lewis. *The Gift: Imagination and the Erotic Life of Property.* New York, 1979.

Jacobs, Wilbur R. *Wilderness Politics and Indian Gifts: The Northern Colonial Frontier, 1748–1763.* Lincoln, Neb., 1950.

Jaenen, Cornelius J. "French Sovereignty and Native Nationhood during the French Regime." In *Sweet Promises: A Reader on Indian-White Relations in Canada.* Edited by J. R. Miller. Toronto, 1991.

———. "The Role of Presents in French-Amerindian Trade." In *Explorations in Canadian Economic History. Essays in Honour of Irene M. Spry.* Edited by Duncan Cameron. Ottawa, Ontario, 1985.

Jameson, J. Franklin. *Narratives of New Netherlands, 1609–1664.* New York, 1909.

Jaquot, Jean. "Thomas Harriot's Reputation for Impiety." *Notes and Records of the Royal Society* 9 (1952): 164–87.

Jehlen, Myra. "History before the Fact; or, Captain John Smith's Unfinished Symphony." *Critical Inquiry* 19 (1993): 677–92.

Jennings, Francis. "The Constitutional Evolution of the Covenant Chain." *Proceedings of the American Philosophical Society* 115 (1971): 88–96.

———. *The Invasion of America: Indians, Colonialism and the Cant of Conquest.* New York, 1975.

Jennings, Francis, M. A. Drake, and D. R. Miller. *The History and Culture of Iroquois Diplomacy.* Syracuse, N.Y., 1983.

Johnson, Edward. *Wonderworking Providence.* Edited by J. Franklin Jameson. New York, 1967.

Johnson, E. A. J. *American Economic Thought in the Seventeenth Century.* London, 1932.

Johnson, Robert. *Nova Britannia: Offering Most Excellent Fruites by Planting in Virginia. Exciting All Such As Be Well Affected to Further the Same.* London, 1609. Reprinted in *Tracts and Other Papers.* Edited by Peter Force. Washington, D.C., 1831.

Jones, Electa F. *Stockbridge, Past and Present; Or, Records of an Old Mission Station.* Springfield, Mass., 1854.

Josselyn, John. *John Josselyn, Colonial Traveller: A Critical Edition of Two Voyages to New-England.* Edited by Paul J. Lindholdt. Hanover, N. H., 1988.

Keenan, Thomas. "The Point is to (Ex)Change It: Reading *Capital*, Rhetorically." In *Fetishism as Cultural Discourse.* Edited by Emily Apter and William Pietz. Ithaca, N.Y., 1993.

Kellaway, William. *The New England Company, 1649–1776: Missionary Society to the American Indians.* London, 1961.

Keller, Arthur S., Oliver J. Lissitzyn, and Frederick J. Mann. *Creation of Rights of Sovereignty through Symbolic Acts, 1400–1800.* New York, 1938.

Knapp, Jeffrey. *An Empire Nowhere: England, America, and Literature from Utopia to The Tempest.* Berkeley, Calif., 1992.

Kopytoff, Igor. "The Cultural Biography of Things: Commoditization as Process." In *The Social Life of Things: Commodities in Cultural Perspective.* Edited by A. Appadurai. Cambridge, 1986.

Krech, Shepard III. "The Early Fur Trade in the Northwestern Subarctic: The Kutchin and the Trade in Beads." In *Le Castor Fait Tout: Selected Papers of the Fifth North American Fur Trade Conference, 1985.* Edited by Bruce Trigger, Toby Morantz, and Louise Dechene. St. Louis, Mo., 1987.

Kuper, Adam. *The Invention of Primitive Society: Transformations of an Illusion.* New York, 1988.

Kupperman, Karen O., ed. *America in European Consciousness, 1493–1750.* Chapel Hill, N. C., 1995.

———. "Presentment of Civility: English Reading of American Self-Presentation in the Early Years of Colonization." *William and Mary Quarterly* 54 (1997): 199–228.

Lafitau, Father Joseph Francois. *Customs of the American Indians Compared with the Customs of Primitive Times.* 1724. Reprint, Toronto, 1974.

Lahontan, Baron. *Nouveaux Voyages de Mr Baron de Lahontan dans L'Amerique Septentrionale. . . .* The Hague, 1703.

———. *New Voyages to North America.* 2 vols. London, 1735.

Langer, Erick, and Robert H. Jackson, eds. *The New Latin American Mission History.* Lincoln, Neb., 1995.

Lawson, John. *A New Voyage to Carolina.* Edited by Hugh Talmage Lefler. 1709. Reprint, Chapel Hill, N.C., 1967.

Layton, Robert, ed. *Conflict in the Archaeology of Living Traditions.* London, 1994.

Leahey, Margaret J. "Iconic Discourse: Aspects of French/Native Language Encounter in New France." Paper presented at the "Communicating with the Indians" conference, John Carter Brown Library, Providence, R.I., August, 1996.

Le Clercq, Chretien. *New Relations of Gaspesia, with the Customs and Religion of the Gaspesian Indians.* Translated and edited by William F. Ganong. 1691. Reprint, Toronto, 1910.

Leone, Mark P., and Parker B. Potter, eds. *The Recovery of Meaning: Historical Archaeology in the Eastern United States.* Washington, D.C., 1988.

Lepore, Jill. "Dead Men Tell No Tales: John Sassamon and the Fatal Consequences of Literacy." *American Quarterly* 46, no. 4 (1994): 479–512.

Levi-Strauss, Claude. *Introduction to the Works of Marcel Mauss.* London, 1987.

Lindholdt, Paul J., ed. *John Josselyn, Colonial Traveller: A Critical Edition of Two Voyages to New England.* Hanover, N. H., 1988.

Long, John. *Voyages and Travels of an Indian Interpreter and Trader.* Edited by Reuben G. Thwaites. 1791. Reprint, Cleveland, Ohio, 1904.

Long, Stephen H. *Narrative of an Expedition to the Source of St. Peter's River.* Edited by W. H. Keating. Philadelphia, 1959.

Lyotard, Jean-Francois. *Libidinal Economy.* London, 1993.

MacAndrew, Craig, and Robert B. Edgerton. *Drunken Comportment: A Social Explanation.* Chicago, 1969.

MacGaffey, Wyatt. "Dialogues of the Deaf: Europeans on the Atlantic Coast of Africa." In *Implicit Understandings: Observing, Reporting, and Reflecting on the Encounters Between Europeans and Other Peoples in the Early Modern Era.* Edited by Stuart B. Schwarz. Cambridge, 1994.

Mackenthun, Gesa. *Metaphors of Dispossession: American Beginnings and the Translation of Empire, 1492–1637.* Norman, Okla., 1997.

Martien, Jerry. *Shell Game: A True Account of Beads and Money in North America.* San Francisco, 1996.

Martin, Calvin. *Keepers of the Game: Indian-Animal Relationships and the Fur Trade.* Berkeley, Calif., 1978.

———. "The Four Lives of a Micmac Copper Pot." *Ethnohistory* 22, no. 2 (1975): 111–33.

Marx, Karl. *Karl Marx: A Reader.* Edited by Jon Elster. Cambridge, 1986.

———. *Selected Writings in Sociology and Social Philosophy.* Edited by T. B. Bottomore and M. Rubel. Harmondsworth, 1961.

Mather, Cotton. *Magnalia Christi Americana; or the Ecclesiastical History of New England from the First Planting in the Year 1420, unto the Year of the Lord 1698.* 2 vols. 1702. Reprint, Hartford, Conn. 1820.

———. *Another Tongue brought in to Confess the Great SAVIOR of the World, or Some Communications of Christianity Put into a Tongue used among the Iroquois . . .* Boston, 1707.

Mauss, Marcel. *The Gift: Forms and Functions of Exchange in Archaic Societies.* London, 1969.

———. *A General Theory of Magic.* Boston, 1972.

McBride, Kevin A. "The Source and Mother of the Fur Trade: Native-Dutch Relations in Eastern New Netherland." In *Enduring Traditions: The Native Peoples of New England.* Edited by Laurie Weinstein. Westport, Conn., 1994.

McGregor, Arthur, ed. *Tradescant's Rarities: Essays on the Foundation of the Ashmolean Museum, 1683, with a Catalogue of the Surviving Early Exhibition.* Oxford, 1983.

Melville, Herman. *Billy Budd, Sailor: An Inside Narrative.* Edited by Harrison Hayford and Merton M. Sealts. Chicago, 1962.

Miller, Christopher, and George R. Hamell. "A New Perspective on Indian-White Contact: Cultural Symbols and Colonial Trade." *Journal of American History* 73 (1986): 311–28.

Moloney, Francis X. *The Fur Trade in New England, 1620–1676.* Cambridge, Mass., 1931.

Montaigne, Michel de. *The Essays of Montaigne.* 2 vols. London, 1935.

Montrose, Louis. "The Work of Gender in the Discourse of Discovery." *Representations* 33 (1991): 1–41.

Morrison, Kenneth M. "'That Art of Coyning Christians': John Eliot and the Praying Indians of Massachusetts." *Ethnohistory* 21 (1974): 77–92.

———. "Montagnais Missionization in Early New France." *American Indian Culture and Research Journal* 10, no. 3 (1986): 1–23.

———. "Towards A History of Intimate Encounters: Algonkian Folklore, Jesuit Missionaries, and Kiwakwe, the Cannibal Giant." *American Indian Culture and Research Journal* 3, no. 4 (1979): 51–80.

———. "Baptism and Alliance: Symbolic Mediations of Religious Syncretism." *Ethnohistory* 37, no. 4 (1990): 416–37.

Morton, Thomas. *New English Canaan.* 1637. Reprint, New York, 1969.

Mullaney, Steven. "Strange Things, Gross Terms, Curious Customs: The Rehearsal of Cultures in the Late Renaissance." In *Representing the English Renaissance.* Edited by Stephen Greenblatt. Berkeley, Calif., 1988.

Munster, Sebastian. *A treatise of the Newe India, with other Newfounde Landes and Ilandes.* Translated by Richard Eden. London, 1553.

Murray, David. *Forked Tongues: Speech Writing and Representation in North American Indian Texts.* Bloomington, Ind., 1992.

Myers, Kathleen A. "The Representation of New World Phenomena: Visual Epistemology and Gonzalo Fernandez de Oviedo's Ilustrations." In *Early Images of the Americas: Transfer and Invention.* Edited by Jerry M. Williams and Robert E. Lewis. Tucson, Ariz., 1993.

Napier, A. David. *Foreign Bodies: Performance, Art and Symbolic Anthropology.* Berkeley, Calif., 1990.

Nelson, Benjamin. *The Idea of Usury: From Tribal Brotherhood to Universal Otherhood.* Chicago, 1969.

Nordhaugen, Even, ed. "... *And the Word was God": Missionary Linguistics and Missionary Grammar.* Munster, 1996.

Olmedillas de Pereiras, Maria de las Nievas. *Pedro Martir de Angleria y La Mentalidad Exoticista.* Madrid, 1974.

Olmedo, Felix G. *Nebrija: Debelador de la Barbarie, Comentador Eclesiastico, Pedagogo-Poeta.* Madrid, 1942.

Parry, Jonathan. "*The Gift*, the Indian Gift and the 'Indian Gift.'" *Man* 21 (1986): 466–71.

Parry, J., and M. Bloch, eds. *Money and the Morality of Exchange.* Cambridge, 1989.

Pefanis, J. *Heterology and the Postmodern: Bataille, Baudrillard and Lyotard.* Durham, N. C., 1991.

Pietz, William. "The Problem of the Fetish." Parts 1–3. *Res* 9 (spring 1985): 5–17; 13 (spring 1987): 23–45; 16 (fall 1988): 105–23.

———. "Fetishism and Materialism: The Limits of Theory in Marx." In *Fetishism as Cultural Discourse.* Edited by Emily Apter and William Pietz. Ithaca, N.Y., 1993.

Pointer, R. W. "'Poor Indians' and the 'Poor in Spirit': The Indian Impact on David Brainerd." *New England Quarterly* 67, no. 3 (1994): 403–26.

Pomedi, Michael M. *Ethnophilosophical and Ethnolinguistic Perspectives on the Huron Indian Soul.* Lewiston, Me., 1991.

Post, Constance. "Old World Order in the New: John Eliot and 'Praying Indians' in Cotton Mather's *Magnalia Christi Americana.*" *New England Quarterly* (1993): 416–33.

Potter, Stephen R. "Early English Effects on Virginia Algonquin Exchange and Tribute in the Tidewater Potomac." In *Powhatan's Mantle: Indians in the Colonial Southeast.* Edited by Peter Wood, G. A. Vaselkov, and M. T. Hatley. Lincoln, Neb., 1989.

Price, George R. "Wampumpeag: The Impact of the 17th Century Wampum Trade on Native Culture in Southern New England and New Netherlands." Master's thesis, University of Montana, 1966.

Purchas, Samuel. *Hakluytus Posthumus, or Purchas his Pilgrimes: contayning a history of the world in sea voyages, and lande travels by Englishmen and others.* 20 vols. Glasgow, 1905–7.

Quinn, David Beers. *The Roanoke Voyages, 1584–90.* 2 vols. London, 1955.

———. *Set Fair for Roanoke: Voyages and Colonies, 1584–1606.* Chapel Hill, N. C., 1985.

Quint, David. "A Reconsideration of Montaigne's *Des Cannibales.*" In *America in European Consciousness, 1493–1750.* Edited by Karen O. Kupperman. Chapel Hill, N. C., 1995.

Quitt, Martin H. "Trade and Acculturation at Jamestown, 1607–1609: The Limits of Understanding." *William and Mary Quarterly* 52, no. 2 (1995): 227–58.

Rabasa, Jose. *Inventing America: Spanish Historiography and the Formation of Eurocentrism.* Norman, Okla., 1993.

Rafael, Vicente L. *Contracting Colonialism: Translation and Christian Conversion in Tagalog Society Under Early Spanish Rule.* Durham, N. C., 1993.

Raheja, G. G. *The Poison in the Gift: Ritual Prestation and the Dominant Caste in a North Indian Village*. Chicago, 1988.

Raleigh, Walter. *The Discoverie of the Large, Rich and Bewtiful Empire of Guiana*. Edited by Neil L. Whitehead. 1596. Reprint, Norman, Okla., 1997.

Ray, Arthur J., and Donald Freeman. *Give Us Good Measure: An Economic Analysis of Relations between the Indians and the Hudson's Bay Company before 1763*. Toronto, 1978.

Reid, J. P. *A Better Kind of Hatchet: Law, Trade and Diplomacy in the Cherokee Nation during the Early Years of European Contact*. Philadelphia, 1976.

Reinitz, Richard. "The Separatist Background of Roger Williams' Argument for Religious Toleration." In *Typology and Early American Literature*. Edited by Sacvan Bercovitch. Amherst, Mass., 1972.

Rich, E. E., ed. *James Isham's Observations and Notes, 1743–1749*. London, 1949.

Richards, David. *Masks of Difference: Cultural Representations in Literature, Anthropology and Art*. Cambridge, 1994.

Richter, Daniel K. *The Ordeal of the Longhouse: The Peoples of the Iroquois League in the Era of European Colonization*. Chapel Hill, N. C., 1992.

Robertson, Karen. "Pocahontas at the Masque." *Signs: Journal of Women in Culture and Society* 21, no. 3 (1996): 551–83.

Robinson, Paul A., Marc A. Kelley, and Patricia E. Rubertone. "Preliminary Biocultural Interpretations from a Seventeenth-Century Narragansett Indian Cemetery in Rhode Island." In *Cultures in Contact: The Impact of European Contacts on Native American Cultural Institutions A. D. 1000–1800*. Edited by William M. Fitzhugh. Washington, D.C., 1985.

Rochefort, Charles de. *Histoire Naturelle e Morale des Iles Antilles del'Amerique*. Rotterdam, 1658.

Ronda, James P. "The European Indian: Jesuit Civilization Planning in New France." *Church History* 41 (1972): 385–95.

———. "Generations of Faith: The Christian Indians of Martha's Vineyard." *William and Mary Quarterly* 38 (1991): 369–94.

Rosenmeier, Jesper. "The Teacher and the Witness: John Cotton and Roger Williams." *William and Mary Quarterly* 25 (1968): 408–31.

Rosenthal, Harvey D. "Indian Claims and the American Conscience: A Brief History of the Indian Claims Commission." In *Irredeemable America: The Indians' Estate and Land Claims*. Edited by Imre Sutton. Albuquerque, N.M., 1985.

Rosier, James. *A True Relation of the Most Prosperous Voyage Made This Present Yeere 1605, by Captaine George Weymouth, in the Discovery of the Land of Virginia*. London, 1605.

Rountree, Helen C. *Pocahontas's People: The Powhatan Indians of Virginia through Four Centuries*. Norman, Okla., and London, 1990.

Rubertone, Patricia E. "Archaeology, Colonialism and 17th-century Native America: Towards an Alternative Interpretation." In *Conflict in the Archaeology of Living Traditions*. Edited by Robert Layton. London, 1994.

Rukeyser, Muriel. *The Traces of Thomas Hariot*. London, 1972.

Sacher-Masoch, Leopold von. *Venus in Furs*. New York, 1965.

Sagard, Gabriel. *The Long Journey to the Country of the Hurons by Father Gabriel Sagard.* Edited by G. M. Wrong. 1632. Reprint, Toronto, 1939.

Sahlins, Marshall. *Stone Age Economics.* London, 1974.

Salisbury, Neal. *Manitou and Providence: Indians, Europeans and the Making of New England, 1500–1643.* New York, 1982.

———. "Religious Encounters in a Colonial Context." *American Indian Quarterly* 16 (fall 1993): 501–9.

Sanchez, Jean-Pierre. "Myths and Legends in the Old World and European Expansionism on the American Continent." In *The Classical Tradition and the Americas.* Vol. 1. Edited by Wolfgang Haase and Meyer Reinhold. Berlin and New York, 1994.

Sayre, Gordon M. *Les Sauvages Americains: Representations of Native Americans in French and Colonial Literature.* Chapel Hill, N. C., 1997.

Schreier, Rudiger. "Take Your Pen and Write. Learning Huron: A Documented Historical Sketch." In " . . . *And the Word was God": Missionary Linguistics and Missionary Grammar.* Edited by Even Nordhaugen. Munster, 1996.

Schwarz, Stuart B. *Implicit Understandings: Observing, Reporting, and Reflecting on the Encounters between Europeans and Other Peoples in the Early Modern Era.* Cambridge, 1994.

Seed, Patricia. "Taking Possession and Reading Texts." In *Early Images of the Americas: Transfer and Invention.* Edited by Jerry M. Williams and Robert E. Lewis. Tucson, Ariz., 1993.

———. *Ceremonies of Possession in Europe's Conquest of the New World, 1492–1640.* Cambridge, 1995.

Shell, M. *The Economy of Literature.* Baltimore, 1978.

Shepard, Thomas. *The Day-breaking, if not the Sun-Rising of the Gospel with the Indians in New-England.* 1647. Reprint, New York, 1865.

———. *The Clear Sunshine of the Gospel Breaking Forth upon the Indians in New-England.* 1648. Reprint, New York, 1865.

Shuffleton, Frank. "Indian Devils and Pilgrim Fathers: Squanto, Hobomok, and the English Conception of Indian Religion." *New England Quarterly* 49, no. 1 (1976): 108–16.

Sider, Gerald. "Why Parrots Learn to Talk, and Why They Can't: Domination, Deception, and Self-Deception in Indian-White Relations." *Comparative Studies in Society and History* 6 (1987): 3–23.

Simmons, William. *Cautantowwit's House: An Indian Burial Ground on the Island of Conanicut in Narragansett Bay.* Providence, R. I., 1970.

———. "Conversion from Indian to Puritan." *New England Quarterly* 52, no. 2 (1979): 197–218.

———. "Red Yankees: Narragansett Conversion in the Great Awakening." *American Ethnologist* 10 (1983): 253–71.

———. *Spirit of the New England Tribes: Indian History and Folklore, 1620–1984.* Hanover, N. H., 1986.

———. "Narragansett." In *History of Indian-White Relations.* Edited by Wilcomb Washburn. Vol. 4 of *Handbook of North American Indians.* Edited by William C. Sturtevant. Washington, D.C., 1988.

Simmons, W., and C. L. Simmons. *Old Light on Separate Ways: Narragansett Diaries of Joseph Fish, 1765–1776.* Hanover, N. H., 1982.

Smith, Timothy J. "Wampum as Primitive Valuables." *Research in Economic Anthropology* 5 (1983): 225–46.

Snyderman, George S. "The Functions of Wampum." *Proceedings of the American Philosophical Society* 98, no. 6 (1954): 469–94.

Speck, Frank G. "The Functions of Wampum among the Eastern Algonkian." *American Anthropological Society Memoirs* 6, no. 1 (1919): 3–71.

Spelman, Henry. *Relation of Virginia.* 1609. Reprint, London, 1872.

Spivak, Gayatri Chakravorty. *In Other Words: Essays in Cultural Politics.* New York, 1987.

Staveley, Keith W. F. "Roger Williams: Bible Politics and Bible Art." *Prose Studies* 14, no. 3 (1991): 76–91.

———. "Roger Williams and the Enclosed Gardens of New England." In *Puritanism: Transatlantic Perspectives on a Seventeenth-Century Faith.* Edited by Francis Bremer. Boston, 1993.

Steckley, John. "The Warrior and the Lineage: Jesuit Use of Iroquoian Images to Communicate Christianity." *Ethnohistory* 39, no. 4 (1972): 478–509.

———. "Brebeuf's Presentation of Catholicism in the Huron Language: A Descriptive Overview." *University of Ottawa Quarterly* 48, no. 1–2 (1978): 95–109.

Still, Judith. *Feminine Economies: Thinking against the Marketplace in the Enlightenment and the Late Twentieth Century.* Manchester, 1997.

Strachey, William. *The Historie of Travaile into Virginia Britannia.* London, 1849.

———. *The Historie of Travell into Virginia Britain.* Edited by Louis B. Wright and Virginia Freund. 1612. Reprint, London, 1953.

———. "A True Reportory of the Wreck and Redemption of Sir Thomas Gates." In *A Voyage to Virginia in 1609.* Edited by Louis B. Wright. Charlottesville, Va., 1964.

Strathern, Marilyn. *The Gender of the Gift: Problems with Women and Problems with Society in Melanesia.* Berkeley, Calif., 1988.

Strong, Pauline Turner. "Feminist Theory and the 'Invasion of the Heart' in North America." *Ethnohistory* 43, no. 4 (1996): 683–712.

Strong, Roy. *Gloriana: The Portraits of Queen Elizabeth I.* London, 1987.

Sutton, Imre, ed. *Irredeemable America: The Indians' Estate and Land Claims.* Albuquerque, N. M., 1985.

Tambiah, Stanley J. *Magic, Science, Religion and the Scope of Rationality.* Cambridge, 1990.

Taussig, Michael T. *The Devil and Commodity Fetishism in South America.* Chapel Hill, N. C., 1980.

———. *Mimesis and Alterity: A Particular History of the Senses.* New York, 1993.

———. *The Magic of the State.* New York, 1997.

Taxay, Don. *Money of the American Indians and Other Primitive Currencies of the Americas.* New York, 1970.

Taylor, Charlotte. "A Frontier Entrepot: The Seventeenth-Century Trading Posts at Cocumscussoc, Rhode Island." Paper presented at the annual meeting of the Society for Historical Archaeology, Vancouver, January 1994.

Thomas, Nicholas. *Entangled Objects: Exchange, Material Culture, and Colonialism in the Pacific.* Cambridge, Mass., 1991.

———. "The Cultural Dynamics of Peripheral Exchange." In *Barter, Exchange and Value: An Anthropological Approach.* Edited by Caroline Humphrey and Stephen Hugh-Jones. Cambridge, 1992.

Thorowgood, Thomas. *Jewes in America.* London, 1660.

Thwaites, Reuben G., ed. *The Jesuit Relations and Allied Documents,* 73 vols. Cleveland, Ohio, 1896–1901.

Tilton, R. S. *Pocahontas: The Evolution of an American Narrative.* Cambridge, 1994.

Tooker, Elisabeth. *An Ethnography of the Huron Indians, 1615–1649.* Syracuse, N.Y., 1991.

Trigger, Bruce G. *The Children of Aataentsic: A History of the Huron People to 1660.* Kingston, Ontario, 1976.

———. *Natives and Newcomers: Canada's "Heroic Age" Reconsidered.* Kingston, Ontario, 1986.

Trigger, Bruce, Toby Morantz, and Louise Dechene, eds. *Le Castor Fait Tout: Selected Papers of the Fifth North American Fur Trade Conference, 1985.* St. Louis, Mo., 1987.

Trosper, Ronald L. "That Other Discipline: Economics and American Indian History." In *New Directions in American Indian History.* Edited by Colin Calloway. Norman, Okla., 1988.

Turgeon, Laurier. "The Tale of the Kettle: Odyssey of an Intercultural Object." *Ethnohistory* 44, no. 1 (1997): 1–29.

Turnbaugh, William A. "Roger Williams: A Key into Narragansett Ethnography." In *Ethnohistory and Archeology: Approaches to Postcontact Change in the Americas.* Edited by J. Daniel Rogers and Samuel M. Wilson. New York, 1993.

———. "Community, Commodities, and the Concept of Property in Seventeenth-Century Narragansett Society." In *Archeology of Eastern North America: Papers in Honor of Stephen Williams.* Edited by James B. Stoltman. Archeological Report 25, Mississippi Department of Archives and History. Jackson, Miss., 1993.

Vaughan, Alden T., and Edward W. Clark. *Puritans among the Indians: Accounts of Captivity and Redemption, 1676–1724.* Cambridge, Mass., 1981.

Waldrop, Rosmarie. *A Key into the Language of America.* New York, 1994.

Wallerstein, Immanuel. *The Modern World System.* Vol. 2. New York, 1980.

Weatherford, Jack. *Indian Givers: How the Indians of the Americas Transformed the World.* New York, 1988.

———. *Native Roots: How the Indians Enriched America.* New York, 1991.

Weddle, D. L. "The Melancholy Saint: Jonathan Edwards's Interpretation of David Brainerd as a Model of Evangelical Spirituality." *Harvard Theological Review* 81, no. 3 (1988): 297–318.

Weeden, William B. *Indian Money as a Factor in New England Civilization.* Johns Hopkins University Studies in Historical and Political Sciences, 2d series, 28–29. Baltimore, 1894.

Weinstein, Laurie, ed. *Enduring Traditions: The Native Peoples of New England.* Westport, Conn., 1994.

Welles, Edwin Stanley. "Some Notes on Wampum." Paper presented at a meeting of the Connecticut Historical Society, Newington, Conn., 1924.

Wertheimer, Eric. "'To Spell Out Each Other': Roger Williams, Perry Miller, and the Indian." *Arizona Quarterly* 50, no. 2 (1994): 1–18.

Whitaker, Alexander. *Good Newes from Virginia.* London, 1613.

White, Bruce M. "Encounters with Spirits: Ojibwa and Dakota Theories about the French and Their Merchandise." *Ethnohistory* 41, no. 3 (1995): 369–405.

White, Hayden. *Tropics of Discourse: Essays in Cultural Criticism.* Baltimore, 1978.

White, Richard. *The Roots of Dependency: Subsistence, Environment and Social Change among the Choctaws, Pawnees and Navajos.* Lincoln, Neb., 1983.

———. *The Middle Ground: Indians, Empires, and the Republics in the Great Lakes Region, 1650–1815.* Cambridge, 1991.

Whitehead, Neil. "The Historical Anthropology of Text: The Interpretation of Ralegh's *Discoverie of Guiana.*" *Current Anthropology* 36, no. 1 (1995): 53–74.

Whitfield, Henry. *The Light appearing more and more towards the Perfect Day.* 1651. Reprint, New York, 1865.

Williams, Jerry M., and Robert E. Lewis, eds. *Early Images of the Americas: Transfer and Invention.* Tucson, Ariz., 1993.

Williams, Roger. *The Bloody Tenent Yet More Bloody: by Mr. Cotton's Endevour to Wash it White in the Blood of the Lamb.* London, 1652.

———. *The Complete Writings of Roger Williams.* 7 vols. New York, 1963.

———. *A Key into the Language of America, or An Help to the Language of the Natives in that part of America called New England.* Edited by John J. Teunissen and Evelyn J. Hinz. 1643. Reprint, Detroit, 1973.

———. *The Correspondence of Roger Williams.* 2 vols. Edited by Glenn W. LaFantasie. Hanover, N. H., 1988.

Winslow, Edward. "Good News From New England." In *Chronicles of the Pilgrim Fathers of the Colony of Plymouth, 1602–1625.* Edited by Alexander Young. 1841. Reprint, New York, 1971.

———. *The Glorious Progress of the Gospel amongst the Indians in New England.* London, 1649.

Winslow, Ola E. *Master Roger Williams.* New York, 1957.

Wogan, Peter. "Perceptions of European Literacy in Early Contact Situations." *Ethnohistory* 41, no. 3 (1994): 407–27.

Wolf, Eric R. *Europe and the People without History.* Berkeley, Calif., 1982.

Wood, P. H., G. A. Vaselkov, and M. T. Hatley, eds. *Powhatan's Mantle: Indians in the Colonial Southeast.* Lincoln, Neb., 1989.

Wood, William. *New England's Prospect.* Edited by Alden T. Vaughan. 1634. Amherst, Mass., 1997.

Young, Alexander, ed. *Chronicles of the Pilgrim Fathers of the Colony of Plymouth, 1602–1625.* 1841. Reprint, New York, 1971.

Index

God's, 67, 160, 163, 167, 168–69, 180–81, 183
and power to give, 20, 51, 55, 60–61, 63–65, 69
specie, 122, 124
Speck, Frank, 134
Spelman, Henry, 67–68
Squanto, 154–55, 181
Staveley, Keith, 103, 112
Steckley, John, 185
Stewart, Susan, 71
Strachey, William, 62–63, 65–67, 84–85, 177–78
Straet, Jan van der, 16, 17
Strathern, Marilyn, 39
substantivism, 30–31, 138
surrealism, 70
syncretism, 169, 190–92, 195

Tambiah, Stanley, 180–81
Tatamy, Moses, 164
Taussig, Michael, 29–30, 46–47, 53, 62, 186
Tempest, The, 22, 24
Teunissen, John J., 96, 97, 104, 105
texts of discovery, 2–5, 8, 72–78, 84, 88–92
word lists in, 79–88
Thanksgiving, 15–16, 17–18
Thevet, André, 72
Thomas, Nicholas, 42, 188, 197
tongues, gift of, 149, 150
tools, metal, 120
trade objects
cultural significance attached to, 70–71, 187–88, 193–94, 195–97
exhibiting of, in Europe, 70–71, 79, 126, 194
as source of power, 139
spiritual objects as, 126–27
use of, by Indians, 76, 190, 193–94, 195
"translation" (term), 9
travel writing, 84. *See also* texts of discovery
Trigger, Bruce, 181, 195, 196
Trosper, Ronald, 45
Tupinamba Indians, 86–88, 89
Turgeon, Laurier, 195–96
Turnbaugh, William, 118

use value, 39
counterposing of, to exchange value, 11, 39–40, 47, 74, 137, 193
expanding the definition of, 39–41, 137, 193

vacuum domicilium, 54, 113
value, 9, 14
difficulty in defining, 11, 13, 39–41, 136–37, 191–93, 195–96
See also exchange value; use value
virginity, 56–57, 73

Wallerstein, Immanuel, 117
wampum, 14, 67, 68, 221–22n.12
European attempts to analyze, 119, 123–25, 127, 128, 129–38
as form of currency, 118, 120, 121–22, 134, 135, 136–37
as form of record keeping, 130–31, 133–34
importance of, in fur trade, 45, 117, 118–19, 125, 136
manufacture of, 118–23, 128, 137, 224n.45
as ornament, 127, 137
overlapping roles of, 9, 120–21, 127, 128–29, 131–33, 135, 140, 191
payment of, as tribute, 118–19
Weatherford, Jack, 18
Weber, Max, 112, 181
Weddle, D. L., 159
Weeden, William, 135–38
Welles, Edwin Stanley, 138
Wequash, 158
Wertheimer, Eric, 98
Wesley, John, 158
Western civilization, as gift, 18, 48
Weymouth, Captain George, 73
Whatley, Janet, 88, 89, 90
Whitaker, Alexander, 88, 144–45
White, Bruce, 42, 193
White, John, 75
White, Richard, 12–13, 26, 27, 62, 131
Whitehead, Neil, 3
Williams, Roger, 13, 116, 127, 177
close relations of, with Indians, 93, 110–11, 114–15, 117, 118